The Gospel of Saving Grace

By Chad Sychtysz

Published by
Spiritbuilding Publishers
9700 Ferry Road, Waynesville, OH 45068

THE GOSPEL OF SAVING GRACE
by Chad Sychtysz

Cover Photo Credit: Larissa Lynch

ISBN: 978–0–9990684–7–2

Spiritbuilding
PUBLISHERS

spiritbuilding.com

Table of Contents

*This book is dedicated to the good memories of
my brother Tracy (1965–2003)*

Acknowledgements

This book is a serious revision of a previously-published book, *The Gospel of Grace* (see my Preface). The original book was largely made possible by two men of high standing in the brotherhood, Bob Owen and Harry Pickup, Jr. (who has since deceased). I believe these men, who put their reputations on the line for an unknown author like myself, still deserve their due credit for launching my writing ministry.

I would also like to recognize Carl "Mac" MacMurray, who owned Spiritbuilding Publishing until December, 2019. He was very supportive of the re-write of my original book, and would have published it himself if I had been able to finish it before his retirement from the publishing business. However, Matthew Allen, who bought Spiritbuilding, has been just as supportive, if not more so, and I appreciate very much his enthusiasm for my work.

Jamey Hinds in Florida has done the layout for all my books and workbooks for a number of years now. I am grateful for his talent in getting my manuscripts prepared for actual printing. Curtis and Patsy Cantwell have been "ghost editing" several of my latest study workbooks, but they also read through the manuscript for this book and offered numerous corrections, improvements, and grammatical changes. Their contribution to this book is substantial.

I also want to thank all those who have been very supportive of me since the 2008 publication of the original "grace" book. Their words of encouragement, praise, and even constructive criticism have made my writing far better than what it used to be. Among my greatest "encouragers" is my wife, Honey, who has been my very best friend for over 30 years.

Preface

In 2003, I wrote *The Gospel of Grace*, my first religious book. For various reasons, this was not published until 2008 by the (now defunct) Religious Supply Center in Louisville, KY. At the time, that book was the best that I could do on a subject that was very detailed, involved, and controversial. The reason why I wrote it in the first place was because there was so little written on "grace" beyond the world of denominational writers and preachers. I felt strongly that Christians—and even non-Christians who are nonetheless seeking the truth—needed a fresh perspective that rested solely on biblical support rather than trying to defend one denominational doctrine or another.

My book was not a big seller, but this was no real surprise. I was a no-name author writing about a subject that most Christians think that they already have figured out. Besides this, I have often said that (most) religious books are in a genre just one notch above poetry in sales and interest. Despite this, my book was well-received by those who read it. Several groups in various churches around the country did in-depth studies on "grace" based upon the content of my work. This was personally rewarding, to be sure, and I am grateful for the many complimentary responses I received.

Even so, I had a nagging feeling early on that I could do better. It was not the subject matter, or my basic approach to it, but it was my writing style that disappointed me. It was wordy, clunky, and a bit unprofessional at times. I did not like the "voice" that I had chosen— one that was intended to be friendly, but that sometimes came across as presumptuous or condescending. Other writing projects forced me to put any further thoughts on *The Gospel of Grace* aside. In the back of my mind, however, I had already decided to one day re-write the book.

What you are holding now is the realization of that back-of-my-mind decision. I spent nearly a year rewriting the entire manuscript of the original "grace" book—every chapter, paragraph, and word choice was weighed, scrutinized, and evaluated. I made many changes, both large and small. I deleted three chapters from the original layout and wrote two completely new ones in their place. I changed the "voice"—the style and diction that narrates the entire work—to something that was more relaxed with a "come, let us reason together" tone. One of the added chapters ("Calvinism and Christianity") deals with a technical subject that was sorely missing in the first book. I also changed the title (slightly) to *The Gospel of Saving Grace*, so as to focus the attention more on grace's role in salvation rather than simply God's kindness (or, benevolence) that He demonstrates toward all people.

If you read the original book, I am quite confident you will enjoy—and benefit from—this one even more. If this is your first journey into the subject of saving grace, then I am equally confident that this will provide you with a biblical overview of this grand topic and will give you much to think about. Feel free to contact me with any feedback: chad@booksbychad.com.

Sincerely,
Chad Sychtysz
(March, 2020)

Introduction

Therefore having been justified by faith, we have peace with God through our Lord Jesus Christ, through whom also we have obtained our introduction by faith into this grace in which we stand; and we exult in hope of the glory of God. (Rom. 5:1–2)

"Grace." This word conveys beauty, kindness, and spiritual enlightenment. Everyone has heard this word, and virtually everyone has *appealed* to its excellence in some way or another. People use "grace" to convey superior qualities of virtue or elegance. Generally speaking, grace is innately recognized as one of the finest of all human virtues. We all want to be shown grace when we fail others, and in our finest moments is when we ourselves are gracious toward others when they fail us.

We call God's grace "amazing," and we are astounded that such a fine gift is made available to us at all. The New Testament in the Bible has a lot to say about divine grace. Preachers regularly cite grace as an essential part of man's salvation; the greatest theologians in the world have devoted a great deal of time and attention to it. Men include grace as a part of their congregation's name, and people typically invoke God's grace as the sole cure for their troubled life. Not surprisingly, then, Christians who have tasted of such divine sweetness write about it, sing about it, and talk about it. As the song says, grace has taken us this far, and grace will lead us home.

With all this pre-existing attention to grace, why then did I feel the need to write a book about it? The short answer is: while many people may understand the basic concept of grace, not everyone understands the theology, dynamics, and implications of it. I speak from experience: I had been a Christian for nearly twenty years before seriously entering into a study of grace. I had never truly understood grace beyond the rather primary definition of "unmerited favor." Grace *is* an unmerited favor, to be sure, but that short definition is by no means an explanation. "Unmerited favor" is vague and over-simplistic, especially for something as important as what we are talking about. We ought to be thinking, "What *is* the favor? *Why* is it a favor, and why must it *be* unmerited? And what am I supposed to *do* with it once I have it?"

On the other hand, since the subject of grace seems ethereal and incomprehensible, people may avoid a deeper study of it altogether. Grace is often assigned to a group of mysterious subjects (like the kingdom of God, the indwelling of the Holy Spirit, how God answers prayers, etc.) that Christians often avoid because we feel we cannot (or simply do not think we need to) define them *absolutely*. To some, grace is a nebulous, metaphysical abstract which cannot be explained except through one's own subjective interpretation. Thus, grace is to you whatever *you* want it to be, and it is to me whatever *I* want it to be. Yet, this approach does not work—not simply because I personally dislike it, but because it reduces the reality of God's salvation to a mere emotional experience. I do not want merely to *feel* saved; I want to know I am saved *in reality*. I cannot teach people my *feelings* about divine grace; I must teach them what God has *revealed* about His grace.

Grace is an inseparable part of God's message of redemption: by it, men are saved; without it, they are lost. This means saving grace must be known absolutely, definitively, and without interfering with or contradicting other aspects of salvation. My personal feelings or convictions concerning grace are irrelevant; what matters is what God has told us in His revealed word (the Bible). Unfortunately, people who write books on grace typically avoid a doctrinal definition and application of it. Many of these merely cater to audiences seeking a particular style of writing—one that gravitates toward heartwarming, sentimental prose rather than an objective exposition of the Scriptures. I have read numerous books filled with wonderful, and often powerful, stories of those who have been deeply affected by God's grace. Such anecdotal testimonies are inspirational, to be sure, but they cannot duplicate or replace what the New Testament actually *teaches* about grace. I dare not trust my relationship with God (and my soul's future) to someone else's subjective experience with grace—nor should you trust yours!

Likewise, a cursory glance into the Scriptures will not do justice in explaining *what grace really is*. One cannot merely cite Eph. 2:8 ("For by grace you have been saved through faith; and that not of yourselves, it is the gift of God") and say, "Well then, there you have it: we're saved by grace and that's all you need to know." First of all, this passage was never intended to be a comprehensive definition of grace. Secondly, this approach is very unsatisfying for the one who wishes to delve deeper into the mind of God, as we who *seek* Him are anxious to do. Thirdly, a superficial approach to grace does not explain *how* it transforms our lives. Many Christians are not even aware they are supposed to do anything *with* grace, but think grace is only something done *to* them. If "by the grace of God I am what I am" (1 Cor. 15:10), then certainly there must be more to grace than just having it applied to my salvation in some mysterious and inexplicable manner. Grace is a gift of God, but He does not give us gifts to horde for ourselves or merely file away in our memory. He gives us gifts to *use* in our service to others, to bring Him glory and honor, and to perfect us in the process. What we do with the gift says a great deal about how we regard the Giver.

Many Christians tend to leave spiritual subjects like grace, justification, or propitiation to the preachers, seminary students, and theologians. Often, whatever conclusion the so-called "clergy" comes up with, we nod in approval and recycle it in our group Bible studies. But the New Testament was never intended to be read and studied only by preachers and theologians. Nor was it written for man-made denominational organizations. Nor was it written for *congregations*, meaning any identifiable, established group of Christians. Nor was it written to be left unread altogether. The word of God was revealed and preserved for you to be read *by* you, and by *us*—common, ordinary Christians.

I say that in a tongue-in-cheek way, since there is really nothing common or ordinary about being a Christian. Christians are blood-bought and soul-cleansed people—each one is a "living stone" in Christ's spiritual temple, His church (1 Pet. 2:5). They have been blessed with a "living hope" (1 Pet. 1:3)—a hope made possible *by* the grace of God—to stand in the very Presence of God in His own heavenly realm. They also enjoy a fellowship with Him that exceeds all physical explanation and defies all attempts to fully describe it. If *you* are a Christian, then this is how you should see yourself. If you are *not* a Christian, then you have every opportunity to become one. The grace of God can *make* you one. God Himself wants nothing less than this.

The saving grace of God is not something men confer upon other men, nor is it something over which churches exercise control. Saving grace comes from heaven; this is its only source. Things that come *from* heaven are defined and governed *by* heaven. Grace is part of God's truth, which is to say that grace is part of God's authority as revealed to man through Scripture. We are not responsible for creating "truth," but we can speak the truth where God has already spoken it. It is not legalistic to speak of saving grace in the exact manner and context in which it is used in the word of God. It is not legalistic to cite God's *law* about how human souls are made right with God. Salvation is not an emotional or subjective experience; it is based upon a *legal process* of justification which includes both human faith (Rom. 5:1–2) *and* divine grace (Titus 3:7).

The Bible was written and designed so that people might believe in God and secure their salvation through a means which is otherwise impossible (John 20:30–31). God's grace is not just part of that means; it *is* the means. But grace—and salvation itself—must not be limited to only one part of a person's life. The kind of believing that leads to salvation does not end with one's conversion. It continues to draw us closer to God in an ever-increasing, ever-deepening fellowship that transforms everything *about* the believer. Thus, not only is his belief system transformed, but so is his heart, his soul, his life, and all of his earthly relationships (one way or another). So, when we talk about grace, we are really not only talking about what we *believe*, but also what we *become*.

The study of divine grace is admittedly an involved one. But, instead of being intimidated by a little extra reading and meditating, you would do well to approach this wonderful gift of God with great anticipation and eagerness. This subject is not beyond us—and it is not beyond you. We are not talking quantum physics here, and you do not need a college degree or seminary ordination to understand it. You just need to approach it God's way, without clinging to pre-conditioned pathways of thinking or pre-formed conclusions. In fact, having an objective approach that is open to new ways of thinking, observing, and implementing is probably the hardest part of the study. The doctrine itself is not terribly difficult. Regardless, saving grace directly affects your eternity; that fact alone makes it an extremely important study.

God wants us—*all* of us—to learn about His grace. More emphatically, He desires that we hunger and thirst for His grace, embrace it fully and completely, and allow it to flood our entire being. Virtually everyone seeks forgiveness of their sins, but many fail to realize that forgiveness is a path, not a destination. You should not seek God's grace merely so that you can be forgiven; you should seek His grace so that, once you *are* forgiven, you can become more and more like Christ. First things first, of course: you cannot become more Christ-like *until* you are forgiven, and you cannot be forgiven until you are "in Christ"—i.e., in a covenant relationship with God *through* Christ. "In Christ" is where God's saving grace and "every spiritual blessing" are found (Eph. 1:3); the doctrinal teaching on this will be explained in the following chapters. The immediate point is: God always operates according to a logical and progressive order of things, and thus we ought to learn to *think* in this same manner.

Christ challenges every person to leave himself (or herself) behind to follow Him (Mat. 16:24). This is a radical and transcendent message, one that is (sadly) foreign to many members in so-called "Christian" churches. Christ's invitation is not one that ought to be taken lightly; He will not accept those who reject it, which is to say that He will not *save* such people. In fact, Christ—not me, and not Christians—divides all of humanity into two groups: those who believe in Him, and those who reject Him (in one way or another) (Mat. 7:13–14). Another description of the two divisions is: those who are saved by grace, and those who have rejected that grace.

Everyone who has sinned is in need of grace; the entire message of Christ's redemption is all about this grace that we so desperately need (Rom. 3:23–24). His gospel is inseparable from and impossible without grace, and vice versa. It is, in a very real sense, the gospel of saving grace.

The gospel of saving grace. This gospel is a message from God overflowing with all kinds of good things, like an armful of beautifully-wrapped packages given to you from a very kind and benevolent admirer. Or, it is like a treasure chest filled with the wealth and secrets of some extremely powerful and wise king, and you are allowed not only to open it, but are permitted to keep whatever is inside—*and no one can take it away from you.* This is how the gospel of grace ought to be appreciated; this is the context in which it must be understood. The apostle Paul actually calls his message "the gospel of the grace of God" (Acts 20:24); he also uses "the grace of Christ" and "the gospel of Christ" interchangeably (Gal. 1:6–7). The gospel of God's saving grace is not only a fine subject, it is one worthy of our time and investigation.

In preparation for your venture into the subject of saving grace, I strongly recommend that you read the books of Luke and Acts in the New Testament. This reading will provide you with the historical and biblical context of Jesus' teaching to His apostles and their implementation of this teaching in the early church. When it comes to the teaching on a biblical subject, I do not have any special information that you cannot have: we can all read the same verses in the same books in the same Bible.[1] I also strongly recommend that you read through *my* book without stopping to look up every biblical citation or endnote. After this, I recommend that you read through it again, and this time *do* look up every citation and endnote. The citations and endnotes are there for a reason, but I do not want you to miss the flowing progression of thought being developed throughout this book.[2]

In order to approach the subject of grace in an organized manner, this book has been divided into three major sections. **Section One** deals with the doctrine of saving grace, where we will examine grace as it is defined and expounded upon in the Bible. I make no apology for appealing directly to Scripture, but I am also sensitive to how people will react when coming face to face with the word of God for what may be the first time. You may even find some disagreement between what you believe personally, or what your church teaches, and what the Bible actually says. Nonetheless, this study regards the Bible *as* the revealed word of God, and (therefore) as our sole and final authority for all matters of salvation.

Section Two deals with the problems people have with grace—what I refer to as people's *resistance* to grace. Just because God offers us something as wonderful as saving grace does not mean everyone approaches it with the proper perspective. Those who resist God's grace will most certainly not benefit from it. The gospel itself is salvation to the one who believes it, but condemns the one who refuses it (John 3:36, 2 Cor. 2:14–16, et al). This section offers an overview of some of these problems, as well as proposed solutions to them.

Section Three reveals where grace is supposed to lead us and what we are supposed to do with it. The ultimate objective of grace is not just to deal with sin (atonement), but to bring us into an ever-deepening, holy relationship with God the Father (consecration). This last section is perhaps the most practical and rewarding of the entire book. It is necessary, however, to first lay the groundwork with the other sections before leaping ahead, just as a chess player does not jump into tournaments before devoting himself to the moves and strategies of the game and its masters.

Our Master in this case is Christ Himself, and He has so much to teach us.

Section One:

The Doctrine of Saving Grace

Chapter 1
The Saving Grace of God

But now apart from the Law the righteousness of God has been
manifested, being witnessed by the Law and the Prophets,
even the righteousness of God through faith in Jesus Christ for all those
who believe; for there is no distinction; for all have sinned and fall short
of the glory of God, being justified as a gift by His grace through the
redemption which is in Christ Jesus . . . (Rom. 3:21–24)

G race" is not necessarily a *religious* word. It only becomes
one when it is used in a religious context. But it certainly is
a very *positive* word. In its ultimate sense, it appeals to a certain
attribute, quality, or state of being that is altogether uncommon and
transcendent. Grace is never used in a derogatory manner, except in
sarcasm or irony. When a girl trips over the carpet or stumbles over
her own two feet, someone is bound to say, "Way to go, Grace!"—
which means she has performed in such a way that is anything but
"graceful."

Grace often implies a connection to the divine—there's that
transcendent aspect—or speaks to a spiritual quality of the thing or
person being described. Thus, people in centuries past hailed kings
and queens as "Your Grace," with the understanding that there was
some divine conferment or endorsement in their having obtained
such royal positions. Historically, grace has been invoked in songs
and national anthems in which people sought a higher blessing from
God than what they could have produced themselves.

The word "grace" is derived from the Latin *gratus*, meaning
"pleasing," and then later *gratia*, meaning "a pleasing quality."[3]
It refers to the beauty of thought, form, or expression; or, that
which is elegant, refined, or attractive. In a moral context, it refers
to that which is right, proper, or decent. When we talk about
graceful motion, for example, we think of ballet, figure skating, or
synchronized swimming. When we talk about graceful talents, this

calls to mind people with artistic ability such as painters, poets, musicians, and the like. When a person is gracious, we understand him or her to be generous, well-mannered, and considerate. Grace is positive, warm, gentle, and courteous. Whether or not we manifest grace to others, we certainly welcome others' grace to us.

The Grace of God

When we talk of God's grace, we imply these same positive, virtuous characteristics, but on a much deeper and more substantive level. God is not merely "nice" or "courteous" to us; His grace extends far beyond such mild or generic definitions. God is not just elegant or refined; while someone may use these terms to describe Him, such words do not fully convey what He does for us. God's dealings with us are gracious, to be sure, but this does not mean He is merely well-mannered and well-pleasing. It hurts our understanding of God and His grace by using limited meanings or inferior definitions to describe them. It would be good for us to allow God's revealed word to define His grace in its rightful and appropriate context.

The word originally translated "grace" from the Hebrew Old Testament usually means "favor," as when one extends kindness to another. It is derived from a root word (*chanan*) meaning "to stoop down."[4] An adult, for example, may literally stoop down to the physical height of a small child in order to speak with him face-to-face. The adult does not do this to belittle the child, but to better relate to him. This is the literal meaning of the word "condescend" [lit., *con-* ("with") + *descend* ("to lower")] and describes what God does to us—He stoops down or condescends to our level. He does not do this to patronize or belittle us, but so that we can have *fellowship* with Him. For example, God came down (or, descended) upon Mt. Sinai for the people of Israel's first meeting with Him (Exod. 19:18). Since there was no way they could have gone up to heaven to meet with Him, He had to come down to them.[5]

This "stooping" action also implies that the one in need of favor is lacking in something that the other (condescending one) possesses. The one who lacks cannot achieve this favor on his own; it must be given to or conferred upon him. Without such favor (or grace) being granted to him, he remains in a deficient or negative light. Apart from the bestowal of grace, he remains inferior to what he *could* be. With this favor, however, he is able to enjoy whatever the giver already possesses. The ultimate "giver" of all good things is God: "The LORD God is a sun and shield; the LORD gives grace and glory; no good thing does He withhold from those who walk uprightly" (Psalm 84:11). He is willing and able to give to *us* who are lacking what *He* already enjoys.

Traditionally, "favor" is often linked with life, while the lack of favor is associated with death. In ancient Oriental empires, such as Persia, if one approached an emperor without having been summoned by him, or in an offensive manner, that person lost his life since he did not find favor with (or, receive grace from) the emperor. However, if the emperor were to "dip the scepter" toward his guest, then favor (grace) was extended toward that person and he lived (e.g., Esther 4:11, 5:2). This is very similar to what believers find in approaching God—or in being denied such approach, as in the case of unbelievers. Again, to approach God in His favor is to enter into fellowship with Him. No one can achieve this fellowship, however, unless God (the "emperor," in this case) grants it to us through His own graciousness.

In the New Testament, the word most often translated "grace" is from the Greek *charis*, which refers to a benefit (of any kind), gift, or unmerited favor.[6] It is often used in reference to what God gives us through Christ (1 Cor. 1:4, 2 Tim. 1:9, et al). In light of this, some mistakenly teach that "grace" is only a New Testament subject and "law" is only an Old Testament subject. This has led some to the false idea that the God of the Old Testament and the God of the New Testament could not possibly be the same God, since they come across so differently! Some of this misunderstanding is based upon passages such as John 1:17: "For the Law was given through Moses; grace and truth were realized through Jesus Christ." Yet, in the Old Testament, divine grace most certainly existed, as exemplified in God's gracious dealings with Israel and other nations, though the emphasis of the Law of Moses was to codify law in order to define *sin* (Rom. 7:7, Gal. 3:19). God's sovereign authority needed to be established up front; law and order among God's people are contingent upon that authority.

In the New Testament, law continues to exist—it is impossible for *sin* to exist apart from *law* (Rom. 4:15, 5:13)—but the emphasis of the gospel is to save *sinners*, not merely define their sins (1 Tim. 1:15). God worked through Moses to bring about an understanding of *law*, but not to the exclusion of grace.[7] God worked through Jesus to bring about an understanding of *grace*, but not to the exclusion of law. Different emphases in different contexts must be taken into account in order to know accurately what is being taught. God will not confer saving grace upon those who willfully and impenitently defy His laws. There would be no *need* for divine grace if there were no laws to break, for then no one could be charged with sin, and therefore no one would need to be saved from anything.

God the Father, like Christ, does not change: He is the same yesterday, today, and tomorrow (Heb. 13:8). The gracious God of the New Testament is also the gracious God of the Old Testament. Different stages of human history, human knowledge, and human spiritual development required God to respond in the way He did in ancient times, just as it requires Him to respond in a certain way in our contemporary world. God is not two-faced, nor did He soften His image in the New Testament. Those who stubbornly remain in rebellion to God today will face the same wrath as was displayed against the stubbornly ungodly nations of the Old Testament. Those who stand in favor with God today, having submitted to His gospel, will enjoy the same unfathomable grace and kindness as He bestowed upon faithful men and women in the pre-Christian era. "Behold then," says Paul, "the kindness and severity of God; to those who fell, severity, but to you [believers], God's kindness, if you continue in His kindness; otherwise you also will be cut off" (Rom. 11:22, bracketed word added).

In what way or manner has God "stooped down" to us? According to the apostle Paul, He did so through His Son, Jesus Christ: "For the grace of God has appeared [in the form of Jesus Christ], bringing salvation to all men" (Titus 2:11, bracketed words added). Jesus is the "Word" who was with God the Father, who *is* a Personage of the Godhead, and who "became flesh [or, human], and dwelt among us" (John 1:1–2, 14). Jesus referred to Himself when He said, "For the bread of God is that which *comes down* out of heaven, and *gives life* to the world" (John 6:33, emphasis added). Jesus *came down* to save us, since there is no way that we could *ascend upward* to Him on our own merit or power (Rom. 10:6–7). He had what we desperately needed—*life in His name*—and therefore came down out of heaven in order to make this available to us.

We will discuss all of this in more detail later, but for now it is important to know that God *did* "stoop down"—He *has* made divine grace available to all men. God did not just talk about stooping down; He did not send a heavenly committee or delegation of angels to represent Him stooping down. Rather, His Son—"the radiance of His [the Father's] glory and the exact representation of His nature" (Heb. 1:3*a*, bracketed words added)—became like us, lived among us, suffered alongside us, and died *for* us so that we might be rescued from our self-inflicted spiritual demise. All this, whether in its parts or its entirety, is nothing less than an act of divine grace.

Something We Do Not Deserve

Someone has defined mercy as God sparing us from what we rightly deserve, whereas grace is God giving us what we do not deserve. This succinct perspective seems most appropriate. When we sin against God—for all sin is truly against God, not merely against (a) law—we fall from innocence and are unable to justify ourselves any longer (Rom. 3:23). Having sinned, fallen, and rendered ourselves unfit for fellowship *with* our Creator, we are condemned to be separated *from* our Creator. We will never *deserve* to be freed from this condemnation—even if someone else does indeed free us. And, we who have sinned against God will never *deserve* to have our fellowship with God restored—even if someone else does indeed restore it. We should not confuse opportunity (to be freed or restored) with *merit* (as if we deserve or have earned something). Simply put, sinners deserve to be destroyed, not saved.

Sometimes our culture interferes with our thinking on these things. In America, for example, we have been indoctrinated with the concept of "entitlement," wherein we feel deserving or entitled to certain rewards, compensations, or privileges just because we are, after all, *Americans.* Our government, we reason, *owes* us something—usually more than we have ever given it—for our having been born in (or naturalized to) this country, paid our taxes, and submitted to its laws. It is typical for a person to mistakenly apply that same logic to God, to the extent that he feels entitled to salvation and all its accompanying amenities simply because he is born under Him, so to speak. Being human is assumed to be, in itself, sufficient for God's favor.

In the spiritual context, we who have sinned against God are offenders, not honorable people. We are law-breakers, not law-abiding citizens. We are in no position to make demands, make assumptions, or negotiate with God. We are the ones who are condemned and in need of salvation, not God. He does not owe us anything; we are impossibly indebted to Him. God is the Giver of life, whether physical or spiritual, and when we offend the Giver of life, we corrupt the image of God in ourselves (Gen. 1:27) and thus are deserving of death. Our spiritual death is the only way such desecration can be legally dealt with. Our good works, good intentions, feelings, tears, disagreements with God, etc., will not change the situation. Left to ourselves, we have no escape from what we have done.

But God has provided—because of His *love* for us—a way of escape: "there is now no condemnation for those who are in Christ Jesus" (Rom. 8:1). Christ has become our only means of overcoming death and punishment—He has absorbed the debt in Himself that we have incurred through our own selfish will. "For Christ also died for sins once for all, the just for the unjust, so that He might bring us to God" (1 Pet. 3:18). We are deserving of death but He has promised us life. We are *not* deserving of life but He has made life possible through the great sacrifice He has made on our behalf. All this is conditioned upon our faith in Him—something we will discuss in due time—but the impossible is now possible, and the unthinkable is now doable.

What God extended to us in order to spare us from what we rightly deserve is called *mercy.* Divine mercy is directly connected to His kindness (Eph. 2:7), patience (2 Pet. 3:9), compassion (Mat. 9:36), and love (John 15:13). In the place of *justice*—which is what we deserve—God offers *mercy* instead. But mercy is not free, and is not offered without expectation of gratitude and reform from the one to whom mercy is shown (Rom. 2:4). God's divine justice does not just evaporate because He (as we would put it) simply feels sorry for us. Justice has to do with what is right, lawful, and consistent with God's holy nature. He cannot violate what is right, do what is unlawful, or deny Himself (2 Tim. 2:13) because then He would cease to be God.[8] He cannot undermine His own holiness in order to save you.

Suppose you are given a speeding ticket, but let's say you *were* speeding because you had to get a severely injured friend to the hospital. In a court of law, you plead your case before a judge. If that judge says, "Regardless of *why* you were speeding, you still broke the law"—that is justice. He has every right to say this, because the law stands regardless of circumstances. You sped, you broke the law, and you deserve the punishment. But if he says, "I have compassion on your situation, and so I am going to strike this infraction from your record"—that is mercy. He has every right to do *this*, too, because he is a fellow human being capable of compassion, and his judgeship allows him such latitude.

In God's world—which is, by the way, where all of us are heading in due time—there is no such thing as simply striking infractions (sins) from the record based on mercy alone. There is only justice, and nothing more or less than this. You say, "But God is merciful—the Bible says so!"—and this is true. But we are not talking (yet) about what God offers to us, only the situation we find ourselves in when we sin against Him. Left to ourselves, we cannot throw ourselves on the mercy of the court, so to speak, because we are not saved by mercy alone. Mercy is a component of God's salvation, not the entirety of it. Mercy spares us from what we deserve *in order that* we might be saved; it does not equal or replace actual salvation. God shows us mercy because He *can*—because His Son, Jesus Christ, made it possible for Him to do so. Since Christ provides a means for salvation outside of our own merit (since we have none), and is not dependent upon us being justified by law (since we have violated it), now God can offer us mercy. If not for Christ, we would have no mercy, and therefore no hope. God would be the Judge who says, "Regardless of your reasoning, excuses, pleadings, and tears, you broke the law—*My* law!—and now you will receive justice." The justice we are talking about here is your paying for your sins through your own punishment. This punishment is more awful than you can even imagine. Indeed, it is the very worst thing that could ever happen to you.

Through the offering of His Son, God not only extends divine mercy, but He also extends divine grace. We must be *spared* (by mercy) in order that we might be *redeemed* (by grace). If God did not spare us from what we do deserve, He certainly could not give us what we do not deserve. Suppose a judge is faced in court with a man who has committed murder, and the man is tried and found guilty of his crime. The judge sentences this murderer to be executed. Out of the audience, another man stands up and says, "If you will take my life for his, then please let him go!" In order for the judge to allow this, he has to first *spare* the murderer of his punishment; then he has to *grant* the murderer his freedom. The man deserves to be punished for his crime; he does not deserve to be freed. Yet, in the case of one who is willing to absorb the penalty of this man's crime in himself, everything changes. The murderer's being spared from death is an act of mercy; his being given his freedom is an act of grace. If the judge had simply ordered the man to his immediate execution, with no opportunity for intervention from the audience, there would be no opportunity for his freedom. In other words, the judge could not show grace unless or until he first showed mercy.

Technically-speaking, mercy *always* precedes grace. Mercy is wonderful—we all want it, especially from God!—but grace is *even better*. Grace is what makes salvation possible; grace *is* salvation. Grace is not merely being saved from punishment, as many people think; it is being ushered into life and fellowship with God. Saving grace—the specific application of divine favor that makes us "partakers of the divine nature" (2 Pet. 1:4) is not any one thing, but can be understood as a package deal, a bundle of spiritual blessings given to the believer upon entering into a covenant relationship with God through Christ.

Saving grace is only achieved through Christ's redemption, and specifically through the blood of Christ. God's offer of salvation is just that—a mere *offer*—until it is brought to life through Christ's blood. Christ, as our holy and righteous Advocate (1 John 2:1–2), intercedes for every sinner who approaches Him with humility, confession, repentance, and the surrender of his soul. Grace necessarily involves God's forgiveness of our sins, but is not limited to that forgiveness. All of this is predicated upon one's obedience to Christ's gospel, for no one comes to the Father except through Christ, no matter how much he tries, prays, or desires otherwise (John 14:6).

A Manifold Grace

We are touching on a number of doctrinal concepts in this brief discussion of grace. My intention is not to overwhelm anyone, but to show how integrated the system of saving grace is with the entire gospel of Christ.[9] But, at this point, it seems necessary to drive home two very important points over which there has been a great deal of misunderstanding.

First, if you are saved—and I mean this in the ultimate sense, as in your actual presence in heaven—it will be because of the saving grace of God. It will *not* be because you merely bear the name "Christian," or because you are an active churchgoer, a good person who does good deeds, a faithful spouse, an excellent parent, or a hard worker. These things are all what God expects you to do, but your having done them will never *earn* your salvation. The power of your salvation rests upon divine effort, not your human effort. Your salvation requires God's active, deliberate, and supernatural *willingness* and *ability* to rescue your soul from an awful destruction—a destruction which, apart from such divine action, *most certainly will happen.*

Second, if you are saved—in the same sense as just described—it will be because of your obedient faith in God's grace. It will *not* be because of your faith in: the Bible; Christ's church; preachers, elders, parents, or friends; your own effort, ability, sincerity, virtue, or deliverance; luck or happenstance. None of these things or people ever *could* save you; your future hope is not secured by these. Your faith in God's grace is absolutely essential for your salvation, just as God's grace in response to your faith is absolutely essential. Saving grace is God's divine response to anyone who comes to him in sincere, obedient faith, since "the righteous man shall live by faith" (Rom. 1:17). Faith is the only thing we can give to God that He has not already given to us; faith is what God most desires from each one of us. Divine mercy spares us from all the horrors of hell; saving grace invites us into glorious fellowship with God.

We will discuss faith in more detail later, but what exactly is saving grace? Certainly, God's grace includes His forgiveness of our sins. In fact, if grace were nothing *more* than this, it would be priceless and amazing. Paul says, "In Him [Christ] we have redemption through His blood, the forgiveness of our trespasses, according to the riches of His grace which He lavished on us" (Eph. 1:7–8). But grace also includes all that God provides the believer *because* of that forgiveness. Grace, as it is depicted in Scripture, is whatever God gives to the one who believes in Him. This "free gift" (Rom. 6:23) is made possible only through the work, worthiness, and mediation of Jesus Christ. Someone had to pay for this grace—it is free to *us*, but not to God—and Christ did so through His sacrifice on the cross. The fact that we are "redeemed" (Col. 1:13–14) indicates a purchase transaction, not simply a declaration from God. Specifically, then, we are talking about *saving* grace—that which is required for salvation—and not merely God's general kindness toward people. There is no question that God is *gracious* to all people by giving them life, health, blessings, and material wealth; He sends sunshine and rain upon both the wicked and the righteous (Mat. 5:45). But such things do not and cannot save anyone.

No specific Bible verse says, "This is what grace is," or, "Here is the official definition of grace." Yet, there are numerous verses that define it by way of deduction. This deduction is not just a good guess (like a hypothesis), but is an inescapable conclusion (i.e., a necessary implication). The next several biblical citations, for example, do not even mention grace, but they do necessarily imply it.

- Jesus told His disciples, "I am the vine, you are the branches; he who abides in Me and I in him, he bears much fruit, for apart from Me you can do nothing" (John 15:5). Think about that: *apart from Him, we can do nothing.* Obviously, the "nothing" refers to our vain attempts at accomplishing God's will through mere human effort. We *cannot* carry out the will of God without Christ's direct help; we certainly cannot save our own souls without Him. But Christ—really, *grace personified*—stooped down to give us what we could not acquire on our own. He makes possible the impossible; He makes doable the undoable. Apart from Him, we cannot be saved, period.

- In Romans 14, Paul wrote about those who may have different convictions—not different *doctrines*, but different *opinions*—concerning their service to God. Yet, he said, "the Lord is able to make him stand" (14:4)—"him" being the one who, despite his private beliefs, could not "stand" otherwise. Think about that: *we cannot stand before God* without His help, no matter how sincere, righteous, pious, or selfless our opinions may be. No one's soul is saved by his (or anyone else's) opinions; he is only saved by divine grace and through his human faith.

- Paul said of himself and fellow ministers, "Not that we are adequate in ourselves to consider anything as coming from ourselves, but our adequacy is from God, who also made us adequate as servants of a new covenant" (2 Cor. 3:5–6). Think about that: *we are not sufficient, fit, or good enough apart from God.* It is God who makes us "adequate," not ourselves, nor our churchgoing, good works, good intentions, or good friends. We are entirely unprepared to stand before God in judgment unless we are *made* prepared through whatever He does for us that we cannot do for ourselves.

- Paul wrote, "I can do all things through Him who strengthens me" (Phil. 4:13). Many people like to quote this passage—and for good reason. It is inspiring, motivating, and edifying. But this is not merely Paul's attempt to sound humble; with regard to his salvation, Paul could *do nothing at all* without divine help to strengthen him. Think about that: salvation is not just difficult apart from divine grace, it is impossible; the problem we face in God's condemnation of our souls is not just problematic *to* us, it is insurmountable *by* us. Christ is not just offering us a helping hand to make our salvation easier for us to accomplish; He *is* our salvation, and we are helpless without Him.

- The apostle Peter wrote, "[God's] divine power has granted to us everything pertaining to life and godliness" (2 Pet. 1:3). Think about that: except for divine favor shown to us in the person and ministry of Jesus Christ (Titus 2:11), we could not have life with God *nor* could we attain to godliness. The context here must be spiritual, since we already have physical life, and godliness is not something one practices in a mere physical realm.

This is just a sampling of passages we could cite on the subject of what God does for us that we cannot do for ourselves. Before we can appreciate the full scope and power of saving grace, we need to abandon the false notion that we are able to *save ourselves.* In fact, Jesus said (bluntly) that if anyone thinks that he *can* or *will* save himself, he will lose everything (Mat. 16:25). Saving grace does not merely facilitate the salvation process, but there can be no process of salvation without it. (We have much more to say on all of this in upcoming chapters.)

At this point, I propose a general but all-encompassing definition of grace that is far more accurate than the traditional and underwhelming "unmerited favor" definition:

Grace is anything and everything God does to deal with our sins and compensate for our human weaknesses, with regard to our salvation.

Or, even more simply:

*Grace is **everything** God does to save us that we cannot do ourselves.*

The context of this definition must always be things pertaining to salvation, since God is not so concerned with things outside of this. Grace will not make you prettier or taller or wealthier, but it *will* be the salvation of your soul, which is infinitely and eternally more important than all other concerns. Grace certainly includes the forgiveness of our sins, but also includes:

- **Joy** over God's having redeemed us through the blood of Christ, and the anticipation of glorious things to come (1 Pet. 1:8–9).

- **Spiritual peace** that comes from knowing we stand justified before God (Rom. 5:1).

- **Confidence** that our prayers will be answered, our souls are prepared for Christ's return, and eternal life itself is secured (1 John 2:28, 3:21–22, and 5:13–15).

- **Anointing** of God's Spirit—not a tangible, physical experience, but a real one all the same (2 Cor. 1:21–22). This anointing or "sealing" (Eph. 1:13–14) provides intercession for our prayers, direction for our spiritual lives, access to God's providential help, and the promise of even more blessings to come (Rom. 8:26, 15:13, and Gal. 5:16–17).[10]

- All the **"fruit"** produced by the Spirit that indwells the believing child of God, for which there is no "law," boundary, or limitation (Gal. 5:22–23). This essentially speaks of the holy life that is made possible only because we have been brought into holy fellowship with a holy God (1 Pet. 1:13–16).

- **Hope** of a future with God because of Christ's redemptive work (Rom. 8:24–25).

These are all things that you need in order to enter into eternal life with Christ, but that you are unable to secure apart from Him. Grace does not invalidate human faith, but is a response to it; grace does not invalidate good works, but gives them meaning and purpose. No amount of human effort, human intentions, or human piety can atone for sins, cleanse the conscience, strengthen the soul, condition the heart to serve in the name of Christ, or prepare a person to stand before God. Your efforts may be *good* efforts, and your deeds may be *good* deeds, but apart from Christ they are *not good enough.* Reading your Bible and assembling with fellow Christians, for example, are expected of believers, but these things cannot redeem one's soul from its condemnation. On the other hand, grace does not remove the responsibility from believers to do those things that they *can* and are *expected* to do. Grace does for you what you *cannot* do, **never** what you are *unwilling* to do. Grace is God's part of your salvation; obedient faith is your part. Even though they are enormously unequal in scope and power, both parts are absolutely necessary.

Saving grace is not a spiritual epiphany, burning in the bosom, or mere heartwarming assurance. It is not a religious experience, church experience, or emotional experience. It is not something that we confer upon each other, the church confers upon us, or we confer upon ourselves. It is not some mysterious and inexplicable "thing" that overcomes the soul and fills the human heart. Rather, it involves God's very real, very powerful, and absolutely necessary activity in the heart and life of the believer. God's grace is God's ability to perform, His willingness to act on our behalf, and His infinite capacity of resources and strength that is applied to the human soul. Grace is an ever-present, ever-working, and ever-transforming power that increasingly brings us into conformity with the image of the Son of God Himself (Rom. 8:29).

Unfortunately, not everyone speaks of saving grace with such good and positive expressions. There are some who do not understand it, do not *seek* to understand it, and actually resist its power and application. There are some who quickly step on top of God's immeasurable grace to talk about things they *can* measure, quantify, and calculate—things of far less importance. There are some who actually resent the grace of God, since it represents to them an ever-increasing debt that they feel obligated to pay.

No, I'm not talking only about sinners who have never committed their lives to the Lord.

I'm talking about *Christians.*

Chapter 2
≡*Grace Is Not a Burden*≡

I am amazed that you are so quickly deserting Him who called you by the grace of Christ, for a different gospel; which is really not another; only there are some who are disturbing you, and want to distort the gospel of Christ. (Gal. 1:6–7)

It is amazing how Christians can take something meant for good and turn it into something difficult. Jesus said, "My yoke is easy, and My burden is light" (Mat. 11:30), but many think true discipleship to be unbearable, and have opted instead for an over-simplified version of it.[11] The apostle John said that God's commandments "are not burdensome" (1 John 5:3), but many find even the most basic commands to be insufferable, and want to reinterpret them as something a bit more palatable.

The fact is, this probably happens more often than any of us want to admit. Left to ourselves, and without keeping God's gifts in their proper context, people—that is, *God's* people—tend to drift toward begrudging divine favor rather than appreciating it.

Sadly, this is not a new phenomenon. Take, for instance, Israel's wandering-in-the-wilderness experience. God gave the Israelites manna from heaven for forty years: He provided them with *free food* and all they had to do was go out in the morning and collect it! They did not have to grow grain, harvest crops, or spend money to buy this food. Yet they did not always appreciate the gift but grumbled and complained about it. The free gift from heaven had become bland and unacceptable in their eyes. "The people spoke against God and Moses, 'Why have you brought us up out of Egypt to die in the wilderness? For there is no food and no water, and we loathe this miserable food [manna]'" (Num. 21:5). This is a most offensive way to talk to the God who had delivered them out of an awful bondage *and* was leading them into the Promised Land!

Some Christians today succumb to this same complaintive mentality. "What am I doing wasting my time going to church? There are others enjoying life to the fullest, without any concern for their moral responsibility to God. I can't believe I left all that behind—and for what?! I loathe this miserable spiritual life!" No one will ever dare use those exact words, of course, but you can rest assured there are some who feel that way. These people look upon God's grace—our spiritual manna—as something that keeps them from enjoying life as *they* want to live it and that interferes with their alleged freedom.

To other Christians, saving grace is looked upon as just another favor to be repaid: as God piles on the gifts and blessings, so He increases their obligation to "do good" and "walk right." Living in the Light is not something to be relished and enjoyed, but is viewed as a kind of spiritual burden. Divine forgiveness is all about releasing us from an unpayable debt, but some see it instead as simply changing the *kind* of debt that is owed, leaving us (still) in a position of always playing catch-up but never making any real progress. In return for being forgiven, now people *have* to go to church, and *have* to make a financial contribution to the church, and *have* to be involved with God's work in a way that is very inconvenient and makes them uncomfortable.

So then, some are unappreciative of the gift of saving grace, and others regard God's gift as a means of control—a way to imprison people by imposing *religious obligation* in place of condemnation for sin. And, while this discussion might seem to fit better under the later section of *resistance* to God's grace, it actually is more fitting here because it illustrates how God's grace can be wrongly *defined*.

An Insurmountable Debt

I want to introduce you to a friend of mine. Actually, she's not just *my* friend, for many people know her and she has a great number of friends. We will call her Linda, and you will find her in every single Christian congregation across the country. She is white, black, Hispanic, Slavic, Italian—whatever you need her to be, whatever makes the visual work for you. She is twenty-something, middle-aged, or a grandmother—whatever you need her to be. She is simple, having only a high-school education, or she is cerebral and complex—an Ivy League-educated woman—or is somewhere in-between. Linda is very pretty—or elegantly beautiful, or she's rather fair, or even downright ordinary. She is tall to some, short to others. She is overweight and shy, or she is petite and bubbly. It really is not important that she is a "she," for she could just as easily be a man, for the sake of this illustration. Her real identity is irrelevant, for Linda is everyone and everywhere, and hers is the story of so many people that it is difficult to talk about her without making reference to millions of other men and women who share her same struggle.

You see, Linda has a serious health problem. No, it's not clogged arteries, diabetes, or cancer. She has a serious *spiritual* health problem. Even though Linda is a Christian, she has a rather skeptical view of God's benevolence toward her. A stifling and oppressive view of heavenly favor is slowly killing her. Sound bizarre? Let me explain how she got to that point.

Before Linda became a Christian, her life was ordinary yet relatively happy. She had a number of good friends, enjoyed a rather carefree life, and thought little of her spiritual condition. Linda thought of herself as a "good person": she (usually) obeyed the laws of the land, stayed away from addictive vices, and kept her distance from bad company. In her mind, God had no right to require of her anything more than this, since she was hardly a serious offender. When she wanted to have a social drink with her friends, she drank; when she wanted to feel good, she smoked pot; when she felt the desire to gratify her longing for physical intimacy, she had sex. None of these things, she explained to herself, amounted to anything that deserved more than a raised eyebrow from God. Surely she would go to heaven when she died, she reasoned, especially since there were so many people in the world who were so much worse than herself.

Then a chance meeting with an acquaintance at work led to a discussion on spiritual matters and moral responsibility. The co-worker was a Christian who, for the time being, looked beyond Linda's worldly behavior to a much more important matter: her alienation from God. This person knew that if Linda did not have a right relationship with God, she would be eternally lost once she left this earthly existence. Not willing to allow that to happen without making considerable effort on Linda's behalf, the co-worker compassionately shared the gospel of Christ with her. Over time, the friend's words began to prevail and the gospel message began working on Linda's once indifferent heart. After one particularly long discussion with her friend over the scriptures, Linda suddenly realized that she needed to respond to God's message of love and forgiveness before it was everlastingly too late. She realized how selfish and careless with her soul she had been until that moment. She understood how her sins, small though they may be in comparison to someone else's, nonetheless warranted divine condemnation. She accepted the fact that no one but Jesus Himself could save her soul. So, that very evening, Linda committed her life to God, was baptized into Christ, and became a Christian.

For the first several months of her "newness of life" (Rom. 6:4), Linda felt overjoyed about her decision. She regularly fellowshipped with other Christians; she eagerly studied her Bible for a better understanding of what God had revealed to mankind; she sought God's providence through prayer. She believed that she stood in a favorable relationship with God. For a while, Linda actually tasted a kind of freedom that she had never known before, one which was nothing like the so-called freedom she had left behind in the world. For a while, all was good and promising, and Linda should never have experienced any digression, except . . .

. . . Except that over that same time, Satan worked double-time to ruin Linda's walk with God and brought back her old perspective to haunt her. The "I'm-a-free-and-independent-unchained-soul" mentality she had come to know so well before now bubbled up to the surface like methane gas belching from a landfill. To God, the stench was foul and offensive, but to Linda it was particularly familiar and therefore she gravitated toward it. She recalled with fondness her carefree days before she had become a Christian and remembered that, if anything was going to get done right, she was going to have to do it herself. Her fierce independence and self-righteous air began to infiltrate her spiritual perspective. Her geometrically-unbounded relationship with God transformed into a very linear, straight-arrow, line-and-vector view of Christianity; she came to view Christianity as a flat world without any spiritual depth. God was no longer Someone to whom she wished to draw near; rather, God was Someone who stood in the way of her own salvation, like a prison guard who tauntingly dangled prison door keys in front of the one behind bars, showing himself to be superior over him. She suddenly found herself relying less and less upon God and more and more upon herself. Over time, Linda fused the gospel of Christ with her own existing beliefs and came up with an entirely new creation: the Gospel According to Linda.

This new gospel has not freed her. It has actually made her more imprisoned, more limited, and more *frustrated* than ever. Her new gospel—which she mistakenly equates with God's—appears fraught with glitches and conflicts, like a computer program that does not interface properly with a certain operating system. On the outside, she has conditioned herself to appear happy and appreciative of Christ's sacrifice for her sins. On the inside, she is filled with turmoil, conflict, and moral confusion. She smiles, shakes people's hands, invites them over to her house for coffee, speaks knowledgeably of spiritual virtues, partakes of communion, says her prayers—all the while, growing more and more dissatisfied with her spiritual life.

What about grace? Oh, Linda's thinks she knows it well. She used to believe that grace was a good thing, before she mentally resurrected the "old" Linda from the dead (having forgotten that whatever has died to the world must remain dead). She's heard it intoned in many sermons, she sings about an "Amazing Grace" in her church hymnal, and reads about being "saved by grace" in the Bible. She knows grace is supposed to be something sweet and fluffy like spiritual cotton candy, or smooth and silky like a fine chocolate truffle. She knows she is supposed to talk about grace in the most sacred and ethereal sense. But after it has been crunched through and spit out of the metal gears of her new reformed gospel, grace means little more than another *debt* she owes to God. He gives grace, to be sure, but she believes one has to *pay* for it. Since there's no such thing as a free lunch, and God obviously thrives on making others suffer dearly for their salvation, it must be worked off. And how does one pay for grace? Good deeds must be done—*more* good deeds. Personal effort is the labor, grace is the paycheck.

So Linda the self-defined Christian lives to justify herself by the Gospel According to Linda. She gets up every morning believing that God demands her flawless attention to detail. She believes her Master to be a hard Boss, reaping where He does not sow and gathering where He scatters no seed.[12] Thus, she lives in *dread* of this Divine Warden. She wants heaven, to be sure, but she realizes that every day is another rung on the ladder to get there. And God, the Supernatural Slavemaster who stands frowning down at her from the top of the ladder, His mighty arms akimbo, will be able to detect the slightest departure from perfection with His all-perceiving eye. So Linda tries harder to be the good servant that she is supposed to be. When she is supposed to be at church, she goes to church. When she is supposed to pray, she prays. When she is supposed to forgive, she forgives—through gritted teeth and with clenched fists, but *she forgives*. She does all this, *not* because she finds any real profit in the experiences themselves, but because she has to, because she is forced to, because Satan has poisoned her mind to believe that God's gospel has commanded her to do so as a form of penance.

Yet, as each day unfolds, she realizes that her mistakes and missteps are more than that for which she can compensate. By the end of the day, regardless of how well she has performed and despite all the good deeds she has accomplished, there is still a deficit—a lingering reminder of her imperfection, a lingering remainder of her debt to God. She lays her head down upon her pillow at night having tried her best (though her best is never good enough) to please the Slavemaster in the Sky, with a *deficit balance* on her justification account. This would not be devastating in itself except she had awoke that *morning* with a deficit balance, left over from the previous day, week, month and year. Deeper and deeper into debt she goes, always trying to pay for her salvation, ever trying to compensate God for the privilege of being saved. Meanwhile, Satan smiles wickedly as he continues to feed her deceptive yet convincing propaganda.

As Linda sees it, the gospel has infected her once-pure heart with its lists of do's and don'ts, laws and ordinances, prescriptions and proscriptions. She sees herself as the link between righteousness and unrighteousness, salvation and condemnation, heaven and hell. Jacob saw angels ascending and descending upon his visionary ladder; in Linda's mind, however, she is the one who daily ascends and descends, carrying loads of penance up to heaven, then wearily going back to earth for more. Heaven will be achieved, she hopes, by every rung she masters. "Christ has paved the way for the *opportunity*," she says with a weary sigh, "but I must be the one who makes it all happen. To be saved, I must be perfect; to be perfect, I must be justified; to be justified, I must work *very hard* at being in complete conformity with every law and commandment God imposes upon me. *I must not fail*, but when I do fail *I must make every effort to compensate for my misdeed.* The Warden of Heaven holds the keys to my future and my salvation (or condemnation) depends on whether or not I please Him with my service. I must be very careful to toe the line, lest I offend Him, and He destroys me in the end. . . ."

Not even Christ understands her suffering (or so she has come to believe). After all, how *can* Christ understand? He never needed grace; He never felt the heavy burden of one day's guilt piled upon the previous thousand days' worth of guilt. Christ, she has come to believe, is no more powerful than a little household idol sitting still and silent upon a shelf in her mental prison. She can share her problems and frustrations with Christ all she wants—she's done this many times—but she has come to seriously doubt His ability to really help her. After all, since He is inside her own confinement, He has no more freedom and independence than she has. As she is trapped by her own set of circumstances (self-imposed as they are), so Christ is equally trapped. The best He can do is offer a weak "Hang in there, believer!—keep the faith!—go with God!" or some other kind of hollow encouragement.

Linda realizes she must be missing something but does not know exactly what it is. She watches incredulously as other people actually *enjoy* being Christians and are bubbling with talk of God's love, intimacy with Christ, and fellowship in the Holy Spirit. She listens incomprehensibly as other Christians talk of how rewarding their relationship is to each other. She cannot understand what it is she is overlooking. Are these people delusional? Are they insane? Are they duped into *thinking* they are happy when in reality they are just as miserable and oppressed by the gospel as she is? After all, they thank God for the wonderful love and *grace* (of all things!) He has *given* them, seemingly oblivious to the tremendous debt they are incurring through such an exchange!

Meanwhile, Linda sullenly and silently suffers in her self-made prison. Who is she going to talk to? No one understands her—or, more accurately, she does not know how to understand anyone else. She cannot talk to people who are like herself for they are just as overwhelmed as she is. She cannot talk to these other "kindred spirit" people, for they obviously live in a surreal world, a kind of spiritual Never-Never Land where people never grow beyond childish fantasies about life with God. What is she going to do, admit that she does not really *enjoy* her relationship with the Lord? "Just to *think* that sounds so *evil*," she admits to herself, "and makes me out to be a hypocrite." She is embarrassed by her failure to overcome her own deficiencies and at the same time she is enraged with the impositions put upon her by this seemingly unremarkable grace.

She tries to convince herself that her situation is normal—it's all those overly-spiritual people who are the anomalies and freaks— so why should she be dissatisfied with it? Yet, she finds herself suffocating under a massive load of guilt which becomes increasingly heavy as every new day's guilt is piled upon it. In her opinion—a view which has been poisoned by Satan—she thinks her good works and service ought to earn more credit than she seems to be able to acquire from the Exacting Accountant in the Sky. She is helpless to act, yet believes no one will be able to help her without putting even more burden and pressure upon her already-fragile situation. She is a human time bomb, waiting to explode—or implode, whichever comes first. Either way, it will either be the end of her or the end of her religion.

"Wretched person that I am! Who will set me free from this living death!?" she cries out to herself, her sad and angry voice echoing pointlessly off of the unfeeling, impassionate walls of her self-imprisoned life. Given her circumstances, how *can* she be free? If the gospel of Christ cannot save her, then what can? She wonders this as she glares at the Christ-idol staring blankly and unblinkingly at her from its proper place on the shelf, offering no real hope and certainly no real answers.

Grappling with Grace

Do you know someone who thinks and lives like this? Someone who thinks Christianity is another word for spiritual slavery and oppression? Have you ever talked to someone who, despite all the joy set before her, feels overwhelmed with the cross she is given to bear? Can you see how crippling this self-determined mentality can be, and how it corrupts all the benefits and beauty of God's gift to man—His Son, the Lord Jesus Christ? One final question, before we move on:

Are you Linda?

Obviously, I exaggerated some of the details in order to emphasize the problem. But the essential message is this: when we live according to a gospel of our own creation, we fail to see things as they really are, but instead adopt a very unrealistic picture of what the true gospel—the gospel of *saving grace*—is all about. God's gospel is not about your or my perceived reality; it is about God's reality which is never biased or blurred by human interference. All of us are limited, in some sense, to a finite perspective. Yet without any outside perspective, we are all blind to reality; left to ourselves, we could never know the true nature of our situation. A person cannot claim that we are blind to our true nature, and then declare authoritatively, "But here is what our true nature is," for that person is just as blind as everyone else.

Christ came from heaven to show us not only who we really are, but also what we *can* be when we follow Him. He has provided us with a heavenly perspective which transcends the blindness of our hearts (John 9:39). He has given us a way of escape from the self-made, self-imposed prisons in which we have unwittingly incarcerated our souls. Thus, the discussion here is not about what we think our condition is (or is not), but *how things really are*. This is God's primary concern; it should be ours as well.

Paul spoke of this reality when he wrote to the Christians in ancient Galatia. He told them bluntly, "I am amazed that you are so quickly deserting Him who called you by the **grace of Christ**, for a different gospel, which is really not another; only there are some who are disturbing you, and want to distort the gospel of Christ" (Gal. 1:6–7, emphasis added). Those Christians had reduced the generous gift of Christ to a system of works and self-righteous human effort. By doing so, they had distorted and thus ruined (for themselves) the entire message of salvation by grace. This is no different than what Linda did.

Paul chastised the Galatian Christians for having been so gullible (Gal. 3:1–3):

> You foolish Galatians, who has bewitched you? . . . This is the only thing I want to find out from you: did you receive the Spirit by the works of the Law, or by hearing with faith? Are you so foolish? Having begun by the Spirit, are you now being perfected by the flesh?

In other words, Paul asked them: "Why did you once look to God for your salvation, but now have taken the whole burden of salvation upon your own shoulders to be carried out by your own strength? This makes no sense. In fact, it is regressive and counterproductive. It defies the message of grace, and even denies the Master who bought you.[13] If you could not save yourself to begin with, then you will not be able to save yourself *ever*." Nonetheless, this mentality is easy to succumb to when we do not understand how grace works. And, when we do not understand how grace works, we do not understand how the gospel works. Satan has bewitched us; we have let him cast a spell upon our heart.

Grace was never meant to be burdensome, but liberating: "It was for freedom that Christ set us free; therefore keep standing firm and do not be subject again to a yoke of slavery" (Gal. 5:1). The one who tries to modify God's divine plan is really saying that he does not *trust* God's grace. (If he *did* trust His grace, there would be no need to change or add to it.) And God's response is, in effect: if you do not trust Me, then you do not have faith in Me, which nullifies grace completely. This is why Paul then says, "You have been severed from Christ, you who are seeking to be justified by law; you have fallen from grace" (Gal. 5:4). He is not talking to people who never had been given grace to begin with, but to *Christians* who had "once been enlightened and [had] tasted of the heavenly gift" (Heb. 6:4).

To be "justified by law" means to have "law" be the absolute standard of one's righteousness.[14] It also means that as soon as one *breaks* that law, he stands condemned *by* it. Law can only do one of two things: justify a perfect law-keeper, or condemn a law-breaker. Law cannot save law-breakers; it has no way to rectify their problem; it cannot reconcile unholy sinners to a holy God. It has no mercy or grace to offer; keeping more laws does not make a single violation of law go away. If a person breaks *one* law, then he is guilty of *breaking the entire law* (Jas. 2:10).

Law does not and cannot change the status of a sinner: according to law, once a sinner, always a sinner. God's grace, on the other hand, *does* change the status of a person so that he is no longer a sinner, but a *child of God*. This does not mean that "child" will never sin, but that he now has divine recourse *for* sin. Grace is what makes such recourse possible in the first place; grace is also what gives him recourse in every necessary instance thereafter.

The Good News of God's Grace

Jesus did not accomplish all that He did just so we could experience a different *kind* of misery or take on a different *kind* of suffering than what we had before. Such thinking not only undermines the gospel of grace but misrepresents it entirely. This means we have no *right* as children of God to bind ourselves (or others) by something to which God does not bind us, or impose upon ourselves (or others) that which God does not impose upon us. We do not belong to ourselves, if indeed we belong to Christ; *you* do not belong to yourself if indeed *you* belong to Christ (1 Cor. 6:19–20).

Therefore, you cannot create your own reality but must accept God's reality as your own. Yet, if you are overcome by your own belief system, then you are a virtual prisoner to it, "for by what a man is overcome, by this he is enslaved" (2 Pet. 2:19).

Only when Linda leaves the darkness of her soul's own making will she be able to step into the Light of God—not the dim glow of the wooden Christ-idol tottering inside her own self-wrought prison, but the brilliant light of the Father of Mercies who desires that all people be saved through the all-powerful, ever-living Jesus Christ (1 Tim. 2:4). Christ is not collecting dust on the shelf of her prison cell but fills the heavens and earth with His glory, majesty, and power. He cannot *be* confined or subdued. If death and Hades cannot contain Him, then certainly Linda will not be able to!

The solution to Linda's dilemma—which may be your *own* dilemma—begins with the abandonment of all pretenses of self-righteousness and self-justification. She must realize that Christ is not a prisoner of her own circumstances or disillusionment; He is on the outside, ready to free her as soon as she asks Him to. He is not dangling the keys to her confinement, smugly taunting her and mocking her enslavement; rather, He cares deeply for Linda (and you!) and desires her salvation. If Linda will trust in His willingness *and* ability to save her—and will allow for no *other* means of salvation—then He will rip the prison cell door off its hinges with supernatural strength and hurl it over His shoulder.

Linda needs to let what had been put to death upon her conversion to Christ *remain* dead and buried (Rom. 6:3–7). She must never attempt to resurrect it. She must leave behind the old nostalgic longing for her former life. She must abandon her ever-demanding but never-fulfilling belief system and let it rust and corrode where it lay. It cannot help her, much less save her, and it never could. She must allow Christ to define His gospel to her, rather than she defining her gospel to Him. She *must* do all these things if indeed she wants to walk with God.

Christianity cannot be (and never was) defined by one's own thoughts, one's past, those who had misguided us, or whatever earthly circumstances in which we find ourselves. Grace is from heaven, and only the Word of God who has come down to us *from* heaven can accurately define and properly portray it (John 1:14–18). Linda must accept Christ's thinking for her own, and His will for her will.

If you wish to be with Christ in glory, *you* must do this same thing.

Chapter 3
⚌*Grace Is a Gift*⚌

*Every one who thirsts, come to the waters; and you who have no
money come, buy and eat. Come, buy wine and milk without money
and without cost. Why do you spend money for what is not bread,
and your wages for what does not satisfy? Listen carefully to Me,
and eat what is good, and delight yourself in abundance. Incline your
ear and come to Me. Listen, that you may live . . . (Isa. 55:1–3)*

Now that we've examined an imaginary illustration (Linda's story), let's turn our attention to a real-life account. The following is a true story.

I know a man—we'll call him "Elliott"—who had been a faithful Christian for decades. Yet, upon hitting his mid-life crisis, he found himself resenting the spiritual predicament he was in. In the middle of this crisis, he would tell me through gritted teeth how unfair it was that God held all the keys to his salvation. He believed that in order to get to heaven, we all have to bow to His whims. When God says "Jump!" we have to cower before him and whimper, "How high, Master?" When God says "Be still!" we have to act like frozen statues, afraid to scarcely breathe. He really believed this whole system of redemption was an imposition upon his freedom to do what he wanted. Why should he have to conform to God's unrelenting commands? Why should everything he did have to be approved before the great God of Only-If-I-Say-So in heaven?

Being an intelligent man who liked to argue his case, Elliott had a battery of answers for those who disagreed with him. (I have found that people who resist God always have ready "answers" to justify themselves.) If given a chance, he would rant about how unfair God was in all these things, and how He just did not make sense to him. Why would a Loving God be so hard on people, so demanding? Nonetheless, he would resignedly comply with the standard Christian duties: go to church, sing the songs, give an offering, etc. This was part of the payment for grace; this is the cross one must bear in order to get to heaven. Everything he did seemed to be a reluctant and heavy-sighed response to God's commands. The more he talked about it, the more bitter he sounded. His cynicism was unmistakable; he was miserable and he made others miserable, too. Christianity might well have been a millstone tied around his neck, so to speak. In that state of mind, this man wouldn't have recognized grace if it had fallen out of the sky and knocked him in the head.

Then Elliott stumbled into a quagmire. His mid-life crisis had convinced him that he needed to reinvigorate his life with a new romance, which he found in an old flame. He looked up a former sweetheart, they began corresponding, they got together, and—well, you know the rest of this episode. Their story is as old as mankind.

The next thing Elliott knew, his world was falling down around him. His wife found out about the affair, his reputation suffered dearly, and he was overcome with guilt and shame. For the next several months—even years—he sought to make sense of his life, his marriage, and especially his faith in God. His involvement with another woman devastated the status quo of his world. Like a person who stares blankly at the ruins of his house after it has been splintered by a tornado, poor Elliott stared numbly at the debris-strewn remnants of his former life. This left him open to a flood of new thoughts and new ideas that he had previously not considered objectively. He stood exposed to the gospel, and the two-edged sword of the word of God finally pierced his calloused heart (Heb. 4:12–13).

Elliott's former, cynical belief system was completely disabled. It no longer worked for him. After all, it was that stubborn, ill-chosen belief system that led him into this disaster in the first place. Yet, paradoxically, it was this very disaster that provided the opportunity to build a *new* belief system. This new system would be nothing like the old one wherein God was allegedly a Prison Warden who held all the keys, but one in which God became a Help in a time of need, where Christ became an Advocate who spoke on his behalf. Elliott was most certainly in need of God, since he had proved to himself and to everyone else that, despite all his intellectual reasoning and smug comebacks, he really had missed the point. Before, he had always had self-serving *answers*; now he was confronted with the *gospel truth*.

Through the process of putting his life back together, Elliott suddenly discovered grace everywhere he looked. His Christian friends who knew of his situation received him back with open arms: *grace*. His wife forgave him and chose to stay with him: *grace*. God, Elliott truly believed, listened to his petitions as he begged for mercy and forgiveness: *grace*. By finding grace, even experiencing it personally and allowing himself to be transformed by it, he eventually learned how to start *showing* grace to others, to *live* by grace. He could not do this before because he had always resisted it. Painfully, but finally, he realized he could not pay for God's grace with his obedience, but that grace is given without a bill of sale.

Now, several years later, Elliott speaks sincerely of his love for God, his compassion on the lost sinner, and his incredible admiration for the Lord Jesus Christ. He freely shares his faith with others and uses his experience of overcoming bitterness and learning how to live by grace as a testimony—and a challenge—to others who are going through similar struggles. Since he had been unwilling to step out of his self-wrought fortress of human dependency on his own, God allowed him to self-destruct. This was the only way the man would listen. Thankfully, he *did* listen. Unfortunately, for every story with this happy ending, there are many more stories of people who (upon self-destructing their own lives) only become more callous and insensitive to grace than before. They just build another dungeon— one stronger and more impenetrable than the first.

Paying for Gifts Received?

Grace is a gift, not a purchase. It is *given* to us; we cannot buy it. Because it is a gift, we are not required to compensate for it; indeed, it is impossible for us to even do so. Yet the fact remains that many well-intentioned Christians overwhelm themselves with unbearable burdens of guilt as they try (and repeatedly fail) to repay God for His grace.

Imagine a child being given a very expensive birthday present and, though he is thankful, he walks away dejected and defeated. "What's wrong?" you ask him, bewildered at such a response. "Well," he says despondently, "I appreciate the gift—I really do—but now I have to go find some way to pay for it, and I have no way to make that kind of money." Imagine this is his response to *every* gift given him, from the clothes on his back to the car purchased for him when he turns sixteen to the college education loans his parents assume later on. What a burden this child will bear! How can he possibly find happiness and contentment in the *gift* if all he sees in it is another debt to repay, with debts piling up year after year, the *least* of which he cannot reimburse?

Such is the situation of those who think God's gift of grace requires compensation. This may be referred to as "debtor's ethic" or "obligatory Christianity."[15] The reality is that we do not compensate God for anything. What can you give to Him that He has not already given to *you*? I have thought long and hard on this for years and can only come up with one answer: **your faith in God** that He is willing and able to do all He has said He *will* do. This is what He requires; this is all you have to offer Him; my faith is all *I* have to offer Him. Everything else—every sacrifice, good work, act of obedience, example of virtuous behavior, etc.—has already been supplied to us by God in some way or another. God has even provided all the evidence necessary *for* our faith. How can we possibly earn what has already been freely given to us?

The only wages we have ever *truly* earned are those incurred through our sins. Here is the deceitfulness of sin: we were conned— by pride, other sinners, our foolish immaturity, and/or Satan himself—to believe that, if we sinned, we would *gain* something. This gain might be financial or material profit, position, prestige, favor in the eyes of others, mastery of our situation, sensual pleasure, etc., or all of these things. The truth is, the only thing we truly gained through sin is spiritual *death* (Rom. 6:23). We signed a contract with death in which we gave away everything we have and everything we *are*, and received only a moment's gratification in return. We mortgaged our soul for an astronomical sum that is impossible to afford.

This is a most foolish transaction, yet *all* of us have engaged in it (Rom. 3:23). Somehow, each one of us thought we would be the first—maybe the only one?—who could defy God with impunity. Yet we have all been utterly and terribly deceived. Apart from the salvation of God's gospel, we will work *for* Satan for the rest of our lives only to die forever *with* Satan in the life to come. This is our only wages; this is all we are capable of earning on our own; this is the reality of our situation regardless of what Satan (or our pride) says otherwise.

So, once we become Christians, do we simply serve a different god and accrue different wages? Not at all. God does not reward believers with heaven as a direct compensation for our service to Him here on earth. He *gives* us heaven because we have given *Him* our genuine faith; "God dispenses gifts, not wages."[16] Remember, the only *wage* we actually deserve is death. "But God, being rich in mercy, because of His great love with which He loved us," rescues us from our self-inflicted death sentence with saving grace (Eph. 2:4–5). "But if it [salvation] is by grace, it is no longer on the basis of works, otherwise grace is no longer grace" (Rom. 11:6, bracketed word added).

The free gift of God's grace does not give us merely the opposite of sin's wages; "the free gift is not like the transgression" (Rom. 5:15). Sin brings death, period; grace, however, gives an abundance of life (John 10:10). Imagine if God, in "saving" us by grace, simply put us on some cold, dark, and barren planet in the universe to live for all eternity without any amenities or provisions beyond the "gift" of a perpetual bleak existence. Imagine God saying to us then, "You should be thankful I gave you anything at all!" or, "Well, I spared you from hell, didn't I? Things could've been much worse!" Instead, He brings us into *His heavenly home* in which are infinite and unfathomable blessings, honor, glory, beauty—incomprehensibly more than I can even describe with my finite comprehension and vocabulary. We are not merely His guests, but are made a part of

His own heavenly family and are thus forever privileged citizens of heaven. His angels will not only be our gracious hosts, but will be our eternal friends as well! Truly, the free gift of God's grace is nothing like the reward of sin, just as Jesus is not merely the opposite of Satan. The two things—and the two personages—are not even comparable.

The Real Cost of Grace

However, we ought never to think that because grace is free to *us*, it is free altogether. "A gift costs everything for the giver, and nothing for the recipient."[17] We see this on the most basic level when we give someone a gift: *we* are the ones who paid for it, not the recipient. Imagine going to a wedding, for example, and attached to every wedding gift is an invoice, the bride and groom being expected to reimburse their guests that amount. This would not only be completely inappropriate, but it would be an offense to the couple. "Some gift!" they would say—and rightly so!

Now let's examine this in a spiritual context. When a person sins, he incurs a loss—every time, without exception. A sacrifice is required to compensate for that loss. Either the sinner pays this sacrifice himself (in hell, through the punishment of his own soul), or something or someone else must be given to compensate for this loss. In the Old Testament, bulls, goats, sheep, and doves were slain *in place of* the execution of the offender. There was never a sin committed among the Israelites that did not require a sacrifice somehow, sometime.[18] Sin *always* creates a loss, *always* causes a breach, *always* corrupts, defiles, contaminates, and destroys *something*. Just because you and I cannot see the damage or feel the pain does not mean it does not exist.

Ancient pagan and polytheistic cultures did not have the same beliefs about a relationship with the Lord that you and I now can enjoy.[19] They often operated in ignorance and selfishness, without seeking God as He had revealed Himself to man (Rom. 1:20–23, Gal. 4:8–9, Eph. 4:17–19, Heb. 1:1–2, et al). The ancients have long believed in the substitutionary (or, vicarious) sacrifice of animals as an appropriate means of spiritual redemption—or, at least, a temporary escape from physical punishment. While their intentions and practices took them away from the God of heaven, substitutionary sacrifice *was* something God permitted in ancient times even among those who "called upon His name" (Gen. 4:26, Psalm 99:6, et al).

This form of sacrifice was even incorporated into the Law of Moses, for several reasons. First, it was all that the Israelites' spiritual understanding could comprehend at the time. They needed the basics first, and God in His wisdom and mercy provided these through the Levitical sacrificial system.[20] But He also made it clear that this was an intermediate step and not the final chapter in the lesson on sacrifice.

Secondly, sacrifice was supposed to teach men that God truly wanted to have a spiritual relationship with man. The core of God's teaching was that sacrifice is a means of *drawing near* to Him. The root meaning of the Hebrew word used for "offering" [*qorban*] in the Old Testament speaks to this (Lev. 1:2, et al).[21] Sacrifices for atonement or ritual consecration were offered as a means of re-establishing or seeking deeper fellowship with God. Appropriately, when Israel agreed to the covenant conditions God laid out at Mt. Sinai, Moses sacrificed animals on behalf of Israel. The blood from these sacrifices was sprinkled upon the written covenant itself as well as the people, in order to unite the two and give life to both (Exod. 24:3–8; see Heb. 9:18–22).

Thirdly, God allowed the death of an animal to symbolically compensate for the Israelite's own death, so that he indeed could approach God in faith. Since God is absolutely holy, no sinful man can draw near to Him on his own merit and live (Exod. 33:20). The implication is that one who approached Him *would have to die*. Yet, God mercifully provided a way for the Israelite to approach Him by way of this substitutionary system of animal sacrifice. Thus, when the Israelite offered his sheep, goat, or bull upon the altar as a sin offering, he understood that *it should be him upon that altar* since he was the one worthy of death. The blood of that animal symbolized its life, and the life of that animal was given in place of the life of the one offering it.

The bodies and blood of mere animals, however, could never *actually* absolve the sins of the sinner for whom they were put to death. The sacrificial system of the Law of Moses was never intended to be God's final answer to the problem of human sin. Not even a river of the blood of animals could compensate for the incalculable debt incurred by even one sinner. For every human sin, a blood sacrifice was required; "without shedding of blood there is no forgiveness" (Heb. 9:22*b*). Blood is the agent of cleansing and atonement for the human soul, but the *source* of this blood must be superior to the one who is being cleansed. In the case of animal blood, the situation is just the opposite: the blood of lesser creatures (animals) was offered for superior creatures (people). This is why "It is impossible for the blood of bulls and goats to take away sins" (Heb. 10:4).

Someone asks, "Why can't God just pardon the sin, pretend it never happened, and be done with it?" The immediate answer is because God does not "pretend" *anything*. God deals only and always with reality; He is a God of truth, justice, and absolutes. But to more fully answer this, we need to appreciate (to the best of our ability) God's holiness. This holiness is not just important to Him; it is inseparable from who He is. When we violate God's holiness—the sacred, righteous, and incorruptible nature of our Creator—He cannot simply sweep that under the rug, pretend it never happened, and "let bygones be bygones." When we defy God's law—whether through profaning His holy name, breaking His holy commandment, or corrupting His holy justice—we defy God Himself. This is equivalent to exalting ourselves as a "god" before Him. Through this act of defiance, we dishonor God *as* God, and we disregard the very source of our life and existence. God has made us "in His image" (Gen. 1:27), and that image—that expression of God within us—cannot exalt itself over the One who gave it, just as the thing molded cannot exalt itself over the molder (Rom. 9:20–21). When we corrupt the soul that God gave to us, God *requires* that soul to pay the penalty of such defiance. This is what hell is: the punishment of those who have defied God but never sought His *redemption* from that punishment through a blood offering.

As stated earlier, God temporarily dealt with the sins of Israel through the ritualistic sacrifice of animals. This was never meant to be a permanent situation, since the *sacrifice* for the loss must be greater than the loss itself. To compensate for an offense, something greater than the offense must be offered—not only to reimburse the loss but also to penalize the offender for having incurred the loss in the first place. While no single Bible passage says all this verbatim, the Law of Moses does teach this concept in the principle of restitution (Lev. 5:15–16). A one-fifth fine or penalty was attached to the compensation (or, reparation) offering and paid to the priests who acted as God's representatives. In a sense, we see this principle of restitution expressed in other ways as an addition to the life of the animal given for the sin itself, usually in the form of a grain offering (as in Num. 15:1–13) or libation (i.e., a drink or liquid offering, as in Lev. 23:13). We see the same thing today in lawsuits: there is compensation for the actual loss, plus a penalty of some kind for the wrongful act itself.

The debt our sins creates cannot be paid for with a mere human sacrifice, even our own, for this would not even be sufficient for what is required. It *equals* the value of the offender (as a human life), but it is not *greater* than the offender. A human sacrifice offers restitution in the form of a life for a life, but no fine or penalty for the crime itself. What God's world of absolutes and perfect justice requires is someone who is a *perfect* human being who is also *more* than human. This someone needs to choose to offer himself in the place of the offender, just as the offender also chose to sin. This someone must provide restitution—a life for a life—but also (because he is *greater* than human) something more than equal to the life of the sinner. This someone cannot not be an animal, since an irrational creature cannot atone for one made in the image of God (Gen. 1:27). This offering cannot not be an angel, because angels are not human, and therefore also cannot fulfill what is required. What is necessary, then, is for *God* to become human, and then offer Himself for the sinner. This offering will be *like* man in every way, but innocent and morally flawless. He will also provide something greater than a mere life for a life, since He is a Divine Being.

Enter Jesus Christ, "the Lamb of God who takes away the sin of the world" (John 1:29). Jesus did not become a sinner in our place, but just the opposite: He provided in Himself a perfect, sinless offering to *redeem* the sinner. God did not *punish* Him for us (just as He did not punish sacrificial animals), for God does not punish the innocent.[22] Instead, it was *men* who punished Him in their hatred and anger for exposing their sins (John 15:18–25). In effect, every one of us who has sinned against God is responsible for His death, inasmuch as it was *our* sins that necessitated it. In absorbing the torture *we* inflicted and the losses *we* incurred, Jesus paid with His own life the debt that we could not ever hope to pay (Mat. 27:33–50). In doing so, He served to represent all those who are accursed because of their own sin (Gal. 3:13).

Thus, even though God condemns sin *and* those who commit it, He offers His own perfect solution for our problem. God's wrath is against all unrighteousness (Rom. 1:18), yet He satisfies (or, propitiates) His own wrath through the vicarious offering of His Son (Rom. 3:23–25, Col. 1:19–22, 1 John 2:1–2, et al). Through Christ, God offers redemption from the very judgment and condemnation that we have brought upon ourselves.

God calls this perfect, timely, and all-sufficient solution *grace.* For grace to be given *to* man, Christ had to give Himself as a sacrifice *for* man. Without His sacrifice, there could be no atonement (or, cleansing; forgiveness) for sin; without atonement, there could be no grace; and without grace it would be impossible for you or me to enter into glory with God in the life to come. In order for our souls to live, the Son of God had to die. There is no other way for us to be saved—there *could* be no other way, and there never *will* be any other way.

But we do not want to leave Christ forever hanging upon a cross. We do not want His bleeding, tortured, and spittle-covered body to be our last image of Him. Since He *is* the Son of God, even death is no match for Him. He overcame death by raising *from* it just as He overcame the world by rising *above* it (John 16:33, Acts 2:24). "Remember Jesus Christ, risen from the dead," Paul wrote triumphantly, even as he faced his own execution (2 Tim. 2:8). Jesus was not defeated on the cross, but quite the opposite: *through* the cross, He has brought grace and hope to a sinful and hopeless world. No longer nailed to a cross in abject humiliation, He is now enthroned at the right hand of God, reigning as both King and High Priest (Acts 2:33, Heb. 8:1). His victory over this world, sin, and death serves as *our* victory over these same things through *His* grace. "For by grace you have been saved through faith; and that not of yourselves, it is the gift of God" (Eph. 2:8). Grace is indeed a free gift to *us*, but it was not free to the One who paid for it with the incalculable cost of His own perfect, innocent, and divine life.

Summary Thoughts

Let's summarize what we have covered so far in this chapter:

- Grace is a gift from God, not something we can acquire on our own.
- Since grace is a gift, it does not need to be paid back and it is pointless to try.
- Our sin incurs a greater debt than we could ever pay in order to reconcile our broken fellowship with God. Apart from God's intervention, we will suffer the wages of sin through eternal punishment.
- No sacrifice—gifts, animals, people, or even ourselves—is sufficient to overcome our debt of sin.
- The sacrifice required for sin must be greater than the one who sinned. A mere human sacrifice is insufficient, since it cannot compensate for the desecration of a human soul. Earthly solutions cannot fix spiritual problems; a sacrifice corrupted by sin is unfit to be presented to God as a solution *for* that corruption.
- The only solution to our spiritual problem lies in God providing an appropriate sacrifice: someone who is human and (at the same time) divine.

- This perfect sacrifice has been realized in Jesus Christ; no one else in all of heaven or human history can equal or surpass His worthiness for this role.
- This solution, and all that it encompasses, is called *grace*.

How are we to pay God back for what we cannot even afford in the first place? Not only can we not pay Him back, but we have no hope of redemption apart from the price *He* has paid through His Son's mediation on the cross. My friend Elliott had to learn all of this the hard way, through his own personal experience. He initially had no respect for the gift since He had no respect for the Giver. Now, however, he realizes just how generous and kind the Giver of grace has been to him, even though he is completely undeserving of it. Thus, he has learned that grace *is* a gift, and that he does not have to spend the rest of his life paying for it.

And, if *you* have received the grace of God, *neither will you.*

Chapter Four
⟫ *The Source of Saving Grace* ⟪

"Do not let your heart be troubled; believe in God, believe also in Me.
In My Father's house are many dwelling places; if it were not so,
I would have told you; for I go to prepare a place for you. And if I go
and prepare a place for you, I will come again, and receive you to
Myself; that where I am, there you may be also. And you know
the way where I am going." Thomas said to Him, "Lord,
we do not know where You are going, how do we know the way?"
Jesus said to him, "I am the way, and the truth, and the life;
no one comes to the Father, but through Me."
(John 14:1–6)

Grace is indeed a free gift. It is heaven's gift of the highest order and the greatest magnitude. It is worth more than all the fortunes of man and earth combined. Nonetheless, there will always be those who try to modify—by reinterpreting, redefining, or customizing—the saving grace of God for various reasons. People love the idea of saving grace, of course, but not everyone is happy with the *source* of it. People love the idea of a "free gift," but many think that "free" means "Nothing is required of me *at all*." People love the idea of God forgiving them, but not everyone cares to live like forgiven people.

Our modern American infatuation with entitlement, "rights," and self-indulgent living has made an objective discussion about "grace" difficult, to say the least. The subject itself is not so hard, but there seems to be a prevailing notion that not only *should* God provide everyone with free grace, but that He should *not* expect any kind of commitment from those who receive it. Many Americans have been indoctrinated with political-correctness, multiculturalism, and "tolerance" dogma. Having to believe in the New Testament gospel and confess Jesus as Lord and Savior is deemed oppressive, intolerant, and even *offensive* to those who want forgiveness and heaven but will not believe in Jesus or the Bible. If God is the loving God that He says He is, they surmise, then His salvation must be just as unconditional as His love.

Denominational theologians call this many-paths-to-heaven philosophy "religious pluralism," a kind of political correctness for the religious community. Not wanting to offend non-Christians, nor wanting to condemn anyone, they have deferred to an ambiguous, all-inclusive version of the gospel that will leave everybody feeling spiritually comfortable and justified. Thus, Catholics believe in Jesus, Muslims believe in Mohammed, Buddhists believe in Buddha, Hindus believe in Vishnu, and everyone else believes in whatever god or savior they choose. Jesus serves as merely a *symbol* of salvation, and not the actual (or only) *route* to salvation. In the afterlife, God will welcome *all* people into heaven, regardless of what they chose to believe here on earth.

It is amazing to hear those who are hyper-sensitive to what offends sinners, but clueless toward (or, simply unconcerned with) what offends Jesus Christ or God the Father. Jesus once told the Jews who refused to believe in Him (despite all the miracles He had performed in their midst), ". . . I honor My Father, and you dishonor Me. . . . It is My Father who glorifies Me, of whom you say, 'He is our God'" (John 8:49, 54). The Jews sought God's favor, but then disregarded His Son. This is no different than what is going on today: people want God's *gifts* and *blessings,* but do not want God's *Son*—in some cases, do not even want God Himself. It is not going to end well for these when they stand before God in the Judgment—and judgment *is coming,* regardless of whether or not one chooses to believe it.

A "Different Gospel"

Ideas that flatly contradict the entire basis *of* Christianity have no place *in* Christianity. And, those who stand opposed to Jesus Christ will ultimately be destroyed *by* Him. Christ Himself promised, "Every plant which My heavenly Father did not plant shall be uprooted" (Mat. 15:13). This means: every person, religious leader, religion, church, gospel, and philosophy that is not consistent with what God has revealed in *His* gospel is doomed to fail. Pluralism, politically-correct-ism, inclusivism, religious globalism—whatever man-made "-ism" one chooses to embrace (and all "-isms" *are* man-made)—these are all shifting sand and offer no spiritual stability for a person's soul.

We either believe God's word is our final authority in all matters of life and godliness, or we do not. Christ and His apostles all adamantly affirm the same thing: Jesus Christ is Lord of lords and King of kings (John 18:37, Phil. 2:9–11, Rev. 17:14, et al). He is not a mere symbol of salvation but is the very substance of it. To maintain otherwise, or to corrupt that fact in any way is to preach "a different gospel" (Gal. 1:6–8). This other gospel does not have to be *entirely* different, but it only needs to violate the core teachings of what has already been revealed from heaven (e.g., Eph. 4:4–6, Col. 1:15–18, et al). The apostle Paul placed a curse upon anyone who would do such a thing. This is a most serious charge, because modifying the gospel of Christ—the gospel in which the *saving grace of God* is defined and explained—is a most serious offense.

The gospel of Christ belongs to Christ. He owns it entirely, not us, not our churches, and not our religion. It is not something we can amend by vote, or re-identify in some sort of religious town meeting discussion. When Peter tried to change Jesus' plans for Him, the Lord turned on him and said, "Get behind Me, Satan! You are a stumbling block to Me; for you are not setting your mind on God's interests, but man's" (Mat. 16:21–23). Jesus called the Jews some pretty awful things, but He reserved "Satan" [lit., adversary] for one of His closest disciples. How dare we think we will get away with doing the same thing, especially when we have far greater information revealed to us than what Peter had at the time!

Later (after Jesus' resurrection and ascension), the same Peter said, "There is salvation in no one else; for there is no other name under heaven that has been given among men, by which we must be saved" (Acts 4:12). The apostle Paul said there is no gospel that can be preached other than the gospel of Christ that he preached; all others are to be rejected. Christ Himself gave Peter and Paul the authority to say such things and underscored their authority with miracles to confirm that their message was from God (2 Cor. 12:12, Heb. 2:1–4). John the Baptist, the prophet who announced Christ to the Jews, said: "He who believes in the Son has eternal life; but he who does not obey the Son shall not see life, but the wrath of God abides on him" (John 3:36). This is a non-negotiable statement, requiring that one either accept it entirely or reject it entirely. There simply is no middle ground.

Jesus, the Sole Savior

The reason why I am pressing these points is because everything we know of the gospel of *saving grace* depends on the absolute nature and identity of *Jesus Christ*. His function as Savior and His saving grace are inseparable; whatever affects the one automatically affects the other. To corrupt Christ's role in the salvation of mankind is to forfeit the grace that comes through Him. Without Christ having done *everything* He was sent here to do—and without Him continuing to do all that He does even now—we would have no grace. Without grace, there would be no forgiveness, no gifts of God, and no promise of heaven. Without Christ (and thus without grace), we have absolutely *no hope*. Thus, salvation is not a multiple-choice issue. One cannot choose Jesus as though He were one of many alternative paths to heaven. One cannot listen to other gospels or choose other religions and hope to be saved (in the end) by Christ anyway. Jesus is the Lord of heaven, the King of God's kingdom. Why would God welcome anyone into His heaven who refuses to recognize this?

Jesus Christ is the very substance of our spiritual future with God. You and I desperately need the grace of God in order to have a right relationship with Him. In order to access that grace, we must recognize Jesus for *what* He really is and for *whom* He really is. Consider what Jesus says about Himself:

- "I am the bread of life" (John 6:35, 48).
- "I am the Light of the world" (John 8:12).
- "I am the door; if anyone enters through Me, he shall be saved" (John 10:9).

- "I am the good shepherd; the good shepherd lays down His life for the sheep" (John 10:11).
- "I am the resurrection and the life" (John 11:25).
- "I am the way, and the truth, and the life; no one comes to the Father but through Me" (John 14:6).
- "I am the true vine, you [disciples] are the branches; he who abides in Me and I in him, he bears much fruit, for apart from Me you can do nothing" (John 15:5, bracketed word added).

Notice how Jesus does not share His role, identification, mission, purpose, etc. with anyone or anything else. No allowance is made for any "Bread," "Light," "Door," "Shepherd," "Resurrection," "Way," "Truth," "Life," or "Vine" other than Him. Christ certainly did not recognize any; His apostles certainly did not recognize any; and the Father did not recognize any. We either believe what the Scripture says about Christ—which includes what Christ says about Himself—or we are just *flying blind* through this life, making up "spiritual" myths as we go, according to whatever tickles our ears (2 Tim. 4:3–4). This is a foolish way to "prepare" for the afterlife and the judgment to come, especially after all that God has done to show otherwise (Acts 17:30–31).

A Necessary Decision

Admittedly, many people today are bothered by the exclusive, non-negotiable, and absolute language of the New Testament. Many believe that Christians are intolerable bigots because they recognize Jesus as the *only* Lord and His gospel as the *only* terms of salvation. Yet, Jesus Himself said, "He who is not with Me is against Me" (Mat. 12:30). Just because someone does not accept Him or His message at face value does not make Him or His message go away or less true. God has given every person the right to choose the destination of his own soul. However, just because we have the freedom to choose our eternal *future* does not mean that any choice we make automatically leads to an eternal *reward*. The freedom to choose and the right choice are not interchangeable ideas.

Someone says, "Yes, but won't God show mercy and grace to those who sincerely believe in Him through a means other than the Christian faith?" Listen to how this sounds to God the Father, after having providing His Son as an offering for our sins (Rom. 8:32). Listen to how this sounds to Jesus, the One who actually died for our sins (Rom. 5:6–8). Listen to how this sounds to the Holy Spirit, who provided all the miracles and prophecies and testimonies to validate Jesus' role as the Savior of the world (John 16:8–11, Heb. 2:3–4). Proposing a means of salvation outside of Christ is not only unbiblical, it is offensive to God (the One who *owns* salvation). There is nothing unfair about God offering only *one route* to receiving His saving grace—especially if it is the only way that *works* and is *needed*. This one way negates every other way.

"But what about God's *love* for us!" someone persists. "Surely He would not withhold His saving grace from those whom He loves!" The problem with this kind of reasoning is the arbitrary use of the word "love." Many define "love" however they want, and then impose their definition on everyone else—including God. To some, "love" means we must give approval to what others are doing, even if it defies God's word. But in God's world—as it has been revealed in His gospel—"love" has an entirely different meaning. It is presumptuous, to say the least, to tell God who *is* Love (1 John 4:8) how He should love us.

Many "love = salvation" proponents are fond of quoting John 3:16—"For God so loved the world, that He gave His only begotten Son, that whoever believes in Him shall not perish, but have eternal life." But this verse does not say that God's love saves everyone from perishing (i.e., losing one's soul). In fact, it says just the opposite: those who do not give their full allegiance to *His Son* will indeed perish, even though God loves them. God's love does not prevent us from perishing, but provides the only way *not* to perish: one who does not accept God's terms for "eternal life" *remains* in a perishing state of being. But to cite God's love as the only thing necessary for salvation (or as a replacement for our obedience) is to misunderstand

and misrepresent His gospel entirely. God cannot forgive those who reject the only means of their forgiveness—His Son. God cannot welcome into fellowship those who refuse the only One who makes such fellowship possible—His Son.

God is a Benevolent Father, Christ is His Servant Son, and the Holy Spirit is the guiding Reason for spiritual life. Together, these three Personages have literally altered the course of history and all of humanity in order to offer *every single person* an opportunity to be with Them. The blessings that God the Father showers upon us in this life are meant to humble us so that we will look to Him for salvation from our sins, as Paul says (Rom. 2:4–11):

> Or do you think lightly of the riches of His kindness and tolerance and patience, not knowing that the kindness of God leads you to repentance? But because of your stubbornness and unrepentant heart you are storing up wrath for yourself in the day of wrath and revelation of the righteous judgment of God, who will render to each person according to his deeds: to those who by perseverance in doing good seek for glory and honor and immortality, eternal life; but to those who are selfishly ambitious and do not obey the truth, but obey unrighteousness, wrath and indignation. There will be tribulation and distress for every soul of man who does evil, of the Jew first and also of the Greek [i.e., non-Jew], but glory and honor and peace to everyone who does good, to the Jew first and also to the Greek. For there is no partiality with God.

The manifestations of God's love—His kindness, tolerance, and patience—require a proper and obedient response on our part. What is at stake here is not one's preference, rights (real or imagined, civil or otherwise), political correctness, or pride. We are not talking about what religion a person chooses to believe in, what church service he wishes to attend, or what lifestyle he wishes to follow. What is involved here is what one's existence will look like—and *feel* like—once he leaves this life and enters into the eternal afterlife.

Summary Thoughts

Nearly everyone looks forward to going to heaven—whatever they view "heaven" to be. Thankfully, many people *will* go to heaven—that is, they will enter into the afterlife on good terms with God and will spend an eternal existence with Him. But these people did not choose a Savior other than Christ, or a gospel other than His gospel. If they had, they would have perished in their sin rather than enjoy fellowship with the Father. Instead, they believed in Christ, obeyed His gospel, and lived by faith in Him until they left this world.

Our sins made God's grace necessary, and His grace makes possible our salvation. We simply cannot be saved apart from the grace that He provides through the sacrifice of His Son on the cross. There is no end to how much grace He can give—to you personally, and to all people—but this must be on His terms, not yours or mine. God will not give His saving grace to unbelievers (i.e., those who refuse to believe in Him, His Son, *and* His gospel). He will not continue to give grace to Christians who refuse any longer to live *like* Christians (to be discussed later). As salvation is conditional, so grace is conditional. Again, we are not merely talking about the kindness that God shows to all people (Mat. 5:44–45, Luke 6:35) but His divine favor which He bestows only upon those who are properly prepared to receive it (also to be discussed later).

Not everyone will accept this. Some have strong opinions otherwise. Many have been led to believe in a version of "grace" that looks nothing like what is actually described in God's gospel. Some people want to believe Jesus is a mystical "symbol" of salvation for those who do not believe in Him. Certainly, those people are entitled to their opinion, but that is all they have—an opinion, and not divine truth (Mat. 15:9, in principle).

This begs the question: at what point does God's truth yield to human opinion? Or, should His truth *ever* yield to human opinion? Men's opinions may sound convincing to some (and especially to themselves), but they cannot change what heaven has already declared. Jesus made no concession for human opinion—especially, opinions which contradicted His teaching—so why should we? More importantly, why should you? Can a person really think that his personal *expectation* of God's grace, or what He does with it, or who He gives it to, is going to change at all the *truth* of it?

If you—or *any* person—wish to receive God's saving grace, then you must listen to what God says about that grace. Let God define it for you, not preachers, pastors, denominational religion, or people whom you admire (but who do not know the gospel). Remember, it is your soul that is on the line here, not your pride, and not whatever you have chosen to believe until now. What matters—what will *only* matter, and *forever* matter—is what God says, not what people say. One of the wisest men who ever lived said this: "The conclusion, when all has been heard, is: fear God and keep His commandments, **because this applies to every person**" (Eccl. 12:13, emphasis added). Here we are, some 3,000 years later, and yet this conclusion has not changed in the least. Truth never does.

Chapter Five
⟹ *The Biblical Teaching of Grace* ⟸

I am the way, and the truth, and the life;
no one comes to the Father but through Me.
(John 14:6)

Authority is rarely a popular subject in pulpit sermons or adult Bible classes. Many ministers prefer to preach on faith or charity than on the (seemingly) dry subject of authority. But this does not mean authority is unimportant to God. Apart from compliance to His authority, one's identity with Christ is impossible—which means his *salvation* is impossible. Authority is essential in establishing what we say and do in the name of God. In essence, we need *permission* from Him to speak about His gospel. His word comes from heaven, whereas ours originates from ourselves; this is a critical difference. One *must* be followed if we wish to be with God; the other is always expendable. These distinctions can never be made interchangeable.

Nonetheless, many people struggle with the need for biblical, doctrinal authority for determining their spiritual beliefs—including beliefs about saving grace. Suppose we first look at the situation outside of a religious context in hypothetical scenarios:

- As you are standing at counter at your bank waiting for your transaction to be completed, the bank teller pulls out a form having the terms to which you agreed when you established your account. Then she begins to rewrite all those terms and expects you to agree to whatever she comes up with—however unreasonable and unrealistic they are.
- A police officer pulls people over at whim and quizzes them on a number of issues important only to him. Those people whose answers disagree with his own personal views and opinions he arrests and throws into prison; those who do agree, he lets go.
- The municipal government of your city decides to double or even triple the taxes of homeowners whom they have chosen at

random. Those who protest this action are immediately fined and stripped of all property, legal rights, and representation.

• Someone finds the deed to your house, rips it to shreds, has a new deed drawn up, and declares himself the new title holder of your house and property. Then he tells you to get out of "his" house immediately and threatens legal action against you if you refuse to comply.

These fictitious scenarios all describe people who are acting without *authority*. All systems of law, government, and society—even families—exist and survive because of the establishment and recognition of authority. In the absence of legitimate authority, no one has the right to act on behalf of others or control them. It takes law and order to have a government that serves the best interests of its citizens; it takes transcendent (or, above-us-all) authority in order to have law and order. The absence of law and order—and especially, the loss of a benevolent government—leads to anarchy. Anarchy means every man for himself, with no rules except "survival of the fittest."[23] Despite all the romanticized Hollywood movies about a post-apocalyptic world, no one really wants chaos or can survive in a completely chaotic world. Anarchy and chaos would be the end of us all.

Whether or not we realize it, we are constantly submitting to the oversight of local and national governments. These agencies which govern our society are only able to do so because of *authority* we have given (or, entrusted) to them. Ideally, we did this so that our society would function properly. Stable societies require stable government, which (again) necessitates law and order, which requires authority to *make* laws and *keep* order. In the different realms alluded to in my earlier hypothetical examples (banking, civil rights, local government, and legal documentation), we depend upon law and order to protect us. Nobody has the right to mess with our personal monetary accounts; no officer has permission to arbitrarily disregard our civil rights; no one ought to tax us without our representation; and our private property cannot be ripped out of our hands without a fight—or a revolution!

We say "Nobody has the right!" but we are not always able to enforce such rights. We are dependent upon other people or governments to *cooperate* with us in order to protect what we deem is ours. Private banking, private property, civil rights, and freedom from being over-taxed are things we all want to enjoy, but in reality, we rely upon a benevolent man-made government to allow these to happen. We hope and pray that our democratic process, and the laws and regulations that arise from that process to protect our rights as citizens, will save us. This is because what we *want* protected is very important to us.

Doctrine and Grace

If we are so concerned about "doctrines" (laws, rights, etc.) that arise from human authority, then imagine how concerned God is about *His* authority. God's authority is *above* every man, government, principality, universal power, or entity, and only His Son has been given "all authority" to act in His name (Mat. 28:18, Eph. 1:22–23, and Col. 1:15–17). We are very defensive of our limited and temporary authority as men; how defensive do you think God is of His *real* and *absolute* authority?

God's doctrine has not been revealed only to tell us what to believe or how to behave. Ultimately, it has been revealed in order to make us better people, and to draw us deeper into fellowship with Him. His doctrine is not a burden to us but is designed to *improve* us. A stream cannot rise above its source; a shadow cannot declare itself greater than the one who makes it; and we cannot overcome our own limitations *with* our limitations. We cannot improve ourselves while being stuck in our own hopeless demise. This is like a man up to his ears in quicksand talking about what a better husband and father he will be in the future when it is clear he has no future!

However, when we appeal to a *transcendent* truth which has been *given* to us from Someone higher and (in every respect) better than ourselves, then we can rise out of the ashes of our own foolish choices and insuperable limitations to *become* someone we could never be otherwise. To attempt anything less than this will only lead us to self-deception. Depending upon our inferior ability does not change the fact that we *are* inferior to God's revealed truth. "A culture that welcomes its own glaring inconsistencies . . . will inevitably suffocate for lack of spiritual oxygen and find human existence devoid of worth and meaning. It is man who dies, not God, when the truth of truth and the meaning of meaning evaporate."[24]

Any departure from proper biblical authority leads to a perversion of sound doctrine. "Sound" indicates that which is healthy, pure, and whole; anything less than this would be, by contrast, diseased, polluted, and incomplete. Paul, having been personally commissioned by Christ to be His apostle, was very clear about this:

- "In pointing out these things to the brethren, you will be a good servant of Christ Jesus, constantly nourished on the words of the faith and of the sound doctrine which you have been following" (1 Tim. 4:6).
- "If anyone advocates a different doctrine and does not agree with sound words, those of our Lord Jesus Christ, and with the doctrine conforming to godliness, he is conceited and understands nothing; but he has a morbid interest in controversial questions and disputes about words, out of which arise envy, strife, abusive language, evil suspicions, and constant friction between men of depraved mind and deprived of the truth, who suppose that godliness is a means of gain" (1 Tim. 6:3–5).
- "Retain the standard of sound words which you have heard from me, in the faith and love which are in Christ Jesus" (2 Tim. 1:13).
- "For the overseer [elder] must be above reproach as God's steward, . . . holding fast the faithful word which is in accordance with the teaching, so that he will be able both to exhort in sound doctrine and to refute those who contradict" (Titus 1:7, 9).
- "But as for you, speak the things which are fitting for sound doctrine" (Titus 2:1).

Such passages indicate that there is a legitimate *standard* that Christians are to follow. Anyone who refuses to follow that standard contradicts God; anyone claiming to be Christian who refuses to follow that standard contradicts the Christ whom he claims to honor. On the other hand, *everyone* who conforms to this standard will most assuredly find favor with Christ *and* the Father. These, and these alone, will be the recipients of saving grace.

God is not indifferent toward His doctrine, nor should we be. The doctrine which determines our relationship *with* God comes *from* Him. He not only has the legal right to make laws for us to live by, He also has the power to enforce them. Both salvation and condemnation belong to God: "There is only one Lawgiver and Judge, the One who is able to save and destroy" (Jas. 4:12a). People cannot save themselves apart from God, but "because of His great love with which He loved us" (Eph. 2:4) He most certainly can offer a means of salvation. This salvation is the doctrine of heaven, a law of Christ, and a gospel of saving grace.

Grace cannot be reduced to a mere spiritual encounter with God that we enjoy apart from divine truth. Instead, grace is made possible only *because* of this truth. Doctrine—the revealed truth for how sinners are able to have fellowship with God—is what *defines* grace. Grace cannot exist in the absence of doctrine; doctrine is pointless (for sinners) in the absence of a grace that saves us from our sins. For example, when Paul says that "being justified by His grace we might be made heirs according to the hope of eternal life" (Titus 3:7), he is speaking *doctrinally* or *authoritatively*. Or, we might say that he is speaking the truth that God *revealed* to him. Whatever instruction the apostle Paul gives concerning our fellowship with God did not come from Paul, but from heaven. This instruction is not Paul's suggestions for believers, but is what allows believers to know *what* to believe and then how to *act* on that belief.

Grace is not an emotional or even spiritual sensation a person "feels" in his heart. Rather, it is the reality of God's forgiveness and Christ's intercession for sinners. It is everything God does for our salvation that we cannot do ourselves. It is a well-defined, unmistakable, and absolutely necessary aspect of God's plan for our redemption. Saving grace is a doctrinal subject, not a conceptual or emotional one. You may *feel* good because of the effect of God's grace on your soul—this is expected and appropriate!—but it is sinful to reduce grace to a mere feeling or religious sentiment.

Defining "Doctrine"

We have been talking a lot about "doctrine" so far, and it is time to define it more directly. Doctrine, in the context of Christ's gospel, is whatever God requires of the believer in order for that person to live in agreement with Him. Jesus said, "If you continue in My word, then you are truly disciples of Mine; and you will know the truth, and the truth will make you free" (John 8:31–32). This is a conditional statement: unless and until the condition is met ("continue in My word"), the promise ("you will know the truth, and . . . free") will not be fulfilled. This is also a sequential statement: continuing in Jesus' word is what *creates* His disciples; the living experience of our discipleship to Him is what deepens our knowledge of His truth; and *all* of this leads to our freedom from condemnation. No one can mess with the order of this instruction, or omit any part of it, without compromising the entire promise.

Jesus' "word" refers to those essential teachings that both establish and maintain one's fellowship with God. His "word" is what defines heavenly truth, and it is only *this* truth—not yours, mine, or anyone else's—that will "make you free." The word that sanctifies us (or, makes us holy through our obedience to it—John 17:17) is also the doctrine that defines us as Christians. Apart from Jesus' words, whether spoken by Him or through His chosen apostles, we cannot have fellowship with His Father (John 15:5). Thus, we can refer to God's word as the doctrine of salvation: by following it, we will know what is true, and this truth leads us straight to God; by rejecting it (or even parts of it), we also reject His truth, and thus we forfeit our fellowship with Him.

There are three aspects of the doctrine of salvation to consider. First, doctrine needs to be properly **defined**. This is God's job, not yours, mine, or ours. We read and obey *what* He has defined; we do not tell Him how *we* have defined (or interpreted) what we have read. This is also true for saving grace: we let *God* tell us what this is and how it works; we do not tell *Him* these things (1 Cor. 14:37–38).

Second, doctrine must be **taught**. It is not something to be left in the pages of a Bible, but is to be accurately communicated to all those who are in need of it (sinners), and especially to those who are already in a covenant relationship with God (Christians) (2 Thess. 2:15, 2 Tim. 2:2). Third, doctrine must be **practiced**. It is not enough to merely know that God's word/truth exists, or even what it says; one who is saved by the truth must also *live* by the truth (Phil. 4:9, Col. 2:6–7).

"Doctrine" often refers to the teachings of God in general (as used in Mat. 15:9, Acts 2:42, and 5:42). (Paul also uses "pattern" or "traditions" to mean this, as in 1 Cor. 11:2, Phil. 3:17, 2 Thess. 2:15, and 3:6.) Teaching in the name of Jesus (as in Acts 5:28) means to teach what is necessary to be in fellowship with Him, which is the same as what is necessary to be in fellowship with the Father. Being in fellowship with Christ is equivalent to being "saved," since no one can be saved unless he has such fellowship, and everyone who *is* saved *does* have this fellowship.[25] When someone asks, "What must I do to be saved?" (Acts 16:30), we must not offer him our opinions, feelings, traditions, or even personal experiences; rather, we must provide him with the doctrine of salvation that necessarily leads a person to fellowship with Christ. This is what it means to "preach Jesus" to someone (as in Acts 8:35).

God's general doctrine of salvation can also be made more specific, as when defining or explaining a specific topic *within* His doctrine, such as justice, mercy, or grace. The doctrine of justification by faith, for example, occupies the first eleven chapters of Romans. (This tells us how *important* this particular doctrine is, and thus the attention we should give to it.) The doctrine of baptism (i.e., immersion in water for the purpose of becoming a Christian) is scattered throughout the entire New Testament.[26] It is my firm conviction that the reason why God seldom gave us concentrations of specific teachings on salvation is because He wanted us to discover these things through study and investigation rather than simply opening up to a certain "list" on a certain page in His word.

Not all doctrinal requirements have to do with specific actions (like repentance) or reactions (like forgiveness of those who sin against us). For example, loving one's fellow brother or sister in Christ is *doctrine,* because one cannot claim to love God and hate the one who has fellowship with Him (1 John 2:11, 4:20). Thus, to love the brethren is *essential* to one's relationship with God (John 13:34–35). We could say the same thing about showing deference (Phil. 2:3–4), showing mercy (Jas. 2:12–13), or withholding judgment (Jas. 4:11–12). While non-specific in nature—i.e., there is not a specific action spelled out for every conceivable circumstance—they are certainly *required* of every person who lives "under grace" (Rom. 6:14). These are not optional for anyone who wishes to become a Christian.

God's truth, as revealed from heaven (Gal. 1:11–12), serves as the doctrinal teaching of salvation. We are not saved just because truth has been revealed, but only when we listen to that truth and rightly act upon it (Mat. 7:24–25, in principle). "Truth," like the doctrine of salvation itself, has certain necessary attributes. Truth is:

- **Timeless.** God's truth—and thus, His gospel of saving grace—does not age, expire, or become outdated over time. It is *always* true and will *never* become irrelevant. Many today think that God's gospel is unable to cope with the Modern Age, but human nature has not changed, the problem of sin has not changed (and needs to be addressed in the same way as in Paul's day), and the gospel of grace is as needed as ever. Just as God Himself does not age or diminish in power, so the "word of the cross" (i.e., the message of salvation through Christ's sacrifice) has not diminished in the least (1 Cor. 1:18).

- **Changeless.** God is the great Constant in the universe; His gospel forever remains the unchangeable message of salvation. Paul laid a strong curse on anyone who would dare alter it; even angels are forbidden to do so (Gal. 1:6–9). Whatever the Holy Spirit revealed through Christ's apostles still applies today (2 Pet. 3:1–2). Time, culture, technology, moral (and gender) confusion, indifference, apathy, etc., cannot modify the "eternal purpose" of God (Eph. 3:11). The limited, short-sighted, and inferior authority of human beings cannot change the supernatural decrees of heaven.

- **Universal.** The gospel of Christ saves all men the same way: by God's divine grace, through obedient human faith (Eph. 2:8). Just as we have all fallen short of God's glory (or, holy nature), so we are all in need of His gospel (Rom. 3:23). Just as we all share the same problem (sin), so we are all in need of the same solution (saving grace). God has one gospel to serve all people who choose to abide by it. For those who refuse this one gospel, there is no other recourse, since "there is salvation in no one else [but Christ]; for there is no other name under heaven that has been given among men by which we must be saved" (Acts 4:12, bracketed words added).

- **Impartial.** God's doctrine does not show favoritism toward one person (or group of people) over another; Christ died "for all," not just for a few (Rom. 6:10, 2 Cor. 5:14–15, 1 Tim. 2:5–6, et al). Every person who seeks God will find Him; "Whoever believes in Him will not be disappointed" (Rom. 10:11). (On the subject [and misunderstandings] of "predestination," in which some assume that God *does* favor some over others, see the chapter titled "Calvinism and Christianity.")

- **Singular in nature.** The doctrine which defines man's fellowship with God has only one possible conclusion for each aspect of that relationship. His doctrine cannot contradict itself and therefore can only produce a *singular, inescapable conclusion.* Any biblical passage for which two or more correct conclusions can logically exist at the same time *cannot* be binding upon all men. Such a passage may be applied in principle (as in 2 Cor. 13:12) or may affect someone personally (as in 1 Cor. 7:25–28), but it is not a matter of salvation. This is where we separate *general* teachings from *essential* doctrine.

Two Categories of Doctrine

Doctrine—Christ's words, apostolic teaching, "the message of truth, the gospel of your salvation" (Eph. 1:13)—can also be applied in two basic categories. The first category can be identified as ***what*** *is necessary in order to establish fellowship with God.* The second category can be identified as *what is necessary in order to maintain one's fellowship with God.* To more fully appreciate all this, we must say something about entering into a *covenant relationship* with Him, but we will save this for the next chapter ("The Access to Saving Grace"), since it is *through* covenant and *because* of covenant that we have access to God's grace.

For now, it is important to appreciate the fact that there are terms and conditions for coming into the context (i.e., a covenant relationship) in which grace is found. Just as someone cannot force his way into heaven, so he cannot receive saving grace without God's consent. Just because one *calls* himself a Christian [lit., Christ-follower] does not mean he is automatically "in Christ"—a phrase used frequently in the New Testament to refer to a covenant with God. A covenant relationship with God *through* Christ must be established in order for grace to be imparted. This is important not only theologically, but practically: if grace is only *found* in Christ, then one must *be* in Christ to receive it. No one who is outside of Christ—i.e., who does not have a relationship with God—will receive divine grace.

Doctrine provides the terms necessary for fellowship with God, which are spelled out in His gospel. (We will cite these in the next chapter.) Fellowship and grace go hand-in-hand: a person either has them both simultaneously, or he does not have them at all. For example, the apostle Paul often opens and/or closes his letters with "Grace to you and peace from God our Father and the Lord Jesus Christ" (Eph. 1:2). Paul wrote to Christians; he could not have said such things to those who remained unsaved. Grace is not possible outside of an established fellowship with God *through* Christ, which is to say, outside of a covenant relationship. Peace works the same way: no one can be at peace with God without being justified (or, made legally innocent) before God (Rom. 5:1–2). Peace is the *result* of a fellowship that has been established with God; peace cannot exist in the *absence* of this. If one wishes to have grace and peace with God, he must be a Christian in the truest sense of the word.

In Eph. 4:1–3, Paul stressed the need to "[be] diligent to preserve the unity of the Spirit in the bond of peace." This is required of covenant-keeping people, and it is impossible for those *not* in covenant with God to do this. Those outside of covenant have neither unity nor peace with God, since they remain "hostile" to Him and "cannot please" Him (Rom. 8:6–8). The only way for anyone to be at peace with God is to be saved by the *grace* of God. Such people *had* to have agreed to doctrinal truths necessary for this grace (Eph. 4:4–6). One who does not agree with these truths cannot enter into a covenant relationship with God, since He will not give His grace to one who is defiant, disobedient, or insubordinate. Whatever He says is necessary in order to have fellowship with Him *must be done*, or the gift of grace (and all that it implies) will be withheld.

The point is: saving grace does not just "happen" to you when you walk into a church building, feel close to God, or tearfully beg Him for forgiveness. Grace is *given* to you when you comply with the terms laid down by God Himself. As the owner of grace and salvation, He has the right to require these. You are not *paying* for grace when you do comply with these terms; rather, you are *preparing* yourself to be a committed and responsible recipient of something priceless and incomprehensibly important. This is analogous to the EULA (end-user license agreement) that you must "accept" before opening and using virtually any new software program. You have to agree to the software company's terms and conditions before you can use their product. If you refuse to "accept," then you are denied access to their program. Similarly, if you refuse to accept God's doctrine—which implies your belief in and obedience to whatever He says—then you will be denied access to His saving grace.

Continuing in a Relationship with God

The second aspect of doctrine is inseparably related to the first, but serves a different purpose. The first aspect—one's initial entrance into covenant with God—is required to establish the relationship. The second aspect—*one's continued observance of the covenant terms*—is required to maintain the relationship indefinitely. This concerns what is expected of the believer (i.e., the covenant participant) in order live in agreement with God. Entering into a relationship is one thing; continuing on *faithfully* through the course of that relationship is another. We can illustrate this with a marriage vow/covenant scenario: anyone can stand at the altar and profess his (or her) desire to enter into a covenant relationship with his wife (or husband). Yet, to remain *faithful* to that relationship throughout the course of his entire life takes the concept to another level. The first question one asks is, "How do I get into this marriage relationship—what terms must I agree to?" The second question is, "Now that I'm in this relationship, what is required of me to uphold my part of this marriage covenant?"

So it is with our covenantal relationship with God. First, His doctrine dictates what is necessary in order to begin a relationship with Him; second, His doctrine describes what is necessary to uphold our part of the agreement. Thus, doctrine not only defines what the relationship is, it also defines how it is to continue. There are several passages in the New Testament to consider with respect to this:

- Jesus' so-called "sermon on the mount" (Mat. 5 – 7) offers a broad perspective of how those in covenant with God are supposed to live. Granted, Jesus' words are directed at Jews (not Christians) who live under the Law of Moses (not the gospel that Paul preached). Nonetheless, the spiritual and moral *principles* set forth in that grand sermon dictate the kind of heart, attitude, and allegiance required of all those who wish to walk with God. Thus, Jesus provides a prescription for life (or, a code of morality and ethics) for all those in covenant with God. All salvation covenants between God and men contain moral expectations of its participants. Morality refers to whatever is consistent with the nature and conduct of God. ("Righteousness" or "godliness" is an appropriate synonym for morality.) What is legally required (as, say, a ritual or specific action) in order to enter into a covenant with God may change as covenants change, but morality *never* changes.[27]
- In the practical application section of his letter to the Romans (12:1—15:13), Paul provides a template of how the believer is to

function in his covenant relationship with God. In that passage is a great emphasis concerning one's proper behavior toward his fellow brother or sister in Christ. One's participation in covenant with God does not exist in a vacuum, separate and apart from interacting with and demonstrating godly love toward fellow believers. Paul does not offer mere suggestions for covenant participants, but doctrinal teachings. To refuse these instructions is to disobey doctrine, which leads to the forfeiture of grace.

- In several of Paul's letters are entire chapters devoted to describing one's life in a covenant relationship with God (e.g., Gal. 5:1—6:10, Eph. 4:20—6:20, Col. 3—4, et al). Again, Paul defines how those who "walk in a manner worthy of the Lord" (Col. 1:10) are to live, since God does not leave this "walk" for you or me to define. His instructions provide moral, ethical, and theological truths specifically designed to keep the believer on the narrow path that leads to life. Such conduct is not limited to one's personal relationship with God, but also necessarily involves one's regard for and treatment of fellow believers—and, in some cases, even non-believers.

- The entire First Epistle of John (1 John) is devoted to defining the believer's walk with Christ, which is synonymous with living faithfully in covenant with God. For example, John wrote, "If we say that we have fellowship with Him and yet walk in the darkness, we lie and do not practice the truth" (1:6). We could reword this as follows, without doing any injustice to the meaning of the passage: "If we say we are abiding by God's covenant with us but choose to live like one who is not in that covenant, we defy both His doctrine *and* His covenant." Or, consider 2:6: "The one who says he abides in Him ought himself to walk in the same manner as He walked." One who has established a covenant with God but later refuses to "walk" in agreement with Christ violates that covenant and thus jeopardizes his salvation. Saving grace is dependent upon a functional, viable covenant standing; it will be denied to one who refuses to participate in that covenant. If grace is necessary for every time we sin (1 John 1:7, 9, 2:1–2), then the covenant in which grace is found needs to be continually honored and upheld.

All said, one's relationship with God requires a legitimate beginning point *and* needs to be properly maintained. Once it has begun, we cannot assume that it will remain intact without continued attention and effort on the part of the covenant participant.

Grace Does Not Work without Faith

As necessary and wonderful as it is, saving grace does not work on its own. In rescuing souls from sin, *God* does not work on His own. His work is immeasurably greater in power, scope, and endurance than ours, but human faith is also a necessary component of salvation. God's grace may be the size of Jupiter and human faith the size of a grape in comparison, but both must come together in order to bring about a "new creation" in Christ (2 Cor. 5:17).

Likewise, just as revealed doctrine defines what saving grace is and how it works, doctrine also defines what human faith must look like and how it is supposed to work. God does not let you define what grace is and what it does, but neither does He let you define what faith is and how you are to live by it. Both of these subjects—grace *and* faith—are essential to salvation, but are also grossly misunderstood in the religious world. Many people choose to define grace beyond or even independent of how God's doctrine has defined it; many do the same thing with faith. It is popular in so-called "mainstream [or, progressive] Christianity" to speak of grace *and* faith guided by human emotions rather than defined by Scripture.

"Faith" refers to an act of human will that is exercised in the absence of full vision, full experience, and full understanding. It is "the assurance of things hoped for" but not immediately received (Heb. 11:1). Abraham was promised by God that his posterity would inherit the land of Canaan, and that his descendants would be innumerable, yet he died before he ever saw either of these happen. Even so, he acted in faith toward God—he "believed" in God—knowing these things *would* happen (Gen. 15:5–7; see Heb. 11:13–16). In Abraham's heart, these promises were sure to be fulfilled; in God's heart, they were already fulfilled the moment He spoke them.

"Faith" is also "the conviction of things not seen" (Heb. 11:1). This does not mean that we are to believe blindly, for blind faith is the religion of fools. Rather, He has provided all the evidence that is necessary to put our faith in His ability to perform. Abraham had not seen everything God was capable of doing—he died long before He rescued Israel from Egypt, for example—but he believed that God was capable of doing what was humanly impossible. If Abraham was promised a son in his old age with his old and barren wife, then he believed it would happen (Rom. 4:16–22). If Abraham was commanded by God to *kill* that son of promise, then he believed that God would, if necessary, resurrect him from the dead (Gen. 22:1–18; see Heb. 11:17–19).

"And without faith it is impossible to please Him, for he who comes to God must believe that He is and that He is a rewarder of those who seek Him" (Heb. 11:6). This speaks of a faith *like* Abraham's, since he is regarded as the father of the faithful (Gal. 3:6–9). When we demonstrate our obedience to God even though we do not see all that He sees, know all that He knows, or do all that He does, *that is faith*. And, when we demonstrate our obedience to God even though we may never see how everything He asks of us will play out in this life, *that is faith*. Even though "we walk by faith, not by sight" (2 Cor. 5:7), we do not walk blindly. We believe that *God* can see everything, and He is leading us based upon what *He* sees and knows rather than us forging our own path. We choose Him, in essence, to be our "eyes" into the future.

"The righteous man shall live by faith" (Rom. 1:17b), but God has always told men what He wants them to do in order to be pleasing to Him. If a person *does* what God says to do, then whatever is done is an act of faith. If a person does *not* do what God says, then his refusal is an act of unbelief. Those who obey God are faithful to Him; those who do not obey God demonstrate a lack of faith in Him. "But to this one I will look," God says, "to him who is humble and contrite of spirit, and who trembles at [i.e., shows reverence toward] My word" (Isa. 66:2b, bracketed words added). Or, we could say, God wants people to be *faithful* to Him; "for such people the Father seeks to be

His worshipers" (John 4:23b). But He never says, "Just be faithful!" without also providing criteria for what He means by this.

Jesus epitomized what it meant to be faithful to God.[28] God the Father told Him what needed to be done, and God the Son willfully, obediently, and gladly did all of it (John 8:29, 17:4, and Heb. 5:8–9). To be faithful, then, is to do the will of the Father—whatever that will requires of us (Mat. 7:21). The only way to *know* the will of the Father is to read what He recorded for us in His gospel, because we cannot know anything for certain about Him *or* His will unless He had revealed it to us (Rom. 12:2, Eph. 5:17, Col. 1:9, 2 Pet. 3:1–2, et al). The many miracles performed by Jesus and His apostles provide the necessary proofs *for* such belief (Heb. 2:3–4). In fact, all the things that have been written and recorded have been preserved so that you *will* believe (John 20:31). The demonstration of that belief is what faith in Him is all about. Faith in God means doing what He said simply because He, having given us every reason to believe in Him and His power, said it.

God does not give saving grace to anyone who refuses to provide Him with obedient faith. In fact, God *cannot* give grace to such people. His entire system of salvation by grace is *through* faith (Eph. 2:8), and does not and cannot function in the absence of it. God does not impart His grace to people "anyway"—i.e., if someone refuses to put faith in Him, He will not go ahead and forgive them *anyway*, help them *anyway*, or save them *anyway*. If He did, then He is not a God of His word, since His *written* word says that there are conditions to receiving grace. If He had said, "Faith is required—unless, of course, you don't *want* to have faith, in which case I will save you anyway," this makes the entire New Testament contradictory and pointless. If the righteous man "lives" by (or, is saved because of) his faith in God, then a person could never be righteous who did *not* live by faith. Faithless, unbelieving, and disobedient people simply will not be saved. Grace can cover billions of sins of a billion sinners, but it will not be given to a single soul that refuses to let God *be* God.

Grace is not on the periphery of our relationship with God; it is at the very core of that relationship. But faith is also at the core of our relationship with Him. These two things—grace and faith—must exist together, function together, and remain together. Take away human faith, and divine grace ceases to be applied; take away divine grace, and the soul dies. The same God who defines saving grace also defines obedient faith. If you believe in God in the way that He expects (because of what He has told you in His word), then you will most certainly be saved by His grace. But if you opt for a customized version of "faith" that seems right in your own eyes but is not what God has asked for, then you have no good reason to believe that you can expect anything from the Lord (cf. Jas. 1:5–8).

Paul puts all of this together for us in Rom. 5:1–2: "Therefore, having been justified by faith, we have peace with God through our Lord Jesus Christ, through whom also we have obtained our introduction by faith into this grace in which we stand; and we exult in hope of the glory of God." To be "justified by faith" means to be made innocent in God's sight *because* (and only *if*) we have made God's will our own. "Justification" is a legal term indicating an exoneration from condemnation because the judicial cost for our crimes has been paid elsewhere—in this case, in Christ's death on the cross ("through our Lord Jesus Christ"; see Col. 1:19–23).

Before we were justified by faith, we were helpless, ungodly, sinners, and enemies of God (Rom. 5:6–10). Once we are justified, we "have peace with God" because we "stand" before Him as innocent souls. Our innocence did not come through our own good works of faith, but through the sacrifice of Christ: His blood takes away our sins. However, even though our works of faith do not save us in themselves, they are necessary *for* our salvation. These works of faith (i.e., our obedience to God's commandments; see 1 John 5:2–3) are proof positive that we really do believe in God, trust His ability to perform, and entrust our souls to His care. Just as God had to prove His love to us by sending His Son (John 3:16, 1 John 4:9–10), so we must prove our love to Him by doing what He says and living in agreement with the terms of His covenant.

We cannot be "justified by faith" apart from grace, but neither can we receive grace without faith. There is no "peace with God" without grace, but (again) there is no grace without faith. We cannot "obtain our introduction by faith," "stand" before God, or even "exult in hope" without grace; but faith is essential in preparing ourselves to receive this grace in the first place. Take grace out of the picture and there is no salvation; take faith out of the picture and there is no picture.

Summary Thoughts

God does not recognize any doctrine but *His*. Thus, God does not recognize any faith but that which *He* defines in *His* word. And, God will not impart saving grace for any reason or under any circumstance other than what *He* has already stated in His word. Man-made, denominational doctrines are no substitute for the gospel of Christ as preached by His apostles. Human emotions or opinions are no substitute for obedient faith. No matter how desperately one desires God's saving grace, it will be withheld from him unless and until he humbly, sincerely, and obediently complies with what God requires of him. And, in the context of salvation, what God requires of one person will be no different than what He requires of *all* people.

You should never mistake spiritual fervor, passionate convictions, or good intentions for obedient faith. While your faith ought to be fervent, passionate, and good, these are not interchangeable for what is being asked of you. God is not as lenient about faith, grace, or religion as so many people think He is. Read His word for yourself to see this. Christ would not have given His life—especially on a cross—for something that could be legally modified by one's personal feeling or interpretation.

Saving grace is God's answer to your sinful dilemma. But He is the One who provided this answer, not you or me, and *we* should never forget this. His grace—as with all of His doctrines of salvation—is not open for critique, review, or negotiation. His gospel is permanent, unchangeable, and irrefutable. Instead of looking for ways to customize it, we ought to be extremely glad that it is solid and unshakable. As is His doctrine, so is His grace: it will never fail us.

We have covered some difficult ground so far—thank you for staying the course. This had to be done, however. Before we can talk about all the benefits that grace provides, we need to know for certain that it is real, legitimate, and founded upon divine truth. You should trust your soul to nothing less.

Chapter Six
⟹ *The Access to Saving Grace* ⟸

For you are all sons of God through faith in Christ Jesus.
For all of you who were baptized into Christ have clothed yourselves
with Christ. There is neither Jew nor Greek, there is neither
slave nor free man, there is neither male nor female; for you are
all one in Christ Jesus. And if you belong to Christ, then you are
Abraham's offspring, heirs according to promise.
(Gal. 3:26–29)

Immediately after the September 11, 2001, terrorist attacks on the World Trade Center and the Pentagon, the military base just outside of Anchorage, Alaska (where I lived at the time), sealed off all its gates from any non-military entry. Prior to this, if my family wanted to join our military friends for an evening or enjoy the base's huge park, it really was no trouble at all. Our friends simply sponsored us at the gate, we acquired a day pass from the MPs, and we were free to travel on base as needed.

Things changed after the so-called 9/11 attacks. It became necessary to present military identification to get on base. As a civilian, I could no longer get past the gate to see our friends, access military facilities, or even visit someone for a Bible study. On the surface, this seemed rather unfair—after all, I am not a terrorist! I am a law-abiding citizen who pays his taxes and looks out for the well-being of his fellow man. The very concept of terrorism is repulsive to me, especially that which is done in the name of religion. So, I might consider it offensive that the military suddenly prohibited my presence on its base(s) simply because of some fanatical terrorists thousands of miles away. Suddenly I was denied access just because I did not have a certain ID card or a little sticker on the windshield of my car. Outrageous!

Well, not really. This is not just about terrorists and ID cards and little stickers. It is about identifying those who *belong* within a certain

place and excluding those who do *not*. I do not really belong on a
military base due to the simple fact that I am not in the military. Since
the military owns the base, it has the authority to determine who will
be permitted access to it and who will be denied access. Since I am
not part of the military community, I am not privileged to enjoy the
benefits of that community. This makes sense, and it is all perfectly
legitimate.

In like manner, if one is a part of God's community, then he has
access to God. If he is *not* a member of God's community, then he
does not. The "community" here refers of course to Christ's church—
not to a physical congregation but to the spiritual body of believers
that belongs to Him, that is, "His body" (Eph. 1:22–23). One is called
or invited into His church through the gospel (2 Thess. 2:14) and is
inducted into His church by divine grace *in response to* prescribed
demonstrations of faith. Once a person is accepted by Christ, he
enjoys a special and very personal identity *with* Him and nothing
in the world can take this away from him. "The firm foundation of
God stands, having this seal, 'The Lord knows those who are His,'
and, 'Everyone who names the name of the Lord is to abstain from
wickedness'" (2 Tim. 2:19). Thus, those who belong to Christ are
known by Him *and* they reciprocate this great honor through holy
behavior.

Paul told the Christians at Philippi in ancient Macedonia, "Our
citizenship is in heaven, from which also we eagerly wait for a Savior,
the Lord Jesus Christ" (Phil. 3:20). Those Christians no doubt
appreciated the analogy, for they understood the importance of
citizenship. Philippi was a Roman colony and many retired soldiers
and military officers lived there. These were Roman citizens, even
though they lived far from Rome itself. Their citizenship with Rome
allowed them access to the rights and privileges that *all* Roman
citizens enjoyed even though they lived among those who were
without Roman citizenship. These latter people could not enjoy these
same privileges; they benefited from Rome's general oversight, but
they had no special status otherwise. They were mere subjects, not
honored citizens.

Similarly, we all live in God's world, and we all share common ground as far as our humanity is concerned. But some of us enjoy a spiritual relationship with the One who owns this world that others do not. (If taken out of context, this could sound pompous and condescending, but it is true nonetheless.) Like Roman citizens scattered throughout the Empire who had a greater status than its general inhabitants, so those who are "in Christ" enjoy a special citizenship that many of our fellow human beings do not. This, not because we are better than they are, but because of the different *choices* we have made when presented with the same opportunities they have had. We are not bragging, then, when we say "our citizenship is in heaven." Rather, we are recognizing the reality of our situation according to God's word and the genuineness of our individual faith.

With this special, spiritual status, we who are "in Christ" have *access* to God that others do not. This does not mean others *cannot* have such access, as though they were prevented from it. Rather, we have already accepted the conditions which govern such access to God and therefore He has granted us this great privilege. Those who have as yet refused these terms (for any reason) do not have this same access. Even if a person *wants* such access, he must have God's approval to draw near to Him. No one can come to the Father except through the Son (John 14:6).

Grace Is Received Only "In Christ"

One who is outside of Christ (i.e., not a Christian) cannot enjoy the saving grace of God. One who *is* "in Christ," however, has access to all the spiritual blessings of heaven (Eph. 1:3). Certainly, God wants all people to be saved (1 Tim. 2:3–4), but salvation must be on His terms. He is, after all, the only source *of* salvation. This is not true only because I believe it; this is true *regardless* of what I believe. This is a doctrinal teaching that comes straight out of God's word, which is always true no matter who believes it.

"In Christ" is not equivalent with "in church" or "in religion" or even "being spiritual." One can be in a church building or involved in a so-called Christian religion without being "in Christ." One can be extremely spiritual-minded or filled with religious conviction and still not be "in Christ." One can say prayers and read the Bible and still not be "in Christ." "In Christ"—a phrase, in one form or another, used prolifically throughout the New Testament—always means *in fellowship with God the Father through Christ the Son*. Belonging to a church family can be a good and rewarding experience, but it does not compensate for having established a relationship with God on His terms. "In Christ" has no reference to church buildings or religious services; it has everything to do with the access to saving grace and, thus, salvation.

For example, consider how the following passages use the phrase "in Christ" (emphases are all mine) and the necessary implications to grace:

- "Therefore if anyone is **in Christ**, he is a new creature; the old things passed away; behold, new things have come" (2 Cor. 5:17). What if someone is *not* "in Christ" but thinks he has a relationship with God anyway? Paul said that he is *not* a "new creature," "new things" have *not* come, and he is still of the "old things" (i.e., of the world), and is still in his sins (John 8:24). One cannot be saved by grace if he has no access to it.

- "Even so consider yourselves to be dead to sin, but alive to God **in Christ Jesus**" (Rom. 6:11). Can one be alive to God *apart* from Christ? Being "dead to sin" is the equivalent of being "alive to God in Christ." Thus, one cannot *be* "dead to sin" if he is *not* "alive to God in Christ." And if one is not dead to sin, then he *lives* in sin— i.e., he remains a sinner. Saving grace will not be given to those who choose to remain in sin.

- "In Christ" means *in God's spiritual family*. Those who are "in Christ" enjoy spiritual benefits; those who are outside of Christ do not. Several passages bring this to light:

  - "[We] are fellow heirs and fellow members of the body, and fellow partakers of the promise **in Christ Jesus** through the gospel" (Eph. 3:6). "In Christ" brings us into fellowship with a great company of people who are also in fellowship with God. This is made possible "through the gospel" of Christ. No other gospel (or, doctrine) provides for this; no saving grace is possible through any *other* gospel.

▫ "[W]e, who are many, are one body **in Christ**, and individually members one of another" (Rom. 12:5). God only recognizes one "body" (church), that of His Son (Eph. 1:22–23). All other "bodies," though they may be religious and spiritual in nature, are not recognized by Him. But those who are "in Christ" enjoy the saving grace that being in that relationship provides.

▫ Paul wrote to "the church of God which is at Corinth, to those who have been sanctified **in Christ Jesus,** saints by calling, with all who in every place call on the name of our Lord Jesus Christ, their Lord and ours" (1 Cor. 1:2). The gospel allows for no other way for a person to be "sanctified" (i.e., set apart for God; made holy) apart from being "in Christ." The only way a person can be sanctified is to be saved by grace through faith; the gospel of grace offers no alternatives to this.

• One who is "in Christ" receives special citizenship privileges:
   ▫ Redemption of his soul (Rom. 3:24).
   ▫ Forgiveness of his sins (Eph. 4:32).
   ▫ The pledge [lit., down payment] of the Holy Spirit (2 Cor. 1:22).
   ▫ Triumph through Christ (2 Cor. 2:14) who has already overcome the world (John 16:33).

• Finally, "God will supply all your needs according to His riches in glory **in Christ Jesus**" (Phil. 4:19). Whenever Scripture talks about what God supplies that we cannot acquire on our own, it is speaking of *grace*. God will *not* supply spiritual help to anyone who refuses the *source* of that help—the One who has made such grace possible. But to whomever surrenders his heart to God and trusts in His ability to save, God will supply *everything* he needs for fellowship with Him.

⌐

Access to saving grace is "in Christ." If one is not "in Christ," then he will not receive saving grace. If he *is* "in Christ," it is only because he agreed to covenantal terms in order to establish a relationship with Him. (Remember, he could not come to God on his own, since he was a sinner who had *zero recourse* but to plead for divine mercy and grace.) Furthermore, if he *is* "in Christ," then he is required to continue to honor those terms and be "faithful until death" (Rev. 2:10).

To further illustrate the situation, consider the following analogy. The state of Alaska has an investment portfolio it calls a "Permanent Fund." This fund was created out of oil revenue from the 1970s but has grown through stock investments to a rather significant sum (billions of dollars). Once you are a resident of Alaska for one year, you become eligible to receive an annual dividend from this account for the following year. If you are *not* a resident of Alaska, then you have no access to that money. A person from Oregon, for example, may earnestly desire to receive such a dividend, but if he is a resident of Oregon and not of Alaska, he is simply not entitled. A person from California may think he is an Alaska resident, and may even act like one (whatever *that* means), and may tell all his friends and family that he is one, but the fact remains that he is *not* an Alaskan and therefore has no right to those dividends. Still another person from Utah may have once been an Alaska resident, during which time he collected a dividend from the Permanent Fund, but having renounced his Alaska citizenship and taken up residence elsewhere, he has also forfeited his participation in receiving a dividend.

In my simple illustration, "Alaska" represents Christ, while "dividend" represents grace. One who earnestly desires to receive God's grace cannot do so without being "in Christ." Another person may *think* he is in Christ (or, a Christian)—and may get everyone else to think he is, too—but unless he is *in fact* in Christ according to God's terms, he will receive no grace for his sins. Still another person may have once received God's grace, but because he has since renounced his allegiance to Christ and has slipped back into the world, he is no longer a recipient of God's grace (2 Pet. 2:20–22). Now, the actual state of Alaska can be (and has been) deceived by those who are not citizens yet portrayed themselves as such, and those people will receive a dividend check fraudulently. But you can rest assured that no one will deceive the Lord, and He will not be fooled by anyone who poses as a true believer when he is not. People can be mocked with deception, but not God (Gal. 6:7).

"In Christ" Means Being in Covenant with God

Before we sinned against God, we were innocent.[29] Law existed, but we did not understand it—and we had not yet "died" because of it (Rom. 7:7–12). Sin was in the world, but we had not yet partaken of it because we were unable to commit sin in *willful defiance* against God. *We* were in the world, but we were not yet old enough or mature enough to be personally responsible to Him. We were responsible only to our parents and/or to those who exercised earthly authority over us.

At some point, we sinned against God on our own cognizance, by our own will, and through our own act of defiance (however subtle it may have seemed to us at the time). Once this act was committed, we fell from our innocence and severed our relationship with Him (Rom. 3:23). In the process, we made sin our master and made ourselves enemies of God (Rom. 5:10, 8:6–8, Jas. 4:4, et al). We could not re-establish our fellowship with God because He cannot have communion with sinners. Something had to be done *about* our sins in order for us to be reconciled to Him, but the problem was beyond our ability to solve.[30]

God's solution for re-establishing fellowship with those who have sinned against Him is through *covenant*. "Covenant" is, in its most basic sense, a binding agreement between two or more parties. In some cases, it is simply a promise one makes to another; this is called a one-sided covenant. An example of this is God's covenant to Noah and all of humankind that He would never again flood the earth with water (Gen. 9:8–17). Such a covenant does not expect anything of the one to whom the promise is given; the promise itself is the covenant, and it is offered without conditions.

In most cases, however, covenants are made between two parties. Sometimes these parties are equals, as in the case of a marriage covenant between a groom and his bride. Both parties are human beings; one is not superior or inferior to the other; both enter into a covenant agreement as equals, but the covenant itself creates an "us"—a sacred union—that did not exist prior to that agreement. People do not have to be married, however, to enter into a covenantal union. David's covenant with Jonathan is an illustration of what might be called a covenant of friendship, in which both parties considered themselves as equals (1 Sam. 18:3).

In other cases, a covenant is made between one *higher* in authority (such as a king) to one *lower* in authority (such as a subject of the king). The king, having the upper hand in every respect, offers terms and conditions of this covenant; the subject has the option either to agree to those terms or reject them. There is no negotiation because the two parties are not equal in status, authority, and power. The king offers his subject something that that person could not have on his own, in order to benefit him somehow (1 Kings 2:36–38, for example).

This is what happens when God comes to us (through His gospel) with an offer of salvation. He is infinitely greater than us in status, authority, and power; we are helpless to receive what He offers us apart from the kindness He extends to us. We cannot negotiate the terms of covenant (as in, "I like *this* term, but I refuse to honor *that* one") because we are in no position to do so. We are doomed sinners; we cannot survive without accepting His offer. He, on the other hand, does not depend upon us for His survival. While He *does* want something out of the agreement—our fellowship—He does not *need* this in order to be God.

We become most familiar with this kind of covenant largely through our study of the Old Testament. ("Testament" is often synonymous with and necessarily implies "covenant.") God brought the Israelites to Mt. Sinai in order to give them an opportunity to enter into a covenant relationship with Him (Exod. 19 – 24). He spelled out the basic covenant terms and conditions to Moses on the mountain, then Moses (as a mediator) repeated this information to the elders of Israel for their consent or rejection. As it turned out, they agreed to it, "and they said, 'All that the LORD has spoken we will do, and we will be obedient!'" (Exod. 24:7). Thus, they entered into covenant with God on His terms, requiring them to do whatever was necessary in order for that covenant relationship to exist *and* continue.

In the New Testament, Jesus serves as the mediator of a *new* covenant. This was not the same covenant as what Israel had, but superseded it. Jesus completely fulfilled all that was required of the first covenant (Mat. 5:17–18, Luke 24:44–47, Acts 3:18, et al), and *at the same time* gave life to a new covenant through His blood (Mat. 26:27–28). God's covenant with Israel dealt with them as an entire people; it was a national covenant. His covenant with sinners today has nothing to do with national, ethnic, or earthly status; it is an individual covenant (Heb. 8:7–13).[31] His covenant with Israel involved land, their physical well-being, and their national fellowship with God; His covenant today involves a spiritual inheritance, our spiritual well-being, and our spiritual fellowship with God (John 4:21–24). What both covenants shared was the fact that *blood* served as the agent of cleansing of sin for the purpose of *allowing* fellowship with God to be possible: "all things are cleansed with blood, and without shedding of blood there is no forgiveness" (Heb. 9:22). This was true under the Old Testament (covenant) as well as in the New Testament (covenant).[32] Blood is absolutely required to make atonement for sin (compare Lev. 17:10–11 and Eph. 1:7). The covenant belongs to God the Father, but it is God the Son who gives life to it. As powerful as God the Father is, He cannot redeem us from our sins apart from the mediatory work of His Son.

It is natural to ask here, "But why 'covenant'? Why didn't God just *say* He will forgive our sins through Jesus' blood and be done with it?" That is not how God—or divine forgiveness—works. The Bible is all about relationships: God's relationship with people, His relationship with Israel, His relationship with other nations, men's relationships with their fellow men, Jesus' relationship with the Father, the church's relationship with Jesus, etc. Relationships are established by covenant, however simple or complex that covenant might be. An agreement is reached, or necessarily understood, by both parties, and this makes fellowship between them possible. In order for God to establish fellowship with sinners, He has to establish a relationship with us in which we are made holy. Covenant provides the context of this relationship.

Covenant does two major things. First, it **defines the relationship**. In order to agree to enter into a relationship with God, we need to know what this looks like, what is required of us, and what we can expect from Him. The relationship needs to have boundaries—where does it begin and end, so to speak; who is included in it; who is excluded; etc. Think of a marriage covenant: it begins with an exchange of vows, and it ends with the death of either spouse (Rom. 7:1–3). Only the husband and wife are participants in that covenant; no one else is allowed to be.[33] It is not children, a house, cars, mutual friends, or a mutual bank account that binds people together, but covenant. The marriage covenant gives definition to the marriage relationship; likewise, our covenant with God gives definition to our relationship with Him. The gospel stipulates the terms of that relationship, and a person either accepts or rejects those terms. He cannot negotiate for different terms, offer a counter-proposal, or only agree to some terms but not others. It is an all-or-nothing proposition—a package deal.

The other thing covenant does is give **functionality** to the relationship. Covenant assigns, in a sense, duties and responsibilities to both parties. In wedding vows, both the groom and bride pledge to *do* certain things for their mate, however generally this may be expressed ("to love in sickness and health," "to have and to hold from this day forward," etc.). Traditionally, the bride will pledge her submission to her new husband, and the groom will pledge to love and protect his new wife. This is very similar to what happens in our agreement with God: we pledge submission to His will, and He promises to serve our best interest and protect us with His providence. In other words, God has His role in the covenant relationship, and we have ours. Our roles are hardly equal—His vastly eclipses ours—but they are both necessary.

A non-functional relationship is inactive and therefore useless. For example, think of an automobile sitting in your driveway which "exists" but has no engine. As a mode of transportation (which is what it was designed for), it is perfectly useless. So it is with friendships, marriages, congregations, laws, and convictions which merely "exist" but are non-functional (or dysfunctional). These are useless; they cannot *do* anything, and therefore they serve no purpose. God does not enter into useless, purposeless, or dysfunctional relationships.

Instead, God has an active part in His covenant with us (grace), and we have our active part (faith). It is irrelevant that God's part contributes enormously more than ours does; it is necessary that *both* parties have something to do. Covenant defines what God will do and what we are supposed to do. Again, grace is what God does for us that we cannot do for ourselves, regarding our salvation. (This includes what it takes to come *into* covenant with Him as well as what is required after this covenant has been established.) Faith is whatever we do for God as an act of faithful obedience to whatever He has told us to do. These two areas of responsibility—grace and faith—work together, but are never expendable or interchangeable. God never carries out our acts of faith, and we can never carry out His acts of grace. Each party in the relationship has a specific and unique role. These roles both converge on the same objective: the salvation of the one who is in covenant with God.

Establishing a Covenant Relationship

The concept of a covenant relationship with God is not difficult for most people to understand, once it is explained to them. Resistance often appears when we start talking about the method of entering into that relationship—what must be promised, what needs to be done, and why it needs to be done. Many people think that merely "asking Jesus into your heart" is a sufficient means of entering into covenant with God, because they have been fed this method from well-known preachers, evangelical religion, and televangelists. This is easy, efficient, and hugely popular.

The problem is—and it is a most serious problem—this "method" is found nowhere in the New Testament. People (largely, *preachers*) just made this up in order to accommodate television audiences, massive churches, and easy religion. Think of the implications: these preachers will tell you that you *need* to be saved because you are in sin. So far, this is true. They say that Jesus is the only Savior whose blood can cleanse your sins—still true. They say that the only way to receive this blood is to turn your life over to God. Provided we let God define what "turning your life" over to Him means, this also is true. Then, at the *most significant point*—the signing on the dotted line, so to speak—they say, "Just ask Jesus into your heart to be saved." This is *not* true. No one in the New Testament ever said it, taught it, practiced it, or believed it.

God's covenant of salvation is the most important relationship into which you could ever enter. The entrance into this covenant—and thus, access to the blood of the covenant, fellowship of the covenant, and "every spiritual blessing" (Eph. 1:3)—is critical. If you do not listen to what God says about entering into a covenant relationship with Him, then you will not *have* one. And, if you do not have such a relationship, then the hope of having your sins forgiven, fellowship with God, and a promise of heaven also does not exist. Simply put, you must never allow *mere men* to tell you how to do *God's business.* You would do well to listen to what God says, regardless of what anyone else tells you.

Even having said that in the plainest language possible, someone will continue to resist. This, not because the biblical instruction is so hard to understand, but because many people want to cling tenaciously to their personal feelings and opinions on the matter. People have a tendency to be very emotional about religion, not always very rational. They assume that God values their feelings as much (and in the same way) as they do. People will listen to some popular preacher tell them how to be saved rather than listen to revealed instructions of the Holy Spirit (i.e., the record of the New Testament). People will listen to family members, friends, mentors, peers, and others whom they respect and trust rather than listening to the One who *owns* life and salvation. People will say things like, "I know it says this-and-that in the Bible, *but* [insert: their own opinion]"—something I affectionately refer to as "But Theology." In other words, such people are not as concerned with listening to the truth as they are with finding a religion that validates their feelings, endorses their pre-existing conclusions, and raises their self-importance. Such people think they are in the driver's seat of establishing a right relationship with God, when in fact they fail to understand what really is at stake. God is not offering us a religion that can be modified, or customized, or accommodative of our feelings. He offers us salvation from our own spiritual ruin—*the very worst thing that could possibly happen to us*—because of His love, through His Son's sacrifice, and on His terms. No one has the right or ability to do otherwise, no matter who he (or she) is or how important others think he is.

Entering into a covenant relationship with God is synonymous with becoming a Christian. Sadly, "Christian" has become such an abused, overused, and misapplied term that we can hardly use it without further clarification. "Christian," in the *biblical* context, means a Christ-follower—not a people follower, popular religion follower, or social media "follower," but one who—regardless of the cost or consequences—*follows Christ*. Ideally, "Christian" and a "disciple" of Christ are one and the same thing. Jesus said, "If anyone wishes to come after Me, he must deny himself, and take up his cross and follow Me" (Mat. 16:24). This is what true Christians do: they accept Jesus' will over their own; they accept the sacrifices required of discipleship to Him; and they follow *His* prescription for life with God rather than trying to add to it, subtract from it, or modify it in any way.[34]

Becoming a Christian is a most serious business. It requires your full commitment, your full allegiance, and the re-prioritization of your entire life. Once you become a Christian (i.e., once you enter into covenant with God), you cannot "opt out" of this. You can choose to be an unfaithful Christian (i.e., live unfaithfully to God's covenant), but you cannot just walk away from it without serious consequence. In fact, it will be far worse in the Judgment for you if you refuse to keep your commitment to God than if you had never made it at all (Heb. 6:4–6, 2 Pet. 2:20–22). One who refuses to keep his hand to the plow, so to speak, is not "fit for the kingdom of God" (Luke 9:61–62).

Christ is not interested in providing for you a nice, comfortable religion in which you can add something "spiritual" to your life. Nor is He offering a quick fix to your spiritual dilemma of guilt, shame, and the dread of the coming Judgment. Nor is He offering you a bunch of theological facts that preachers and seminary students quibble over but have no practical value to you or anyone else. Rather, Christ focuses on what needs to be done—or, if you are presently outside of covenant with God, what *you* need to do—in order to establish a relationship with God that will transcend this life and usher you into *eternal* life. This is a most serious decision, and thus requires your serious attention to detail.

How One Gains Access to Grace

Becoming a Christian, entering into a covenant relationship with God, and being saved are synonymous actions. If one is happening, then the others *must also* be happening. This does not mean that if you *call* yourself a Christian, you *are* in covenant with Him, or that you *are* saved. The method by which a person becomes a Christian is equal to the method by which he (or she) enters into covenant with God, which also must be equal to the method by which he is saved. No one can truly become a Christian (or enter into covenant, or be saved) by a method that did not originate with God. He alone has the right to tell us how this is to be done. (For ease of explanation in what follows, I will speak to "you" as if you were the one in need of salvation, which in fact may or may not be the case.)

The first thing that is required is this: you need to hear the gospel message. Human faith in God is based upon hearing the word of Christ (Rom. 10:17). Every single person's conversion story in the book of Acts began with him (or her) hearing the message of salvation preached by the apostles or someone else. This message was rooted in the Old Testament prophecies, for in these were the predictions of the Savior of the world (e.g., Acts 17:1–3). People cannot have faith in something they know nothing about; truthful information provides the basis for intelligent decisions. The apostle John summed it up best (John 20:30–31): "Therefore many other signs Jesus also performed in the presence of the disciples, which are not written in this book; but these have been written so that you may believe that Jesus is the Christ, the Son of God; and that believing you may have life in His name." Without such information, we are flying *blind*, so to speak— and no one can or will be saved by blind faith.

There were no denominational churches in the time period covered by Acts. What became known as Roman Catholicism was hundreds of years in the future; most modern denominations were another *thousand* years beyond that. Thus, the gospel that people heard at that time was the one that the apostles taught. The only proper method of response to this gospel at that time was also the one that the apostles taught. This remains the only gospel and method of conversion worth listening to today. (It is true that soon afterward, Judaism, Gnosticism, and a number of other "isms" began masquerading as "the gospel," but all of these are soundly refuted by the same apostolic authority by which the original gospel was preached.)

Once you hear the gospel message of salvation, you have a decision to make: believe it or reject it. To "believe" in the gospel means more than simply giving your intellectual nod to the truths and facts that it contains. To "believe" means to *obey* what the gospel says to do. In a sense, "believe" has to do with the mind (or, rational thought); "faith" has to do with the heart (or, human will); both of these actions are required. Once the mind believes in the truth that will "make you free" (John 8:32), the heart can be surrendered in faith. Many people quote John 3:16 ("For God so loved the world, that He gave His only begotten Son, that whoever believes in Him shall not perish, but have eternal life") and assume that all you have to do is just believe that Jesus died for you. But that is not what Jesus actually said, and it is impossible to act in faith unless and until you do something *about* your belief—something God told you to do, not something you came up with on your own.

Believing in the gospel of Christ means believing in Christ Himself. This means that you agree that He is smarter than you, He is more powerful than you, His will is better than yours, and He alone can save you.[35] To believe in Him also means to give your *love* to Him. Love, in this context, refers to the devotion, loyalty, and adoration of your heart. You do not only want what Christ has to offer, but you want *Him*, and want to be where He is. With such admission, something is demanded of you as proof of your love and belief. This proof is demonstrated in the form of obedience: "If you love Me, you will keep My commandments" (John 14:15). (The commands that came to us through His chosen apostles are still *His*, since these men were given authority to convey them to us.) No one can truly "know" God who does not or will not love and obey His Son (1 John 2:3–6).

Furthermore, your belief in Christ needs to be confessed, which means that it needs to be openly and publicly declared to those who serve as witnesses of your faith. To "confess" Christ means to speak in agreement with Him. This is required with regard to what He has said is true about Himself (recall His "I am" statements from an earlier chapter) as well as what He said is true about *you*. If Christ says that you are a sinner, then you must agree to this; to do otherwise is to call Him a liar (1 John 1:8, 10). (When He declares that you are forgiven, then you must agree to *this*, too; otherwise, you are *still* calling Him a liar.) Confession is most appropriately offered at the time of your conversion, but it also refers to the life (or "walk") that you pledge to lead from that point forward. It is in this latter sense to which Christ refers in Mat. 10:32–33.

To enter into covenant with God through Christ also requires of you an acceptance of the cost of discipleship. Many people want what has been called "cheap grace"—a salvation in which God does all the work and the "believer" does virtually nothing. But Jesus spoke of self-denial, self-sacrifice, and *dying* to "self": "If anyone wishes to come after Me, he must deny himself, and take up his cross and follow Me" (Mat. 16:24). To "deny" yourself means to put His will ahead of your own—not merely when it seems agreeable or convenient for you, but at all times. To "take up [your] cross" means to accept the difficult and even sacrificial life as Christ's disciple. While your allegiance to Christ may not literally take your life, it *must* cost you everything, and many have suffered martyrdom because of it (Mat. 10:21, Luke 14:25–33, and Rom. 8:36). You do not have to "hate" your loved ones *literally* in order to follow Him, but they all *must* be put second to Him. You may not have to literally give up all your possessions to follow Him, but all your possessions *must* be surrendered to Him, and nothing can be more important than your allegiance to Him. Your covenant with God—and thus, your *soul*—must not be compromised by anything in this world (Mat. 16:25–26).

Also, to become a Christian, you must repent of your sins. Repentance seems to be one of the most avoided subjects in modern Christendom. Yet, God is very serious about repentance, and the gospel of Christ is a message *of* "repentance for forgiveness of sins" (Luke 24:44–48). In fact, the very first instruction ever given by an apostle to those who asked what they must do in order to escape God's condemnation was to *repent* (Acts 2:38, 3:19). God cannot and will not enter into covenant with someone who refuses to let go of his (or her) sin!

To "repent" means to change one's mind, change one's heart, and thus change the spiritual direction that he (or she) is heading. It is not just saying "I'm sorry," for words cannot replace action. It is not the same as feeling sorry, for feelings do not produce real change. It is not mere regret (usually, for getting caught), for regret is only what those who remain in the world have (2 Cor. 7:10). Repentance is a kind of conversion: it is a letting go of one thing in order to pursue its opposite. Thus, repentance lets go of sin in order to pursue righteousness (Titus 2:11–12). ("In order to" always implies a purpose-driven, goal-oriented action, not a thought or feeling.) This is what must be done upon your conversion, but it also must continue as God exposes sin in your life thereafter. John says it bluntly: "the one who practices righteousness is righteous, just as He [Christ] is righteous; the one who practices sin is of the devil" (1 John 3:7–8).

And finally, to come into contact with the blood of Christ, you have to die *with* Christ. The apostle Paul explains how this is accomplished (Rom. 6:3–7):

> Or do you not know that all of us who have been baptized into Christ Jesus have been baptized into His death? Therefore we have been buried with Him through baptism into death, so that as Christ was raised from the dead through the glory of the Father, so we too might walk in newness of life. For if we have become united with Him in the likeness of His death, certainly we shall also be in the likeness of His resurrection, knowing this, that our old self was crucified with Him, in order that our body of sin might be done away with, so that we would no longer be slaves to sin; for he who has died is freed from sin.

Christ does not put law to death, but He puts the condemnation of law to death, so to speak—He takes it out of the way.[36] Sin does not die to you, but *you* are the one who dies to sin—in essence, you die to your allegiance to sin. Sin rules over us as long as we are sinners; in order to escape that domination, we must die to sin's lordship. This allows us to profess a *new* allegiance to a *new* Lord—Jesus Christ (Rom. 6:12–23).

Thus, one must become *united with Christ in the likeness of His death.* Paul makes it clear that uniting with the death of Christ is accomplished through baptism (immersion) in water. In this way, you must "die" to your former allegiance to sin, be buried (immersed) completely in water, and rise out of the water (resurrection) in order to "walk in newness of life" (regeneration).[37] We do not "die" *like* Jesus, we die *with* Jesus. He died a literal death, was literally buried, and then literally rose from His actual grave. Your "death" in water is obviously symbolic in nature, but this does not make it any less important if indeed it is required for establishing a covenant with God. Your baptism serves as the historical event that separates your *old* life in sin from your *new* life with God. You cannot do this by "just asking Jesus into your heart" or imagining yourself into a Christian.

Someone says, "Yes, baptism may be important, but it is not *necessary*." Jesus says it is necessary (Mat. 28:19); so does Peter (Acts 2:38, 1 Pet. 3:21); so does Paul (Gal. 3:27, Col. 2:11–12); and so does the Holy Spirit—the One who inspired, recorded, and preserved all these citations. Just because something is symbolic to God does not make it optional or expendable. The Passover sacrifice was filled with symbolism, but Israel was commanded to observe it. Likewise, the Lord's Supper is symbolic in nature, but Christians are commanded to observe it. We cannot, on the one hand, gladly accept the death of Christ on our behalf, but on the other hand refuse to demonstrate our own change of allegiance through the very method that He said to do. It cannot be called "faithful obedience" if we refuse to act in faith or be obedient to what is taught in Scripture. If a person does not die with Christ, he has no reason to believe that he will live with Him (2 Tim. 2:11).

Baptism is the visible act of faith required for entering into a covenant relationship with God. The cleansing of our "evil conscience" takes place at the same time that "our bodies are washed with pure water" (Heb. 10:22)—an expression that can have no other meaning in reference to salvation than to baptism in water. Peter says that "baptism now saves you—not the removal of dirt from the flesh, but an appeal to God for a good conscience—through the resurrection of Jesus Christ" (1 Pet. 3:21). The act of baptism itself does not cleanse the conscience, since water cannot atone for sins. But baptism is an act of faith—just like repentance, self-denial, taking up one's cross, and confessing Jesus' name are also acts of faith.

Faith is our part of the equation; grace—and thus, forgiveness—is God's part. Through the blood of Christ and the power that it takes to resurrect someone from the dead, God forgives the sin of the believer who calls upon His name for salvation (Rom. 10:11–13) and brings him into a covenant relationship with Him. Baptism is, in a very real sense, one's signature on the dotted line of God's covenant terms and conditions.

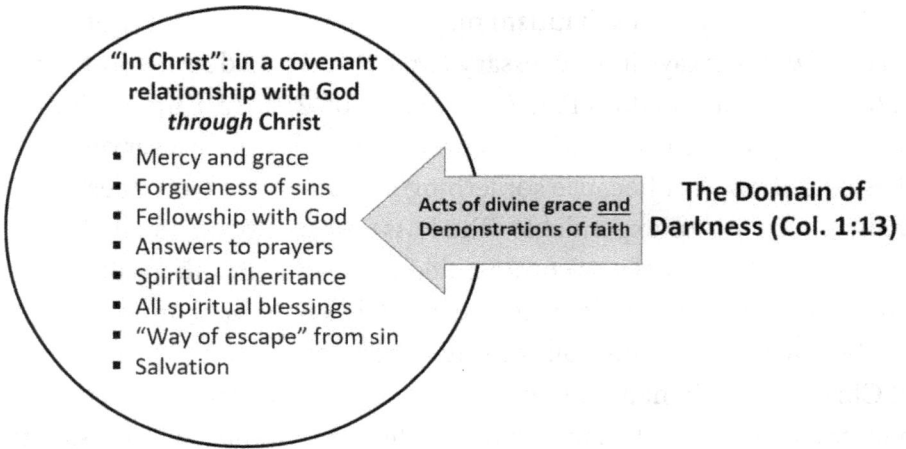

"In Christ": in a covenant relationship with God *through* Christ
- Mercy and grace
- Forgiveness of sins
- Fellowship with God
- Answers to prayers
- Spiritual inheritance
- All spiritual blessings
- "Way of escape" from sin
- Salvation

Acts of divine grace <u>and</u> Demonstrations of faith

The Domain of Darkness (Col. 1:13)

Let's summarize what has just been said with regard to becoming a Christian, which is equivalent to entering into a covenant of salvation with God through Christ:

- You must know Christ's message of salvation in the first place.
- You must believe that Jesus the Man is Christ the Son of God—the God-sent Savior of all mankind. This belief must be accompanied by obedient acts of faith toward whatever God requires of you.
- You must make a confession that publicly supports that belief.
- You must be willing to deny your self-serving life, take up the sacrificial life of a Christ-follower, and actively *follow* the Lord.
- You must repent of your sinful thoughts and behavior. In other words, you must "lay aside the deeds of darkness and put on the armor of light" and at the same time "put on the Lord Jesus Christ, and make no provision for the flesh in regard to its lusts" (Rom. 13:12, 14).
- You must be baptized into Christ as a symbolic re-enactment of His own death, burial, and resurrection. In effect, you must die *with* Christ in the likeness of His own death.

These represent your agreement to the *terms and conditions* of your fellowship with God. God will not give His grace to anyone who deliberately refuses to comply with His terms; such a person is simply not prepared to receive this priceless gift. Salvation will be given to those who comply *in faith* with what God has instructed; it will *not*

be given to those who know the right thing to do but refuse to do it
(Jas. 4:17). Just as the military will not allow a single civilian upon
its restricted property who is lacking in credentials, so Jesus will not
admit a single soul into His community of believers who lacks faithful
obedience to Him.

Most people are fine with all of this except for the part about
baptism. This is not because the biblical instruction is hard or
confusing, but because they have been listening to denominational
creeds and evangelical ministers rather than reading the Bible. These
creeds and ministers claim that, since baptism is a work of faith, and
we are not saved "as a result of works, so that no one may boast"
(Eph. 2:9), therefore baptism is not necessary. These same creeds
and ministers have no problem with mandating prayer (especially
a "sinner's prayer"), church attendance, tithing (their word, not
mine), supporting various ministries, and a lifetime of good works.
Suddenly, inexplicably, and hypocritically, baptism has been singled
out as the one "work" of faith that is forbidden, but all other works
of faith are required for salvation. This is not the Bible talking, but
is religious bias, human ignorance, and the vain attempt to defend
a denomination over and above the sound doctrine of the New
Testament. Your soul must not be a follower of these hopeless things,
because they are guaranteed to disappoint you when you stand before
God.

It is true what Paul says: "For by grace you have been saved
through faith; and that not of yourselves, it is the gift of God; not as a
result of works, so that no one may boast" (Eph. 2:8–9). Paul is by no
means forbidding baptism as a necessary work of faith—remember
that Paul himself was baptized in order to become a Christian (Acts
9:18, 22:16)—and most of the New Testament instruction on baptism
comes through him. What Paul *is* doing is emphasizing the actual
source of saving power. Works of faith, however necessary, are
not the power behind salvation; it is the *grace of God* that actually
redeems the human soul. We are not saved by faith alone, but neither
are we saved by grace alone. Rather, we are saved *by grace*, and our
access to that grace is *through faith* (Rom. 5:1–2). This is what Paul

said; this is what must be taught; we have no right to teach otherwise. Works of faith are not a separate issue *from* obedience; they are the necessary demonstration *of* obedience.

To refuse baptism (or any other action required by God) because it is a "work" ignores the fact that anything we do as part of our salvation is a work—even saying a prayer and living a morally pure life. If we were truly saved by grace *only*—meaning, apart from *any* human participation—then we would not have to do anything at all, not even ask Christ to be our Savior or beg for the forgiveness of our sins. We would not even have to believe in God, for belief itself is a work (John 6:29). God would just save us, and we would be—in fact, *must* be—oblivious to the entire experience. If that sounds ridiculous to you, then you understood my point and, whether you realized it or not, you just agreed with what has just been said about baptism.

Summary Thoughts

All of God's gifts to us—mercy, forgiveness, peace, joy, and eternal life itself—are free, but are most certainly conditional. (The only exception is love itself, which is free *and* unconditional, for God loves us *regardless* of our response to Him.) The "condition" always boils down to one's sincere faith in God's saving grace, nothing more or less. We do not pay for gifts *with* our faith, but we do prepare ourselves *in* faith to receive them. We do not earn gifts, but we do submit to whatever is required in order to gain *access* to them. Grace is God's free gift to us, but we must first demonstrate our faith in the One *offering* it. Thus, we are not saved by works of faith, but we are not saved without them, either. When the grace of God is *united with* the human faith of the believer, a "new creature" is born (2 Cor. 5:17; see Eph. 2:10) and that soul is reconciled with his Creator in holy fellowship.

Sometimes people make things harder for themselves than God has made them. At other times, people take things more lightly than God has meant them. Genuine followers of Christ do not worry about what others say, but they simply do whatever God has instructed *them* to do. A lot of people can give you answers concerning what you should believe, why you should believe it, and how you should live your life. What you need for your salvation are not other people's answers, but *the truth*. Man-made religion will not save your soul; people's opinions will not save your soul; *your own opinion* will not save your soul. The access to saving grace—and life with God—is found through listening to heavenly truth and then complying with what it has said to do.

Is this what *you* have done?

Chapter Seven
⟩Law and Grace⟨

. . . [S]in is not imputed when there is no law. . . . [And] the Law [of Moses] came in so that the transgression would increase; but where sin increased, grace abounded all the more, so that, as sin reigned in death, even so grace would reign through righteousness to eternal life through Jesus Christ our Lord. (Rom. 5:13, 20–21, bracketed words added)

Remember "Linda" about whom we talked earlier who was trying to justify herself within the confines of her own thinking? Let's return now to her scenario to illustrate more of what causes such self-righteousness and how to get beyond it. God's word is not about creating spiritual problems, or perpetuating them, but is all about providing excellent and heavenly solutions for otherwise insurmountable problems. The solution is not always easy, but it is *always* possible (Mat. 19:26).

Linda cannot enjoy God's saving grace as long as she relies upon trying to rectify her sins through law-keeping (i.e., doing what she believes to be right, being a good person, going to church, saying her prayers, etc.). God will not give help to anyone who refuses to trust in His ability to perform. Linda's heart is convinced that more law-*keeping* will be the answer to all of her law-*breaking*. Christ's response is, in effect, "Your attempt to save yourself is hopeless. Until you come to Me fully believing that I alone am your only hope, you will die in your sins."[38]

Linda cannot save herself; you cannot save yourself; I cannot save myself. *We cannot save ourselves.* If we could, we would not need God, Christ, the gospel, or anything else *besides* ourselves. People who try to save themselves are playing "God," since they are attempting to do what He alone is capable of doing. God obviously does not take kindly to such arrogance, no matter how well-intentioned it may be. People like Linda are not heinously wicked, but they do not trust God's grace largely because of one of two reasons. First, they are too proud to admit how dependent they are upon God to save them. (We will cover this in an upcoming chapter.) Second, they *do not understand how His grace works*—something we need to talk about right now.

What It Means to Be "Justified"

The key to understanding Linda's problem—and thus her solution—is found in Gal. 5:4: "You have been severed from Christ, you who are seeking to be justified by law; you have fallen from grace." Many people (including Christians) are intimidated by big words in Scripture like "justification." While there is no attempt being made here to oversimplify the subject, its basic premise is straightforward enough. God's justification of our souls translates to His having removed our guilt through the blood of His Son. This means: He looks upon His Son's death on the cross as payment for the debt we have incurred through our having sinned against Him.[39] We are justified not just because this solution to our problem exists, but because we have actively demonstrated our *faith* in that solution. Thus, we are "justified by faith" and "have obtained our introduction by faith into this grace in which we stand" (Rom. 5:1–2). We walk by faith (2 Cor. 5:7), but we stand before God in His grace.

"Justified by law" means to make "law"—things to do, promises to fulfill, and commandments to obey—serve as the absolute standard of one's righteousness. In the passage cited earlier (Gal. 5:4), "law" specifically (or, contextually) refers to the Law of Moses, but it can by extension refer to *any* legal system a person uses to calculate his righteousness *based upon his own human performance*. Thus, "law" generically refers to any system of justification or righteousness which is dependent ultimately upon human effort rather than divine grace.

If you are a perfect law-keeper, then law justifies you. In this sense, law declares you to be innocent of sin (because you have not violated it), and therefore it does not condemn you. If you are a law-*breaker*, then law can no longer justify you (because you *have* violated it), and therefore it *does* condemn you. "Justified" means to be declared righteous, innocent, and "just" before law and, in particular, the law-giver. One who trusts in law-keeping may *appeal* to Christ in seeking His stamp of approval, but he relies more upon his personal righteousness than the grace of God.

This is what Linda does. She gauges her righteousness not by what God imparts to her as a free gift but by what she (thinks she) has earned as a religious accomplishment. She trusts in law—specifically, *her* law, or her *keeping* of law—more than she trusts in Christ's intercession for her. The trouble is, any violation of "law" makes her no longer a law-*keeper* but a law-*breaker*. Law does not care about people; it does not care how well you have performed in other areas; it only sees how you have failed in any *one* area. Likewise, it does not care how well you did in the past; it only sees what you have done *wrong*. Thus, law cannot look upon the law-breaker as anything other than a *sinner*. In effect, Linda stands condemned not only by God, but also by her own system of law-keeping.

Law did not create Linda's problem, *Linda* did. Law—and especially God's law—is not the problem, but Linda's trust in law to deliver her from her sins is the problem. Paul, after acknowledging that he "died" when he sinned against the Law of Moses (Rom. 7:7–11), nonetheless declared (7:12–13):

> So then, the Law is holy, and the commandment is holy and righteous and good. Therefore did that which is good become a cause of death for me? May it never be! Rather it was sin, in order that it might be shown to be sin by effecting my death through that which is good, so that through the commandment sin would become utterly sinful.

Linda's sin against law was her problem, not the legal commandment itself. Likewise, our sin against God's law is our problem, not the commandment itself. God's commands are not meant to destroy us, but to show us how we are to walk in fellowship with Him. Even so, when we break even one of His laws, we break *the law* (Jas. 2:10). The guilt we incur in doing so cannot be removed by tears, good works, good intentions, churchgoing, or more law-keeping. Once we are guilty, we cannot be justified by human effort. Faith is necessary in order to address the problem, but divine grace is necessary in order to *solve* the problem.

Paul told the Galatian Christians (in Gal. 5:4) that seeking to be justified by law not only contradicts living by grace, but forfeits the effect of grace altogether. This does not mean that the power of God's grace is diminished in the least. Rather, it means that those who put their hope in something *other* than His grace will lose the benefit of it altogether. Trusting in something (or, someone, including oneself) other than God is tantamount to idolatry, and is an act of unbelief in Him, not faith. Throughout the Bible, God condemns idolatry and unbelief, and He has not softened His position on these now.

Living by Law

While a "law-keeping" scenario may sound foreign to you, there are *many* people—church-going, Bible-reading, hymn-singing, potluck-attending, well-intentioned *Christians*—who live like this. These people believe in God, but with a measure of reservation. They know that they *need* God, but not in the way that they *should* need Him. God, for them, is just someone whom they have to please with service and good works, not someone to love and fully depend upon. They read the gospel through the filter of their own expectations. They have a wrong perception of God, and therefore have a wrong perception of what He offers them.

Wrong perceptions *of* God can lead to wrong actions in people's relationships *with* God. By not trusting in His all-sufficient grace, people instead rely on insufficient human effort. They try to solve spiritual problems with earth-bound solutions. Instead of basking in the warm fellowship of God's love, they spend their lives trying to appease God's anger toward them. Such people live by *law*, not by *grace*. They have created their own "law" (i.e., standard of self-righteousness) and make great efforts to conform to it.

In speaking about his unconverted countrymen (the Jews), Paul said, "For I testify about them that they have a zeal for God, but not in accordance with knowledge. For not knowing about God's righteousness, and *seeking to establish their own*, they did not subject themselves to the righteousness of God" (Rom. 10:2–3, emphasis added). These people were not intentionally or maliciously trying to supplant the Law of Moses. Instead, they claimed to be very zealous for God and His Law but pursued righteousness with their own customized version of justification. They had zeal, to be sure (just like so many Christians), but lacked a proper view of God's *grace* (again, like so many Christians). They believed that justification was attained through strict and meticulous compliance with laws and regulations. They prided themselves on all the laws and traditions they kept, not realizing that righteousness was not found through law-keeping but through Christ (Rom. 10:4).

This describes Linda. It describes many church members.
It describes me, as I used to be (and, honestly, as I struggle to resist even now). Maybe it describes *you*, as you are now. But once we learn the gospel more accurately, we have no good reason to remain in that condition.

Living by Grace

Let's compare this rigid, legalistic, and unworkable system of living by law with the gospel's prescription for living by grace. In sharp contrast to Linda, I want to introduce you to a wonderful Christian woman named Frances. Frances does not see God as a hard master who reaps where He did not sow, but as a merciful and forgiving Father who has tapped the depths of heaven and eternity to secure atonement for her sins. She knows that this Father chastises and disciplines, but He does so out of love because He does not want to lose her (Heb. 12:6–11, Rev. 3:19). She knows that He expects obedience to His commandments, but He also provides the means to compensate for her human weakness and failure (1 John 5:2–3, 2:1–2). Her service to God is not an endurance of terrible suffering, but she willfully accepts temporary losses in order to gain eternal rewards (2 Cor. 4:16–18).

Frances sees God's commandments as refreshing and rejuvenating. Rather than burden her, His commandments provide direction to her soul and give life to all who love them (John 6:63,

12:50). She understands that her completion comes not through her own worthiness, but through all that Christ accomplishes *through* her, He being the Advocate who speaks on her behalf (Col. 1:28, 1 John 2:1–2). She does not see a frowning God standing in her way, foot tapping in impatience, arms folded in disapproval, sighing with disappointment, blocking her path to heaven with unrealistic demands and expectations. On the contrary, she adoringly *worships* God with all of her heart, and looks forward to being with Him in His heaven. She does not confess Christ incidentally, as the need arises, but her whole *life* is a confession of her love for and desire to serve Him (Mat. 10:32–33). She understands that justification is by grace through faith, and that human effort by itself is unable to save anyone.

Comparing the Two Belief Systems

Living by law is a checklist religion. In Linda's case, for instance, she has a list of what she must do to be justified and spends her day or week or life trying to complete it (like a chore list). She may be oblivious to the existence of this "list," but it exists all the same—she updates and references it all the time. Having enough checkmarks translates to qualifying for heaven, as though Christianity were some kind of Olympic-grade obstacle course.

Living by (Self-Made) Law

Linda believes (consciously or not), "If I . . .
- ✓ pray enough
- ✓ read enough
- ✓ pay enough
- ✓ help enough
- ✓ attend enough
- ✓ forgive enough (etc.)

. . . then I will be justified before God, and He will admit me into heaven."

One who lives by grace, however, sees things very differently. For example, Frances does not trust her own meritorious works to absolve her of guilt—that is something only Christ can do through His atoning work on the cross.[40] Having accepted this, she recognizes her role in her salvation is not that of justifier, for no one but God can justify sinners. Frances has no checklists, no legal hoops to jump through, no need to struggle with past failures while at the same time wrestling with perfectionism. She does good works, to be sure, but for completely different reasons than Linda does. She understands obedience is required by God as a demonstration of *faith*, not a means of *qualification*. She is justified by grace through her faith, and that not of herself, for grace is the gift of God, "not as a result of works, that no one should boast" (Eph. 2:8–9).

Living by Saving Grace

Frances believes, "Since I am a child of God, I will . . .
✓ pray without ceasing
✓ read the word of God
✓ pay whatever is owed
✓ help in whatever way I can
✓ attend without forsaking
✓ forgive as often as I am asked (etc.)
. . . and having been justified by His grace, God will welcome me into His heaven."

Linda lives by law in an attempt to be justified before God. Frances lives by a faith that relies on God's gracious forgiveness for imperfect law-keeping. In a sense, Linda serves God with her head, with a human logic and a legal perspective; Frances, with her *heart*, with trust in God's pardon and participation in heaven's glory. Or we could say: Linda serves God like a cynical, world-weary *adult*, whereas Frances serves God with the open heart and trusting faith of a *child* (Mat. 18:1–3). Linda approaches Christianity like many people approach life: we follow rules and regulations; if we obey, there is praise and reward; disobey, and there is judgment and the need for compensation. Do well and all will be well, generally speaking; mess up, press the wrong button, or fail to press the *right* button, and there are reprimands, fines, and punishments.

It is not uncommon for Christians to have this mentality. It is likely that *all* of us begin our walk in Christ in this way: do well, and all will be well; mess up, and there will be hell to pay—literally. Concepts like mercy, grace, and forgiveness do not always get past the point of being *concepts* for us. We struggle with how to put these concepts into real-life applications. Living as a true *child of God*, however, means we do not focus on our faults and dwell on our inadequacies but seek to honor our Father by giving Him our very best and trusting Him to compensate for wherever our "best" has failed. This paradoxical, child-like approach is exactly what God wants of us. Even though we may all begin with living by law (in some form or another), we ought to "leave behind" such elementary understandings and "press on to maturity" in Christ (Heb. 6:1).

One who lives by law may end up performing the exact same actions and practicing the exact same habits as one who lives by grace, but for entirely different reasons. Both Linda and Frances will pray, read the Bible, regularly participate in congregational worship, give generously, and engage in active Christian lifestyles. Yet, they both do these things with entirely different motives, and motive means *everything* to God. Linda is motivated by fear, while Frances is motivated by love. Linda lives by law because she fears an ultimate punishment and retribution for her sins; she does not understand what absolute forgiveness means or how to obtain it. Frances lives by grace because of God's love for her, and her love for God. She serves Christ because she loves Him, not because she fears His punishment. In fact, she does not have to worry about punishment at all, since "perfect love casts out [the] fear" of punishment (1 John 4:18). Linda is enslaved to fear—a slavery Christ came to *remove*, not magnify or perpetuate (Heb. 2:14–15). Frances lives in *spiritual freedom*—she is not enslaved to fear, dogma, human expectations, or God's frowning disappointment. Linda fears going to hell; Frances dreams about being in heaven.

God's people worrying about going to hell is offensive to the gospel of grace, and undermines the mediatory work of Christ. While we may wrestle with these kinds of thoughts early on in our walk as a Christian, to continue in this thinking manifests unbelief, not faith. This is like saying to God, "I don't think You are willing or capable of reconciling me to Yourself through Christ like you said You would." Unbelief takes many forms, but this *kind* of unbelief is particularly insidious because it can so easily reside in the hearts of unsuspecting and well-intentioned Christians.

Living without fear of going to hell does not mean that the *possibility* of hell no longer exists. Christians *can* lose their souls, if indeed they "[fall] from grace or are "severed from Christ" (Gal. 5:4).[41] At the same time, it is wrong for us to *fear* being lost if indeed we are walking by faith and (thus) are being saved by grace. Those who *cease* to walk by faith abandon the "narrow" path and choose instead the "broad" path that leads to destruction (Mat. 7:13–14). God does not foreordain any person's destiny. One's destiny is *chosen* through the decisions that he (or she) makes in this life—especially his decisions concerning God.

Minimums and Maximums

Often what accompanies the "living by law" mentality is what we might call a minimum-and-maximum approach to Christian duty. Such people (like Linda) do not experience the great freedom to live, love, and serve "in Christ," but they only experience a life limited and stunted by legalism. Linda, for example, says (consciously or not), "I will do *this much* [minimum requirement] for the Lord, but I am not obligated to do any more than *that* [maximum requirement]." You might picture her holding out her hands as though she were showing you the size of a fish she just caught. Her spiritual relationship with God is forced into a rigid, box-like framework. This is similar to the stereotypical labor union mentality: as Linda sees it, everyone has their assignment in the church. To carry out your assignment is your own responsibility; but go beyond this and you step over the line and infringe upon someone else's responsibility—and this is deemed unacceptable. Imagine Linda saying, in so many words, "I feel it is my responsibility to go visit the sick and hospitalized. Doing so will justify me as a 'good Christian' for today. But I do not see the need to encourage fellow Christians or talk to others about my faith. We have elders and preachers and Bible class teachers for that."

Imagine now a preacher trying to motivate a congregation filled with people who subscribe to Linda's minimum-and-maximum mentality. Imagine him every Sunday trying to explain to them the "whole purpose of God" (Acts 20:26–27) and talking about each disciple's responsibility to themselves, their families, the church, and the lost. Meanwhile, the members are nodding their heads and murmuring "Amen," but are saying to themselves, "Nope, that's not *my* responsibility—I've already got my assignment(s). I agree, those other things must be done, but someone else will have to do it."

The fallacy of choosing our "assignments" and ministries that fit neatly inside our comfort zones is this: *we have chosen them.* We have not let God choose them for us. Our having chosen them limits our capacity to serve God because of self-determined interests and agendas. This is not discipleship; it is a form of smug self-righteousness. It assumes that we can define our Christian walk, label it "worship" or "service," and offer it as "an offering and a sacrifice to God as a fragrant aroma" (Eph. 5:2). This is all very backward from the kind of reverent, humble, and submissive people He expects us to be—and what we promised to be in our baptism. We would never hear Christ say such things to God. We cannot imagine Him saying, while pantomiming with His hands, "Father, I'll do *this much* for mankind, but *no more.*" If *He* would never say such things, those who follow Him must never say them, either.

Living by Law: Establishing "Minimums" and "Maximums"

"I will do this much . . ."   **". . . but I will do no more than this."**

|---|

MINIMUM   **MAXIMUM**

Paul calls all such minimum-and-maximum law-keeping a "yoke of slavery" (Gal. 5:1). The Pharisees were famous for their meticulous calibration and strict measurement of service to God. They were careful to keep the very technical requirements of law, but refused to give the much greater offerings of the heart, such as justice, mercy, and faithfulness (Mat. 23:23). If a *Christian* chooses to live this way, he severs himself from Christ and falls from grace (Gal. 5:1–4). All it takes to forfeit God's saving grace is to live by one's own standard of perfection—to become one's own justifier apart from Christ.

This self-defeating approach robs a person of great spiritual blessings—peace, joy, contentment, patience, freedom, etc. It brings Christianity down to a humanistic, even secular, level; it implies that we reach heaven by climbing a ladder of human effort, every rung being another meritorious accomplishment. Heaven is still the goal, but it is not God who takes us there. At best, He is like a cheerleader on the sideline who applauds our successes but turns His back to us in shame when we fail to make the play.

By limiting what we will do, we limit how God will perform His work through us. Works do not save us, but God's works are most certainly accomplished through His people—according to His will, not ours. The apostle Paul wrote: "For we are His workmanship, created in Christ Jesus for good works, which God prepared beforehand, that we should walk in them" (Eph. 2:10); and, "it is God who is at work in you, both to will and to work for His good pleasure" (Phil. 2:13). It is not left up to us to decide what "good works" look like, or how we are to carry them out. This is God's business, and the more we "understand what the will of the Lord is" (Eph. 5:17), the better we will know what He wants us to do.

What will be the extent of these good works? That's the beautiful part: *there is no extent.* There are no minimums or maximums for God's people; there are no self-appointed, self-determined, or pre-fixed parameters to legislate. No one has to keep track of how much or how often or how little anything is done—no bookkeeping, no calculating, no juggling of facts and figures. Instead, every believer simply does what needs to be done, to the best of his (or her) ability. This is not a workaholic Christianity, in which there is no moderation; rather, it simply removes the need for having to pay attention to "how much," "how far," or for "how long" something has to be done. We act out of love and gratitude, not bound to a legalistic code.

Love without Limits

There are no ladders to heaven. We participate in our salvation, but we are not the reason for it, nor do we have the power to make it happen. The "word of the cross"—the message of what *Christ* has accomplished, not us—rests upon "the power of God," not human effort (1 Cor. 1:18). It is not about us climbing up to heaven. Rather, it is about God reaching down with all the tenderness of a caring Father, *lifting* us up out of our dungeon of hopelessness, and *carrying* us up to heaven in the cradle of His hand. That is saving grace. All He asks is that we not let go of His hand and trust in His power to deliver us. That is obedient faith.

Frances, who walks by faith and trusts in grace, not only allows God to carry her but thoroughly enjoys the experience. She does not have to worry about putting limits or boundaries on her service to God. She serves God with her entire *life*, not with incidental chores or assignments. She is not under contract to God to perform certain works. Instead, she has entered into a covenant with God in which she is free to engage in good works and spiritual virtues without end and without calculation. "The fruit of the Spirit is love, joy, peace, patience, kindness, goodness, faithfulness, gentleness, self-control; against such things *there is no law*" (Gal. 5:22–23, emphasis added). There is no quantification of or limitation to godly virtues. Frances, like all who live by grace through faith, pursues this "fruit" as often as she chooses. In fact, the closer she draws near to God in faith, the more she *wants* to pursue it.[42]

Because this "fruit" is spiritual in nature, it cannot be hindered by people, laws, circumstances, or timeframes. For example, no one can stop you from showing godly love—there is no limit or extent to which this can be done. No one can limit how often you will forgive a person. No one can put boundaries around how much internal joy or patience or faithfulness you choose to exercise. *There is no law against such things.* No person or church can legislate how much or how often these things must be done, nor can any person or eldership or congregation place limits on them. Living by grace through faith gives us *freedom* to let God's spiritual work be carried out in us without our needing to quantify, measure, or regulate it. No one can stop us from letting Christ live and breathe and work in us, as long as we accept by faith His gospel of saving grace fully and completely (Gal. 2:20).

Living by Grace: Recognizing no Limits or Boundaries to Service
"I will do whatever is necessary out of faith in God and gratitude for His grace."

$\longleftarrow \hspace{5cm} \longrightarrow$

LOVE WITHOUT LIMITS

Linda limits her love, while Frances loves without limits. This describes Frances' love for God *and* her love for her fellow human being. Likewise, she forgives without limits, shows kindness without question, demonstrates patience without being prompted, rejoices in the Lord without reservation, and offers mercy to whomever is in need of it. Because of this, she knows the peace of God "which surpasses all comprehension" (Phil. 4:7), partakes of the "divine nature" of God (2 Pet. 1:4), and realizes that He has granted her and all true believers the opportunity to be "filled up to all the fullness of God" (Eph. 3:19). While Frances' outward actions may be very similar—and, in some cases, exactly the same—as Linda's, her heart works on a completely different wavelength and she is motivated by an altogether different incentive.

What about Works?

Someone might be thinking, "With all this abundant grace which God gives so freely, why be concerned about law at all?" Being saved by grace does not mean we are exempt from law. Likewise, while we must avoid being *legalistic* in our approach to the Christian life, this does not mean we are to avoid *legalities* (laws). Legalism is a mindset that demands conformity to one's own perception of how things should be done; laws of God demand conformity to what He says is right, true, and *must* be done. Legalism serves to gratify an individual person's expectations; laws of God serve to define the acceptable behavior of one who is in covenant with Him. Legalism is based on human commandments; laws of God are divine commandments.

Our attention to grace must never rub law out of the picture. Law and grace do have a relationship, for the one (grace) actually demands the presence of the other (law). In the absence of *law* there cannot be a charge of *sin*, since sin is a violation of law (Rom. 4:15); in fact, "sin is not imputed [or, charged; blamed] when there is no law" (Rom. 5:13, bracketed words are mine). If we have no law, then we cannot sin; if there is no sin, there is also no need for grace. Saving grace is God's direct response to human sin. Those who claim to be saved by grace but not bound by law simply do not understand what necessitates grace in the first place. There is no reason for God to give saving grace to a perfect, sinless person. This is like healing a person who is not sick, or rescuing a person who is not perishing.

Some think that we need grace *up front*—in other words, in order to become Christians—but then *after* this, we are no longer bound by law because we live under grace. This comes from a misunderstanding of Rom. 6:14: "For sin shall not be master over you, for you are not under law but under grace." "Under law," in the context of Paul's writings, means: under the *condemnation* that law brings for having violated it.[43] To be "under grace" means: we receive forgiveness *through* grace when we fail to keep God's law (and take the necessary steps to rectify this). Thus, we are no longer condemned by law *when* we are forgiven by grace. "The commandments of God are not negligible because we are under grace. They are *doable* because we are under grace."[44]

Grace is not a replacement for law (works). Grace simply restores what our violation of law has corrupted. Paul told the Ephesian Christians, for example, that before they were saved by grace they were "dead" to God (Eph. 2:1). A Christian who shows no faith in God is *also* "dead" to Him (Jas. 2:26); so is an entire *congregation* that fails to fulfill its obligations of faith to God (Rev. 3:1). A Christian demonstrates his faith through obedience, but there cannot *be* any "obedience" unless there is some law to obey. Instead of our "works" being unnecessary (as some have wrongly concluded), God saves us by grace in order to give *meaning* to our works. All the works of faith in the world cannot remove a single human sin—this takes an act of God. But, the one who *has* been cleansed of his sin by grace is now able to render acceptable and priestly service to Him (Rom. 12:1–2). "For we are His workmanship, created in Christ Jesus for good works, which God prepared beforehand so that we would walk in them" (Eph. 2:10). We cannot possibly perform "good works" if they have all been nullified by grace, nor can we "walk" in "good works" if they are not required of us. Such reasoning contradicts what is written.

The fact that we *need* divine grace necessarily implies that we *have* sinned. It also implies that God is both able and willing to save us *from* our sin—not only when we first call upon His name (Rom. 10:11–13), but every time we approach the "throne of grace" in humble faith thereafter (Heb. 4:16). With every sin, there must be sufficient grace to cover it; with a multitude of sins, there must be an abundance of grace. No one can "out-sin" God's grace. In other words, no one can sin so much or so grievously that His grace will be incapable of reconciling that sinner to Himself through Christ.

While this speaks to the great generosity of God, it must never be construed as a license to sin. To willfully sin while banking on grace is an abuse of our covenantal relationship with God. Paul addressed this rhetorically: "Are we to continue in sin that grace might increase? May it never be! How shall we who died to sin still live in it?" (Rom. 6:1*b*–2). In our baptism into Christ, we "died to sin" (Rom. 6:3–7).

The decision to die with Christ in baptism relinquished any right to engage in the practice of sin. Christ appeared in the world "to take away sins," not to perpetuate them. We cannot simultaneously dabble in sin *and* be saved by grace. There is no "gray area" here: one either walks with God in righteousness, or he walks with Satan in wickedness and deceit (1 John 3:6–9). There is no walking the fence here, either, because (as someone has once said), "The devil owns the fence."

Summary Thoughts

Linda, like so many of us have done, is missing the balance between grace and works. She thinks that God set her on the *path* to heaven, but the rest of the journey is up to her. She is trying to marry justification by grace (Titus 3:7) to justification by law. This creates an unholy union: it will not work for Linda or anyone else. Thankfully, her misunderstanding of grace is not a birth defect; it can be resolved. With some biblical education and a desire to learn the truth, she can re-learn grace as God intended her to know it. However, she is first going to have to admit that her present way is the wrong way—and *abandon* it altogether.

Others think that grace is a replacement for works (i.e., human demonstrations of obedience to God), but this also contradicts New Testament teaching. No one will receive God's grace who does not demonstrate faith in Him, and no one can demonstrate such faith apart from obedience to His commandments. Grace is not a license to escape "law" any more than it is a license to practice sin. God is very clear on the matter; we must not let religious dogma, traditional thinking, or appeals to human emotions change what is written. Paul exclaimed triumphantly, "Therefore there is now no condemnation for those who are in Christ Jesus. For the law of the Spirit of life in Christ Jesus has set you *free* from the law of sin and of death" (Rom. 8:1–2, emphasis added). This does not mean we are free from law's obligation; it means we who are "in Christ Jesus" are free from its condemnation.

Linda has a legalistic, short-sighted, and unfulfilling view of grace. Frances, however, does her best to keep God's laws but also trusts in

His grace to overcome her inadequacies and deal rightly with her sins. Perhaps there is a little bit of Linda in all of us, even as we are trying to live more like Frances. Even so, if you are a Christian, God wants you growing ever-closer to Him through conformity to His Son, the Lord Jesus Christ. This serves God's best interest, your best interest, and the best interest of everyone in your circle of influence.

Section Two:
Resistance to Grace

Chapter Eight
⟹ *The Problem of Unbelief* ⟸

*"It is the Spirit who gives life; the flesh profits nothing;
the words that I have spoken to you are spirit and are life.
But there are some of you who do not believe."* (John 6:63–64a)

People may be at the same time both skeptical and gullible. We may resist what is most obvious, yet accept what is most unbelievable. For example, someone says, "I don't believe that a supremely-intelligent Being created the world," yet chooses to embrace the Neo-Darwinist explanation of our present existence that defies human logic, natural science, natural laws, and statistical probability.

Someone else says, "The Bible is just a bunch of men's writings, so why should I trust the words of mere people?" Yet he listens to propagandist media, social media, and select political pundits, and he blindly accepts whatever these sources tell him. He unquestioningly follows his stockbroker's advice. When scientists tell him that Evolution just "happened," he believes it. When intelligent men decorated with doctorates and Mensa memberships tell him there is no God, he shrugs and says, "Works for me."

Still someone else says, "I don't have to be responsible to God— I'm my own person, and I live my own life." This sounds liberating and independent up front. Yet, this person fails to see how his life is dictated, limited, conditioned, re-directed, enslaved, and sometimes even destroyed by numerous things that remain out of his control. These include: other people, society, governments, wars and conflicts, financial markets, environmental factors, weather, natural catastrophes, time, and death itself. He is filled with self-importance in a world that does not care about his self-importance and that will, in due time, steamroll over his utopian dreams.

Many people believe in UFOs, the Bermuda Triangle, a highly-advanced "lost continent of Atlantis," and intelligent alien life. We lap up stories about ghosts and paranormal activity, listen wide-eyed to urban myths, nod in amazement at unverifiable stories of miracles performed in some remote (and possibly non-existent) village in Africa, and embrace as fact unprovable theories about how intelligent life once arose out of non-living space dust. Scientists find a rock in Antarctica and it somehow proves life existed on Mars. Paleontologists find a piece of skull in Mongolia, or Africa, or the Bronx—it really doesn't matter—and suddenly all the previous "facts" about the origin of human life on earth are revised, recalculated, and replayed over and over in on all the "science" channels. Other scientists tell us the world is in imminent danger of being destroyed by pollution, or the shrinking ozone layer spells doom for all of us, or if we keep using our Weber barbecues and Craftsman lawnmowers, the world will heat up, melt all the icecaps, and everyone below Denver will drown.

People have been conditioned to believe what "scientists" and "leading experts" and even "unnamed sources" say, often without any form of fact-checking or critical thinking. People have also been conditioned to believe—by the same human authorities that led them to believe the things just mentioned—that the Bible is old, outdated, irrelevant, full of myths, and contradictory. Our congressional leaders contradict themselves frequently (or simply manipulate data and statistics to reach a desirable conclusion), yet people keep voting them into office, willing to overlook or simply tolerate their hypocrisy. But when someone hears a distant rumor about some vague "contradiction" buried deep within the pages of the word of God, he pitches the entire gospel of salvation aside without further investigation. "See?" he says smugly, condescendingly, and even irrationally. "You just can't trust the Bible!"

People have been conditioned to question—and, often, *reject*— whatever is in the realm of Christianity. There are several reasons for this.

- First, Christianity seems optional, expendable, and (at best) customizable. Because it *can* be rejected, it appears to have little inherent value; because it *can* be customized, it seems to be absent of any single, authoritative truth.

- Second, Christianity, as a religion, has been placed on par with all kinds of other religions (Judaism, Islam, Hinduism, and all kinds of other "-isms"). Take your pick—believe whatever you want, practice it however you choose, but don't take any of it too seriously. If you are unhappy with one religion, you can always jump ship to another.

- Third, denominationalism—another "-ism"—has so misrepresented and fractured the New Testament *pattern* for Christianity that it makes people cynical about the pattern itself.[45] We are led to believe that a singular gospel allows for dozens of "Christian religions" that all separate themselves from, contradict, and condemn each other. This makes a mockery of "the truth"; this makes God out to be a source of confusion (despite 1 Cor. 14:33).

- Fourth, the Bible requires time and effort to study, learn, practice, and share it with others. The mass of humanity chooses the path of least resistance (what Jesus called the "broad" way that "leads to destruction"—Mat. 7:13-14), while believing in divinely-revealed truth requires following the path of *most* resistance. In other words, many people will devote countless hours to learning sports statistics, video games, pop culture references, and computer apps, but are intellectually lazy regarding the most important aspect of their existence—the future of their own soul.

That is the short list. But the real reason why people roll their eyes at Christianity and easily dispense with it has nothing to do with informed decision-making, a thorough investigation of the New Testament gospel, or even an intelligent quest for "the truth." It comes down to something far less noble—something that often masquerades as something else. It comes down to an unwillingness to make a serious investment in something that will completely and forever alter how one lives from this point forward. It comes down to the lack of *commitment*.

Belief, Commitment, and Sacrifice

We are, more than ever before in American history, a commitment-phobic society. Marriage requires commitment, and thus it is often postponed, avoided, abandoned, or simply replaced by some other social convention. Many of our modern sitcoms revolve around the neurotic and predictable charades of superficial characters trying desperately to maintain an immature relationship but avoid marriage. These people will have sex with each other, move in together, have children together (as an extension of their own egos), and intertwine their lives—this is all seemingly normal and acceptable. But marriage is not on the table, is a topic of tension or conflict when it *is* on the table, or is simply avoided like the plague.

Being a patriotic American citizen requires commitment. It requires a person to stand for one given nation, one set of values, and one system of government, not a variety of these. It also requires a person to *reject* whatever person, ideology, or conduct that threatens this one nation, set of values, and system of government. Yet, many modern Americans have become commitment-phobic with regard to any sense of patriotism, which is another way of saying that they have become so *spineless* that they feel compelled to give away all the precious value of our citizenship to whoever walks on American soil, even if that person came here through illegal means. The modern American is, ironically, unwilling to commit to what it means to *be* an American. Left unchecked, this will not end well.

Fear of commitment drives people's refusal to believe things that *should* be believed for their benefit, preservation, and spiritual welfare. Believing in evolution, aliens, ghosts, news media, social media, and nearly anything that is found on the internet is easy. Such beliefs involve very little brain activity. The "Big Bang" theory, alleged paranormal activity, scientific speculation, the opinionated rhetoric of late-night talk show hosts, and modern folklore do not really require anything of us. Believing that marriage is unnecessary, expendable, or can be customized to one's liking requires no responsibility toward why God *gave* us marriage in the first place.

Believing in a citizenship that has no definition, no singular value system, and nothing to defend or even die for requires no commitment *to* citizenship. A society without commitment is certain to fail. Being commitment-phobic may be a convenient path of least resistance, but it also sows the seeds of our own destruction.

Where there is no meaningful belief, there will be no commitment. And, where there is no commitment, there will be no sacrifices made toward achieving anything more than self-serving, indifferent, and purposeless survival. And, where there is no sacrifice, there can be no improvement, advancement, or preservation. Those who choose to believe in hopeless things have *no hope* of any betterment, because hopeless things cannot produce a hopeful and productive future. Instead, things are certain to decline; loss, pain, and suffering are inevitable.

Likewise, one who refuses to believe in God's gospel has *no hope*. The Bible speaks pointedly and unapologetically about this (John 8:24, Eph. 2:11–12, 4:17–19, 1 Thess. 4:13, et al). Mercy, grace, forgiveness, and being unafraid of the judgment to come all require a firm, resolute, and well-defined *commitment* of the believer. The alternative is bleak, awful, and hopeless. The Evolutionist, for example, believes—because his dogma allows for no other conclusion—that he has no purpose for his existence, no meaning to his life, no soul, and no afterlife. Since he has no "God" but so-called "blind forces of nature," he has sucked all the "life" *out* of his life. He has no spiritual allegiance, no otherworldly devotion, and no transcendent perspective. He thinks he has a "good life," but there is really nothing good about being self-deceived, living in self-delusion, and being cast into "outer darkness" (Mat. 25:30). There is nothing hopeful in an artificial happiness that is built upon a satanic lie.

A person can reject God's revealed truth if he wants to, but this serves no good purpose. By rejecting all that is written in the New Testament, he discards all the evidence (i.e., teaching, miracles, eyewitness testimonies, and historical accounts) that it has to offer. Even though he refuses to believe in God, he still believes in *something*, but has accepted this other belief with far less evidence and substantiation than what Christ's gospel offers him. Thus, he chooses to reject the evidence of his own Creator—evidence provided and preserved *by* his Creator—for something incalculably inferior *to* his Creator. This is not only illogical, but it is a decision that will, if left unchanged, haunt him long after this world has passed away (1 John 2:15–17).

On the other hand, one's agreement with God's revealed truth will force a change in his belief system, transformation of his heart, and improvement of his moral behavior. His beliefs require commitment, and his commitment requires sacrifice. But, instead of believing in useless things, he believes in the truth; instead of avoiding commitment, he voluntarily submits to it; and instead of avoiding sacrifices, he willingly makes these. He does all this because he values the truth, believes in the source of truth (John 14:6), and wants what the truth promises him (John 8:32, 12:50). While it would be much easier for him *not* to believe in God and all that He has revealed, it is far better that he *does* believe. God has not only given him a reason *to* believe, but He promises amazing rewards *for* his belief (Mat. 19:29, John 14:1–3, Jas. 2:12, et al).

The Suspension of Disbelief

What does all this have to do with grace? *Everything.*

Saving grace is not something you can visibly see. Even so, God has given you every *reason to believe* that it most certainly does exist. "[W]e walk by faith, not by sight" (2 Cor. 5:7)—which means, you should not plan on *seeing* God's grace being given (like an aura surrounding you, or maybe a golden halo over your head), but you do have sufficient reason to *believe* that He has imparted it to you, if indeed you walk by faith in Him. And, if God's grace is real, then your commitment to Him should be real, and the sacrifices you make to Him should also be real.

Belief, commitment, and sacrifice all rise or fall together. If you truly believe, you will commit; if you truly believe and commit, you will make sacrifices consistent with your beliefs and your commitments. Many Christians have a bad habit of separating these things ("Just because I'm not committed as I should be doesn't mean

I don't *believe*!"; or, "I *am* committed, but I don't feel like I should have to sacrifice my happiness just to prove it"; etc.). But, for now, we will focus on the *believing* part, because this is what sets everything in motion. A person will not truly commit *or* make meaningful sacrifices if he does not really believe in what he is committing to or making sacrifices for.

People tend to believe in other *people* (or companies that people operate) more than they do in God and His promises. This is understandable, from a purely earthly point of view: we can *see* people; we can engage in active business with their companies. Thus, a Christian may believe that a car manufacturer will honor a 100,000 warranty on its vehicles, but may question whether God (who cannot lie—Titus 1:2) will honor His promises to him through Christ. Or, a Christian believes that a painted yellow line on the asphalt will keep oncoming cars from plowing headlong into him, but may grapple with believing in God's providence, even though He has mastery over the entire universe (Col. 1:16–17). Still another Christian may believe his stock portfolio will give him residual income in some 20 or 30 years, but may struggle with believing that an all-powerful God is capable of giving him eternal life (1 John 2:25).

Let me explain this problem another way. When a person watches a fictional movie, he typically has to pretend to believe temporarily in its ridiculous premise. Take the blockbuster movie *Jurassic Park* (1993), for example. In the movie, a filthy rich scientist raises a bunch of dinosaurs on a remote island. He did this by combining ancient dinosaur DNA with modern reptilian DNA and manipulating this process into, um, dinosaurs! (Never mind that this ancient dinosaur DNA is supposed to have been altered during the last "millions of years" to *create* modern reptiles.) Not only this, but the dinosaurs quickly learn how to breed by adapting their sexual orientation to meet the needs of their existence—because, as Jeff Goldblum's character puts it, "Life . . . finds a way." Amazing! Evolution allegedly took "millions of years," but these dinosaurs have genetically adapted themselves before you can even finish a bucket of popcorn. Anyone with a sixth-grade education can see the scientific pitfalls, but that does not stop us from watching it with a certain amount of fascination. (Besides, the special effects are *awesome*.)

Thus, ridiculous as the premise is, *we choose to believe it*. Well, we do not *really* believe it, but we choose to do so for the purpose of allowing ourselves to be entertained for a couple of hours. Film critics call this temporary acceptance the "suspension of disbelief": for the duration of the movie, the viewer agrees to suspend his disbelief in an unbelievable premise in order to be entertained. Otherwise, the viewer will immediately recognize the stupidity of the premise, plot, script, actors, etc., and will never watch the movie at all.

In a sense, a Christian may succumb to this "suspension of disbelief" with regard to his faith in God and His gospel of grace. That person may believe in grace as long as he has to—say, for the duration of spiritual discussion with a fellow Christian, or a sermon, or a church service. He does not really believe in grace, inasmuch as his life has not been transformed *by* grace. His commitment is tepid and his sacrifices are lacking in the absence of *real* belief, but at least he "believes" for the purpose of making a good show, putting on a good front, or keeping other Christians off of his back. Maybe he really *wants* to believe, but there are too many doubts, stumbling blocks, and/or distractions in the way for his belief to develop into something meaningful and life-changing. He temporarily believes in grace to accommodate the moment, but he has not internalized what God's grace really ought to mean to him.

People may suspend their disbelief concerning dinosaurs or in highly-accelerated and inexplicable adaptation for the sake of mere entertainment. No one should take any of this seriously; this is just a harmless diversion. But Christians ought to take God, His saving grace, and their soul's salvation *by* that grace very seriously. To claim to believe in His grace but refuse to let it transform one's heart and dictate one's behavior is to be "double-minded" and "unstable in all his ways." Such a person "ought not to expect that he will receive anything from the Lord" (Jas. 1:5–8).

On the other hand, one who genuinely believes in God's grace is made a "new creature" (2 Cor. 5:17) and the life that he now lives, he lives to Christ. He realizes that "by the grace of God I am what I am" (1 Cor. 15:10), and therefore owes his identity, existence, and promises of future glory to God's having given him a gift he could never earn or repay. He does not merely suspend his disbelief in God for a brief period of time, but he truly lives by divine grace. He is the same person at home, at work, at play, and everywhere he goes, as he is while sitting in the midst of a worship service. His belief in God never changes, except to grow stronger over time.

Belief in God is a package deal. Real belief trusts all that God says and has revealed.[46] God does not have to prove His grace independent of Himself; if He is real, then what He promises also is real (Heb. 11:6). Remember, everything you know *factually* about God comes to you through His revealed word. If you believe in His word to learn who God is, then you can believe in that same word to know what He says is true. You cannot logically or biblically separate what God *says* from who He *is* or what He *does*. You cannot say, for example, "I know that I have a soul in need of redemption, but I'm not certain that God is capable *of* redeeming me." The same Bible that revealed to you that you have an eternal soul also reveals the power He has to *save* your soul through His divine grace. It is entirely inconsistent to believe in one revealed truth but not another, especially when both truths come to us from the same credible source. Because God exists, His love exists, because "God is love" (1 John 4:8). And, because God exists—because He *is* love—He will serve your best interest when you respond rightly to His love. The most loving thing that God can do for us is to save us from our own foolish choices through His all-sufficient grace. All of this has been revealed to you and me from the same source: His word. We either believe all of this, or we really do not believe any of it.

The Proof of Grace

Such is the conceptual argument. But there is tangible proof of God's grace as well. This is manifested in what He did for Israel in the Old Testament—all the *grace* He showed them. The children of Israel were a bunch of slaves held captive in Egypt when God came to deliver them. Did these people deserve to be delivered? There's no good reason to believe they were any more deserving than any other captive people. Did God show grace to them *in* His deliverance? Absolutely—it was a free gift, an expression of His heavenly grace (Deut. 7:7–8). Likewise, His providential care for them in their wilderness wanderings was a gift they did not deserve and could not repay (Deut. 8:2–4). His having brought them into the Promised Land (Canaan) was a gift for which He was entirely responsible (Deut. 32:49). The covenant He entered into with Israel gave them a special relationship with Him that no other nation enjoyed (Exod. 19:5–6). Every time He forgave an Israelite, He showed grace. Every time He forgave the nation of Israel, He showed grace. Every time He did *anything* for Israel that they could not do for themselves (with respect to their prosperity and survival), He showed divine grace.

It is true that such acts of grace were not in the same context as what we have been discussing—i.e., His having "saved" the nation of Israel is not on the same level as a soul being saved by grace through faith in Christ. Yet, God has proved His willingness and desire *to* save people from whatever would destroy them *when* those people put their faith in Him. This is as true in a physical context (with Israel) as it is in a spiritual one (in our case). With specific regard to spiritual salvation, *every soul that has ever been delivered from divine condemnation* has been saved by grace through faith.

The greatest proof of God's grace is revealed in the person of Jesus Christ. "[T]he Word [Christ] became flesh, and dwelt among us, and we beheld His glory, glory as of the only begotten from the Father, full of grace and truth" (John 1:14). The way Jesus lived, the words He spoke, the miracles He wrought, and the magnificent sacrifice He made for mankind are all manifestations of God's grace. We could not have reached up into heaven to bring divine grace down to us, nor could we raise ourselves from the deadness of our condemnation to stand before God. But Christ descended from heaven *and* ascended from the grave on our behalf. Both actions are gifts of God that are critical to our salvation but were impossible for us to have done for ourselves (Rom. 3:23–24, 10:5–10).

Christ has made redemption (as yet, an unseen thing) *real* and *believable* to the one who accepts the proofs He has provided in His own physical life, death, and resurrection (Acts 17:30–31). Because He lived and "dwelt among us," one can believe that "the grace of God has appeared, bringing salvation to man" (Titus 2:11). God has condescended to us in His Son in order to save us from ourselves. Jesus' sacrificial death proves how far God was willing to go in order to make grace *real* and *available* to all who believe in Him. Jesus' resurrection from the dead proves that God is willing and able to raise us from *our* "death" (the result of our being condemned for our sins) (Rom. 6:4–5). By the same power by which Jesus ascended to heaven, so the believer will also one day ascend to heaven (Phil. 3:20–21). Jesus Christ is our proof of God's grace: as He has lived, so we can live; as He has died, so we die with Him in our baptism; as He has been raised to glory, so we are raised—first, in faith (symbolically, in our baptism), but someday in fact (upon our bodily resurrection).[47] When someone says, "How do we know that God's grace really exists?" we direct them to the Lord Jesus and show them grace in the flesh.

But, of course, it does not matter what God or Jesus or the apostles say to the one who refuses to believe it. "For this is the will of My Father," Jesus said, "that everyone who beholds the Son and believes in Him will have eternal life, and I Myself will raise him up on the last day" (John 6:40). But Jesus also said that "unless you believe that I am He [i.e., the Messiah sent from God for our salvation—MY WORDS], you will die in your sins" (John 8:24). To believe in Jesus means to obey Him. It is not enough merely to agree with who He is and what He said; it is necessary also to respond to this agreement with demonstrations of faith. No one is saved for merely having a belief, but everyone will be saved who hears Jesus' words and responds accordingly (Mat. 7:24–27).

Putting Belief into Action

Belief in God's grace depends upon a conviction in Christ and His gospel. A "conviction" is a belief that is so strong, it demands action and moves us forward. There is nothing half-hearted or incidental about a genuine conviction. Jesus had it; the apostle Paul had it; every man or woman who lived by faith in God had it; every person who chooses to follow Christ *must* have it. One of the (big) reasons why the world is in such moral confusion today is because so many people lack moral conviction—the strong, driving desire to do the right thing, no matter what the cost or consequences. Sadly, many Christians who *once* had this have since lost it.

There is nothing wrong, however, with admitting that our belief is not yet where it should be, or that we are struggling to maintain it, especially in the face of very difficult trials. There are strong beliefs, and then there are developing beliefs; likewise, there are strong convictions, and then there are developing convictions. A developing belief is not only growing, but it *seeks* to grow—it does what is necessary to grow. Unbelief, on the other hand, refuses to accept the truth, or will not act on the truth, or will not grow according to the truth. Many Christians think "unbelief" only describes the disposition of atheists, agnostics, and irreligious people. Yet, Paul described himself as having manifested "unbelief"—even while he was passionately religious—when he refused to listen to God's truth (1 Tim. 1:12–13). Any Christian today who knows *what* to believe but deliberately refuses *to* believe is not living *like* a believer. Instead, he acts just like those who are outside of Christ who live in darkness and rebellion to God. Sadly, there are many unbelievers sitting on church pews across the country on any given Sunday.

In all fairness, some unbelief is due to a misunderstanding of God's word, or one's failure to grasp the big picture. For example, we can read of an account of a man who begged Jesus to heal his demon-possessed son (Mark 9:14–29). "[I]f You can do anything," the man cried, "take pity on us and help us!" Jesus gently chastised the man in order to make a point. "'If You can'? All things are possible to him who believes"—to which the man immediately responded, "I do believe; help my unbelief." It was not as though this man did not believe in Christ at all, for he was imploring Him to use His divine power to heal his son. Instead, he was admitting to Jesus that his belief did not have the depth or maturity that it should have had. He believed with his head, but he struggled to believe with his heart.

I am certain that all of us who are striving to believe—and are confronting pockets of unbelief within ourselves—can relate to this man's statement. We understand his frustration; we have experienced personally his spiritual struggle. It is not that we do not believe at all, but our belief is not yet as strong as it could be—hopefully, as it *will* be. We intellectually agree with Jesus that "all things are possible to him who believes," but we still wrestle with our own spiritual immaturity. God knows that we do this, so do not be afraid to admit it to Him, or to yourself. "I do believe; help my unbelief" should be our own plea to Jesus whenever He has promised us something in which we *ought* to believe, but we have not yet *perfected* that belief.

Summary Thoughts

If you are "in Christ" and are doing your best to obey Him, do you believe that God has truly forgiven you? Do you believe that God will do everything for your salvation that you are unable to do yourself? Do you believe that God is working in your life in ways that you do not have to know and that He does not have to explain to you? Do you believe in God's grace?

Saving grace sounds too good to be true. If it remains dependent upon what you are able to bring to the table, it *is* too good to be true. Apart from divine help, it is absolutely *impossible*. But God makes the impossible *possible* and the undoable *doable*. If your salvation were left up to your own strength, you would not have a chance. But God's grace does not work with "chance"; it operates according to truth and reality. If you believe in His grace, then it is *true* that He *really will* save your soul. Nothing in the world can stop this from happening except one thing: your *unbelief* in it.

While formerly he "acted ignorantly in unbelief," the apostle Paul gave his head, heart, and soul over to Jesus Christ. At the end of his life, as he faced his own martyrdom, he said confidently, "I am not ashamed [of suffering for the Lord—MY WORDS]; for I know whom I have believed and I am convinced that He is able to guard what I have entrusted to Him until that day" (2 Tim. 1:12). Later he declared, "the time of my departure has come. I have fought the good fight, I have finished the course, I have kept the faith; in the future there is laid up for me the crown of righteousness, which the Lord, the righteous Judge, will award to me on that day; and not only to me, but also to all who have loved His appearing" (4:6–8). Paul believed in Christ because Christ gave him every reason to believe in Him. He trusted in divine grace because a Savior as virtuous and powerful as Christ could never disappoint him.

What about you?

Chapter Nine
⇒ *The Problem of Guilt* ⇐

"Wash yourselves, make yourselves clean; remove the evil of your deeds from My sight. Cease to do evil, learn to do good; seek justice, reprove the ruthless; defend the orphan, plead for the widow. Come now, and let us reason together," says the LORD, *"Though your sins are as scarlet, they will be as white as snow; though they are red like crimson, they will be like wool"* (Isa. 1:16–18)

There is a man in nearly every congregation—we'll call him "Allen"—who ought to do more than he is doing, contribute more than he is contributing, and serve more than he is serving. Allen is very capable and resourceful. He is skilled in a number of different areas. He gets along with people exceptionally well, and is highly respected among his peers. He has a beautiful family, a good job, and a comfortable income. Allen ought to be a church-appointed deacon and seems to be an excellent candidate for a future elder.

Strangely, however, Allen's participation is that of a casual churchgoer. He refuses to teach any classes, although he appears completely qualified to do so. He turns down every nomination for being a deacon, although he appears to be naturally fit for such a responsibility. He seems to want to associate with the group and yet, while smiling and friendly, he always maintains a certain distance and disconnectedness from fellow believers. We think he is just being modest, or that he is a very busy man, or perhaps he feels uncomfortable in leadership positions. This is what we think, and he is content to let us think it.

The reality is this: Allen is wrestling with a terribly powerful, asphyxiating guilt over something he has done—possibly even something he is still aching to do, or is still doing—and yet he refuses to divulge it to anyone. Allen has a well-disguised drinking problem, or a covert drug addiction. Or, he has a penchant for pornography, or even a strange sexual fetish which he can only have fulfilled in the seedier parts of town. Or, he has had an affair and, even if the sexual encounters are over, he does not *want* it to be over, or he cannot bring himself to deal with his indiscretion. Or, he is still reeling from incidents that happened a long time ago in which innocent people (like himself?) were hurt and for which he feels personally responsible. Any of these things might be going on in Allen's *head*, regardless of what is actually happening in Allen's *life*.

To be fair, let's assume that Allen has made efforts to overcome his private issue, whatever it is, and has asked God's forgiveness a thousand times over. But, given the distance he keeps from fellow Christians, he still feels that gnawing, aching, suffocating, dead weight of *guilt* pressing down on his soul every single day of his life. This is why he will not participate in his church any more than he has to: he feels too guilty, too unworthy, too hypocritical to go any further. Quite frankly, it is all he can do just to show up for Sunday worship.

The Nature of Guilt

One common and debilitating reason why Christians—yes, *Christians*—will not surrender to God's saving grace is, ironically, because of the enormity of their guilt. I say "ironically" because God's grace is all about *removing* guilt, not perpetuating it. Even so, many well-intentioned believers allow personal guilt to stand in the way of a fulfilling and rewarding relationship with the Lord. While no external forces can separate us from Christ (Rom. 8:38–39), what goes on inside *can* destroy us—if we let it. Nothing in the world can be as tormenting as the monstrous guilt that haunts one's every waking moment. An army of soldiers—even all the demonic forces of hell—cannot force us to compromise our convictions, but a subtle and sinister force called guilt can take us down without a shot being fired, so to speak.

Guilt is something we can all appreciate. We all know what it is like to feel guilty. We have all seen a guilty look; we have all observed people's hesitations due to the guilt they were experiencing. We have all *felt* guilty for something we did not even do or for which we were not even responsible. For example, a woman may feel guilty for delivering a still-born child. A man may feel guilty for being "downsized" from his job. A child (perhaps a young Allen?) may feel guilty for the breakup of his parent's marriage. Many people bear upon their shoulders crosses that do not belong to them and they were never meant to carry. Guilt is a common human reaction to one's personal perceived failure to control a given situation. But just because guilt is common does not mean it is healthy, or is necessary, or will not completely destroy a person.

As God sees it, real guilt is not a mere feeling, a philosophical concept, or a theological state of existence. Guilt is the perilous state of being of one who has sinned (or, transgressed; violated) any of God's moral or written commandments (Jas. 2:10). Guilt exists when one has broken a law, whether it is a law of God, a law of the land, or even the "law" of one's own conscience (Rom. 2:14–15, 14:23). Being "guilty" is, in essence, the legal status of one who is convicted of a particular sin. Guilt and shame often coexist, but they are not interchangeable. Guilt may exist regardless of whether one is shameful for what he has done; shame can also exist regardless if one is actually guilty for having committed a crime against God. Technically speaking, "guilty" is what you *are* when you have sinned; "shame" is what you *feel* when that sin is known by others (including God). You feel shame when you experience your own or another's condemnation for what you have done, whether or not God condemns you.

Not everyone who breaks the law will be prosecuted (in this life) for his crime, if his action remains undetected. He may feel guilty about what he did, but as long as he is willing to live with his guilt, he can masquerade as an innocent man. For most people, however, the pain of their guilt leads them either to confess their crimes or seek some way to cope (often, through some form of narcotics or medication). Some attempt to run away from their guilt (as if they could); a few choose suicide. The point is: most people who truly are guilty know that they deserve to be punished. Many are tormented by the anticipation of that punishment.

Unlike America's imperfect legal system, where the guilty may be set free and the innocent may be wrongly imprisoned, God's legal system is flawless and entirely impartial. No crime, however small, escapes His detection; "And there is no creature hidden from His sight, but all things are open and laid bare to the eyes of Him with whom we have to do" (Heb. 4:13). No one bluffs his way past God's moral justice; He will ultimately "judge the secrets of men through Christ Jesus" (Rom. 2:16), for He knows what is in each person (John 2:25). God holds all people accountable for their sins, however private or difficult to prosecute in a human court of law they may be. God knows even the sins of the heart which no mortal man can possibly know except the one who committed them. In His sermon on the mount (Mat. 5 – 7), Jesus spoke of murderers who did not kill anyone, adulterers who never illicitly touched another woman, and treacherous husbands who divorced their wives according to the technical requirements of the Law of Moses (Mat 5:21–32). Yet, in each case, the hearts of those involved were corrupted with anger, greed, or lust—and God *sees* this.

Those who committed such sins under the Law of Moses stood guilty before God. Likewise, we who are under the law of Christ are guilty of unseen and otherwise undetected sins of the heart. Apart from God's means of dealing with these sins (by grace and through faith), it is impossible to have them removed. Thus, one who is not cleansed by the blood of Christ remains guilty of his sins. If he dies in this state, then he will pay for his crimes for the rest of his eternal existence. This person will stand before God's heavenly tribunal— surrounded by God's army of angels—and hear God's thundering condemnation of his soul: "Depart from Me, accursed one" (Mat. 25:41). These words are the worst thing to hear from God; this is the worst thing that could ever happen to any person! For millions and millions of souls, this will be the last thing they hear before they are cast into the outer darkness where "there will be weeping and gnashing of teeth" (Mat. 8:12) from the pain of their torment as well as the horrible pain of regret over missed opportunity.

Guilt Is a Debilitating Force

Knowing that you are guilty before God is (and should be) a terrifying experience. Until this is properly dealt with, it takes an enormous toll on your spiritual life. Real guilt anticipates real punishment; as real as your sin is, so is the eternal punishment for that sin. Real guilt is when the reality of eternal separation from God, the outer darkness of the damned, and all the horrors of hell *touch your very soul.* Such thoughts are the stuff of nightmares. It is no wonder, then, that some people literally go insane over the guilt they experience.

There is no good reason for a Christian—one who is "in Christ" and therefore has access to God's covenant terms of forgiveness—to live as a guilty person. Even so, many Christians do just this: they live in fear, knowing full well that "God is a consuming fire" (Heb. 12:29) and that they have become the object of that fire. The guilty Christian knows that, despite his best efforts to conceal his guilt from others, it remains ever-present before the Lord. Instead of dealing with his sins, he wrestles with guilt, and the weight of divine condemnation crushes him into a spiritual dwarf. His Christian convictions appear to him as shallow and ineffective. His conversations about spiritual matters and the business of heaven are few and forced. He cannot look others in the eye, he cannot level with his wife, he cannot *be* what he knows he ought to be. Instead, he walks around tending outwardly to his responsibilities but knowing inwardly he is a fraud, an impostor, a hypocrite. (This is where Allen is, and this is why he remains aloof.)

Having experienced this incapacitating guilt personally, I can speak of it with graphic clarity. I am certainly not proud of admitting this, but I did not want anyone to think that I am describing this in merely clinical terms. The moral pain I have felt when avoiding spiritual responsibility for my sins cannot be put into words. There is a kind of *hell* that a person goes through when confronted with the overwhelming horrors of divine condemnation—especially when that condemnation becomes a very real possibility.

All such behavior—I shamefully allude to my own past experiences—betrays what the Christian professes to believe. Purposely remaining (for any reason) in a state of guilt questions God's forgiveness, the Spirit's intercession, and Christ's work of redemption. That person feels worthless, even though Christ would never die for a worthless cause. He remains in sin, even though Christ died "to take away sins" (1 John 3:5). He doubts in the system of saving grace, even though Christ has shown the power of that grace through the power of His own resurrection (1 Pet. 1:3). He remains unclean, even though God promises to cleanse him with the blood of Christ if he would but show *faith* in His forgiveness rather than shamefully *avoid* it.

Satan loves to see God's children drowning in their own guilt and shame. The children of God are supposed to be wise to his schemes and wary of his wicked disguises (2 Cor. 2:11, 11:14). But Satan has been very successful in deceiving many a Christian into accepting his message of doom and defeat. Even though Christians were once convinced of and converted by God's gospel of grace, Satan has converted a number of them back into the fearful, quaking, and useless slaves of sin that they once had been. As Steve Farrar (in *Point Man*) rightly concludes, Satan does not care if one goes to church, talks about spiritual things, goes through the motions of a believer, and calls himself a Christian—as long as he is not *effective*.[48]

A child of God that is debilitated by self-wrought and self-perpetuating guilt is actually more useful to Satan than a person who has never made a commitment to God in the first place. This is because he not only destroys his own spiritual life, but he will likely be very instrumental in destroying other Christians who are influenced by his half-hearted, negative, and duplicitous treatment of the gospel. He advertises, consciously or not, "God's gospel of grace may promise spiritual deliverance, but look at me—I believed it, and *I am miserable*. And, likely, you will be, too." The Christian who will not trust in God's gospel of grace becomes an evangelist for Satan's message of hopelessness and failure. Thus, this demoralized messenger of good news is more demoralizing than a good messenger of bad news.

Satan Cannot Hold You Prisoner (Unless You Let Him)

Though Satan may gloat over how many prisoners he has, such imprisonment is actually self-inflicted. Satan's claims and accusations are based upon lies and deceit—false conclusions that people *believe* are real. The only time Satan can exercise power over our hearts is when we *give* him this power. Satan feeds on our guilt, our shame, and our fear; it is through our self-imposed weakness and naïve gullibility that he gains dominance over our heart. When we draw near to God, we actively resist the devil and he has no choice but to *flee* from us (Jas. 4:7–8). He does not flee because of our power, but because of *God's* power that works through us (Phil. 2:13, Heb. 13:20–21). Satan can resist us easily enough—we are no match for his clever manipulations and wicked deceptions—but he is no match for God. Sadly, not everyone believes this. Not all *Christians* believe this.

As an illustration, recall when the apostle Peter was imprisoned by King Herod Agrippa I (Acts 12:1–11). Peter was kept in an inner prison, guarded by armed Roman soldiers, his hands chained to two of these guards. (The apostles had escaped prison before, while under the watch of Jewish officers [Acts 5:17–25], so Herod took measures to make sure that they would not escape *Roman* imprisonment.) But an angel of God visited Peter at night and roused him from his sleep. As Peter stood up, the chains fell off his hands. As he walked out of his cell, locked doors of the prison opened automatically and guards were rendered powerless to stop him. This is a great illustration about faith in prayer, the limitations of men, and divine deliverance.

Just as the grace of God delivered Peter from prison, so He can deliver *us*. Picture a guilty Christian who believes he is confined to a dungeon of hopelessness and failure. Satan gladly plays the role of the prison warden, posts his demonic "guards" all around, and shackles this child of God between them. The guilty Christian languishes there in the darkness, miserable in his condition, having nothing to look forward to but his spiritual execution. Suddenly, a glorified Jesus, bathed in brilliant light, presents Himself before this person and says,

"Get up quickly!" Translated, this means, "What in the world are you *doing here*? I have died a horrible, torturous death on the cross to *free you from this very situation,* and here you sit in the middle of your prison! Now *get up,* for I am your Savior. Satan has no power over you except what you have given him." When that person obeys the Lord's command, he will indeed stand up. Chains fall off his hands. Prison doors open automatically. Demons and Satan himself flee, for the Lord Jesus Christ is more powerful than any or all of them.

How pathetic it is when God's people allow Satan to wield power over them! How awful it is when they languish in prison, even though Christ has moved heaven and earth to free them *from* prison! Christ has *already* defeated Satan in His victorious sacrifice on the cross.[49] He has *already* "rendered powerless him who had the power of death, that is, the devil," that He "might free those who through fear of death were subject to slavery all their lives" (Heb. 2:14–15). So then, *what in the world are we doing there*, all of us who find ourselves being crushed with guilt, suffocating with shame, and living in the unspeakable dread of being condemned to hell? This is not only a manifestation of unbelief, but it is entirely unnecessary—and therefore inexcusable.

Grace versus Guilt

God's grace is capable of removing our guilt—not just some of it, but *all* of it. He promises in His covenant that He "will be merciful to [our] iniquities" and "will remember [our] sins no more" (Heb. 8:12). This does not mean that He will literally forget all that we have done—because He *is* God, He cannot literally forget *anything*—but that He will not condemn us for sins that have been forgiven.[50]

You are not unique in that you have sinned, for *everyone* has done this (Rom. 3:23). In fact, if you say that you have *not* sinned, you make God out to be a liar (1 John 1:10). But when you deal with sin in the manner which God has prescribed (to be discussed shortly), then your sin no longer exists. This means you no longer bear the *guilt* of that sin and thus will not have to answer to God for it. This means sin's shackles have fallen off, prison doors have been supernaturally opened, and you are a free person—free to walk in God's light (1 John

1:7). You need not fear future punishment by God for sins that have been forgiven; you cannot be innocent and guilty at the same time. If you belong to God in Christ, "There is no fear in love; but perfect love casts out fear, because fear involves punishment, and the one who fears is not perfected in love" (1 John 4:17–18). God removes your fear when He removes your sins.

Listen, because this is very important: God knows that all those who strive to follow Him are going to have difficulties, doubts, times of weakness, and even periods of despondency. He even knows that we are going to sin. (I am just being realistic here, not giving permission.) There are times when we are going to beat ourselves up pretty badly for the foolish, inexcusable, and immature things we have done. I am well acquainted with this. I have sinned against God without making much effort to resist temptation; I have failed to trust in His love without realizing it; I have slandered His holy name in ways that make me cringe and lower my head to think about it. Maybe you are more spiritually mature than I am, or maybe you can relate. Either way, my point is: God's grace is not meant to intensify our guilt; it is meant to *remove it entirely.*

The apostle John says (1 John 3:19–22): "We will know by this that we are of the truth, and will assure our heart before Him in whatever our heart condemns us; for God is greater than our heart and knows all things. Beloved, if our heart does not condemn us, we have confidence before God; and whatever we ask we receive from Him, because we keep His commandments and do the things that are pleasing in His sight." John is *not* saying, "Don't sweat whatever is tormenting you, it's no big deal." Whatever is troubling your soul *is* a "big deal," and may cause you tremendous grief. Rather, he says, essentially: Do not think that just because you are struggling with sin, or wrestling with imagined guilt, or trying hard to overcome some stumbling block in your life, that God has abandoned you. God does not abandon people; people abandon God. As long as your attitude is to serve Him and you are doing your best to "keep His commandments and do the things that are pleasing in His sight," you can still "have confidence before God," knowing His grace is able to overcome your periods of doubt, despondency, and failure. "God is greater than our heart"—His grace is capable of handling your feelings of guilt, shame, and despair.

What Needs to Be Done

But here's the other side of this: you cannot assume God's grace will cleanse you of your sins without any action on your part. Grace never works alone; it always works in conjunction with human faith. (Just because it is incomprehensibly greater in power than human faith does not change this fact.) Grace never gives anyone license to sin—a kind of "Get Out of Jail Free" card. Dietrich Bonhoeffer calls a doctrine that justifies the sin and not the sinner "cheap grace."[51] We must never cheapen saving grace in order to justify sin, make sin easier to commit, or be careless about our spiritual responsibility toward God.

Saving grace must never be assumed into existence. If you are not in a covenant relationship with God, or if you will not show humble faith *in* God, or if you will not "walk in a manner worthy of the Lord" (Col. 1:10), then you will not receive His grace. You cannot *assume* God's grace will save you if you fail or refuse to do what is necessary to receive it. While *earning* grace is impossible, it *is* necessary to prepare the heart to receive God's gift. Grace will not be applied automatically; it must be *asked* for, as a demonstration of your faith in the One who provides it.

If you are already a Christian, all of this is done through a relatively simple but absolutely necessary process:

- You must **acknowledge** (or, confess) your sin—to God, yourself, and (if applicable) the one against whom you sinned (1 John 1:8–9, Acts 19:18, et al). This has to do with taking personal responsibility for what you did. God will not forgive anyone who refuses to admit his sin. To "confess" in this context means to be in agreement with whatever conclusions God has about you. Thus, if His gospel declares you guilty, then you need to be in agreement with that verdict (and act accordingly). It also works the other way: if God declares you righteous, then it does not matter who brings a charge against you (Rom. 8:33)—you are found innocent before Him.

- You must **repent** of the sinful action or lifestyle that you engaged in (Acts 2:38, 3:19, 26:20, 2 Cor. 7:9–10, et al). This requires a change in *attitude* as well as a corresponding change in *behavior*— never one or the other, but always both. Repentance is not merely a change in direction; it is a commitment to the *right(eous)* direction. No one is truly repentant who does not allow Christ's gospel to direct his way to the Father.

- You must **petition** God to remove your sin through an appeal to the sacrifice of Christ (Mat. 6:12, Acts 8:22, Jas. 5:16, 1 John 2:1–2, et al). This requires that you believe in the process of petitioning (prayer) as well as in the One whom you are petitioning (God). Since all petitions for forgiveness can only be made through prayer, you can see why Satan does not *want* us to pray. If you refuse to pray to God because you feel so guilty for your sins, you cut off access to the very means by which that guilt is removed. (This creates a vicious circle: first, "I won't pray because I feel guilty"; then, "I feel guilty because I won't pray." And around and around it goes, accomplishing nothing, but becoming increasingly worse as time goes on.) God wants to hear your prayers so He can forgive your sins. Prayer is a manifestation of faith in His forgiveness; refusing to pray is tantamount to refusing to have faith in God.

Such is the biblical prescription for how Christians are to deal properly with their sins. If you have never been baptized into a covenant relationship with God through Christ, then this process will not work for you until you have done so. (This has already been covered in detail in Chapter Six, "The Access to Saving Grace.") Saving grace is not available outside of the context in which the blood of Christ is applied; sinners who remain outside of this covenant also remain disconnected from the source of their salvation. The good news is: *all this can change.* And, if you are not a Christian, you would be very wise to make this change.

Summary Thoughts

God's grace is designed to overcome the sinner's guilt, not to ignore, suppress, or marginalize it. Neither the quantity nor intensity of his guilt is relevant; God's grace is able and sufficient to take care of it all. What must be avoided at all cost is succumbing to Satan's insinuation that our sin is too great for God's grace or keeps His grace at bay. Grace will not be denied the humble sinner who turns to God for help—grace is His divine and direct *response* to our sin. Grace does not run away from sin in revulsion, but is designed to eliminate it. God does not turn away from the contrite believer in horror and disgust—He cleanses him and then *embraces* him!

Have you sinned against God and are still wallowing in guilt and feelings of worthlessness? If you are a Christian, there is no need for this. Remember "Allen," whose story opened this chapter? There is no good reason to live like him. Allen is allowing his guilt to drive his life into the ground rather than allowing grace to *lead him home*. Allen has access to divine grace, but prevents himself from benefiting from it. He portrays himself as a true believer, but in reality, he lives like an unbeliever. He has great potential, but unless he turns that potential into action, nothing will ever happen because his situation will never change.

What are *you* doing?

If you have prayed to God for forgiveness, do you believe He has removed your sin? If so, you are no longer guilty *of* that sin. Do you still feel guilty, even though you keep praying over and over for God to remove your sin? If so, with all due respect, you really do not yet understand how God's grace works. Go back and re-read this chapter. Better yet, read the New Testament—you will find it simply does not support your "feeling." But if you have sinned against God, have taken the appropriate steps to be reconciled with Him, and *trust* that He has indeed forgiven you, then you can bask in the warmth of fellowship with our Lord.

"How blessed is he whose transgression is forgiven, whose sin is covered!" (Psalm 32:1).

Chapter Ten
⟹ *The Problem of Abuse* ⟸

*To the pure, all things are pure; but to those who are defiled
and unbelieving, nothing is pure, but both their mind and their
conscience are defiled. They profess to know God, but by their deeds
they deny Him. . . . But as for you, speak the things which are
fitting for sound doctrine.* (Titus 1:15–16, 2:1)

S aving grace is a priceless, beautiful, and most excellent gift of
God. It is something Christians should be talking about—*a lot.* It
should be a regular part of our conversations with fellow believers. It
should be something we want to share with those who are lost. We
ought to be gushing with gratitude for this truly amazing blessing that
we cannot earn, cannot repay, and have never deserved.

But just because we "should" or "ought" to do these things does
not mean we *are* doing them, or that we feel comfortable doing
them. There are various reasons for this. One of these is this: some
"Christians" (both real and imaged) have abused this gift, in one way
or another. For example, their teaching about grace is unbiblical.
They say things about God's grace beyond or different than what God
Himself has said. They misrepresent the application of grace; they
claim that it is unconditional; etc. Many have turned grace into an
emotional experience rather than a practical one. Modern "Christian"
music, for example, often portrays grace as an almost magical force
field that makes us euphoric, god-like, and invincible.

So much abuse of such a good thing is very upsetting to those
striving to maintain the sound doctrine of Christ's gospel. In recoiling
from the abuse of the teaching and application of grace in the so-
called Christian community, upset believers tend to go to the other
extreme. Since being too vocal about grace—whatever *that* means—
appears to create a negative association with those who abuse grace,
these others have chosen to remain largely silent on the subject. This
is a strange—and completely inappropriate—way to promote a gospel
that is entirely predicated upon God's saving grace.

The Charismatic Experience

Conservatism is all about protecting the status quo—not always necessarily what is *true*, but what is *believed* to be true. Jesus protected the Law of Moses because it *was* true (Mat. 5:17–18); the Pharisees of His day protected their long-held traditions because they equated these *with* the truth (Mat. 15:1–6). (Jesus soundly condemned the Pharisees' position—but that is another discussion.) Many conservative-minded Christians believe that religious subjects and practices that conflict with what *they* believe to be "the truth" are to be avoided. This is not to say that this avoidance is always right or wrong, but that it happens. For example, Baptists allow their members to give vocal "testimonies" of their faith during worship services; Catholics practice confession (to priests), confirmation, and exorcisms; Mormons baptize for the dead; and Seventh-day Adventists observe Saturday as the God-ordained "Sabbath." Most conservative Christians reject all of these beliefs or practices. In fact, most will not even *talk* about them.

Charismatic religion, for example, makes many references to God's grace.[52] Seldom, however, will the preacher of charismatic religion allow the Bible to define saving grace in its proper context. Charismatic religion is characterized by emotionally-charged and "Spirit-filled" worship services which allegedly involves the direct physical manipulation by the Holy Spirit, speaking in tongues, and even faith-healing. I have attended some of their so-called "faith healing" services, and so I speak from personal observation and experience.

To the uninitiated, these services can be intimidating, even overwhelming. Through a slow build-up—often through the use of songs, music, singing, clapping, stirring testimonies, and prayers—a preacher of magnetic personality leads his group to the threshold of spiritual euphoria. Often at this point, people in the audience will stand and raise their arms in the air, rhythmically swaying to the smooth sound of the music and the undulating and hypnotic voice of the preacher. While he alternates between quietly cooing and then exploding into fiery praises and interjections of alleged prophecies from the Holy Spirit, the audience becomes mesmerized and transfixed. Some people start crying out in spiritual ecstasy, others start speaking incoherently in what is claimed to be angelic tongues, while others fall to the ground in spasmodic convulsions, claiming to be overtaken by the Holy Spirit. All this may be followed by a "healing" session in which people are said to be miraculously cured of problems, diseases, demon possession, etc.

I respect a person's right to believe whatever he (or she) wants to believe. Even so, the worship experiences I just described are completely foreign to the Scriptures. The apostle Paul never whipped his audience up into a frenzy in order to have a "faith healing" session. Christians in the early church never lost control of their senses—or their bodies—in a moment of epiphany at the cue of the preacher. We do have New Testament accounts of people speaking in tongues by the power of the Holy Spirit, but never in languages that were unintelligible or untranslatable. Quite the opposite, they spoke fluently in known languages (Acts 2:4–11). The apostle Paul instructed, "Let all things be done for edification. If anyone speaks in a tongue [in the assembly—MY WORDS], it should be by two or at the most three, and each in turn, and one must interpret; but if there is no interpreter, he must keep silent in the church; and let him speak to himself and to God" (1 Cor. 14:26–28). And no angel in the Bible ever spoke in a tongue different than the native language of those to whom he was speaking.

The world scoffs and rolls its eyes at Christians—and those who think they are Christians—whose beliefs are based on confusion, chaos, and misunderstanding. Such scorn is well-deserved. People who claim to be enlightened by an intelligent God have no right to practice blind faith and cheap grace. Faith that rests upon anything less than divinely-revealed knowledge and factual evidence is nothing more than an opinion. Those who abuse God's grace (through erroneous teaching, misapplication, or just sheer ignorance) are following human passions, human appetites, and human opinions (Phil. 3:17–19). By invoking God's Spirit, divine favor, and divine grace in ways that defy New Testament teaching they bring shame to the gospel of saving grace. God has no obligation to respond to—much less *save*—those who decide to pray, teach, perform, and worship according to their own desires. There are many in the world who think that they will be heard by God for their many words, but are terribly mistaken (Mat. 6:7–8).

Fear and Safety

In case anyone thinks mine to be an unfair and overly-critical assessment of others, let me now turn the tables and examine "conservative" Christians. For the sake of argument, I will include myself in this group. We do tend to look down upon the people I have just described with an attitude of self-righteousness. We tend to be quicker to *condemn* such people than to give them any benefit of doubt. Our reason, of course, seems justified enough: the undignified use of God's grace in charismatic circles (and other religious movements) *bothers* us to the core. Instead of engaging in meaningful dialogue with them over the Scriptures, we tend to distance ourselves from them altogether. We treat them as if they are a contagion: if we get too close, they might corrupt us. We think that if *we* openly appeal to the same divine grace to which *they* appeal, then people might start associating *us* with *them*, and then we will need to convince everyone that we are *not* them, and they are *not* us.

Instead of isolating the problem of their teaching on grace (because not *all* of their teaching on grace is in error), we tend to downplay the subject of grace altogether. We focus instead on much "safer" subjects like "the one true church," "apostolic authority," or "justification by faith." Thus, when someone confesses their sins and petitions God for His divine favor, we will speak officially of forgiveness and restoration as though we were discussing the stock indexes of the Wall Street Journal. We will admit—as-a-matter-of-factly, without too much emotion or feeling, since we do not want to appear *charismatic*—that, yes, God has forgiven so-and-so and our fellowship with this person has now been technically restored, but we may have a hard time actually using words like grace or mercy or

Spirit. Or, if we *do* use them, we may offer a disclaimer about what such words mean ("scripturally") and what they do *not* mean, in case anyone thinks we are going, well, "charismatic."

Of course, we will *sing* about grace. This is harmless enough. We are not committing ourselves by merely singing lyrics to songs—especially when they are classics. So then, we sing about "Amazing Grace" and "Matchless Grace" and how "His Grace Reaches Me," but since these are only *songs,* they remain in safe territory. If anyone dare accuse us of singing the same songs as those "charismatic people," our response might be something like, "Yes, but they sing them much more *charismatically* than we do," which paints us as a bunch of prudish, priggish, pickle-faced "pew people" who are unwilling to enthusiastically extol God's grace simply because of what other people have done! We claim not to be servants of men but of God (Gal. 1:10), but here we are, allowing other men to dictate how we are going to worship the God of heaven. Why would we do such a thing?

Because, in reality, *we are afraid.* (Maybe *you* are not afraid, but many of us *are.*)

We are afraid of complicity with those with whom we disagree. We are afraid of appearing too modern or contemporary for fear of our church traditions being compromised—or altogether lost. We are afraid we will be criticized by our elders and the older generation of believers, many who have been brought up in a strict, starchy, and static way of thinking that is largely intolerant of change or new ideas (as though talking freely about grace was a "new" idea). We are generally afraid of change altogether, or of any perceived threats to what we do, how we speak, our church vernacular, or how we regard people of other religions. Some of us have become so ingrained with conservative thinking that we are blind to our own insular attitudes. Some of us will not entertain any new information or allow our beliefs to be challenged by any perspective other than our own. In a sense, we have built a wall around our churches in much the same way as individuals (like Linda) build a wall around their own lives. In an extreme sense, we have created a collective box-like mentality with its translucent walls filtering out everything that does not agree with our own well-rehearsed belief system. *Our* system is not open for discussion, critique, or enlightenment.

We who travel in "conservative" circles have a tendency to talk openly only about those practices and conclusions which we deem "safe" and therefore allegedly superior. We assume that, as long as we remain in the "safe" zone, we have arrived: we have the truth, anyone who is outside our "safe" zone does *not* have the truth, and we feel justified in critiquing *them* even though we do not want to hear their critiques of *us*. A typical segment of our conversation will run like something like this: "Well, brother Joe, you have a good point there, but, you know, we want to take the 'safe' course of action, which means doing what we've always done." Or: "We need to maintain our present course of thinking, otherwise, we 'open the door' to all kinds of potential abuse, and *before you know it*, we will be in the middle of apostasy."[53] (The "before you know it" phrase is a favorite of the slippery-slope rhetoric. The idea is: if we do anything differently than what we are doing now, doom is inevitable.)

But being safe in *this* context necessarily implies that we are afraid. The safe route usually means we are afraid of all other routes. The safe manner of worship services usually means we are afraid to try anything different than what we have practiced and supposedly perfected for years and decades. The safe conclusions we have drawn from Scripture means we are afraid to consider all other conclusions. Because we think we have the safe way, course, direction, method, etc., we tacitly imply that we have tried and tested every *other* way, course, method, etc. and have found them lacking in some way, which further implies that our safe way is the superior one. Now in some cases we may actually *have* a superior approach in one way or another, but this is often an assumption and not a proven fact.

We have a tendency to confuse "safe" with "proper," "fitting," and "protective." Likewise, we tend to think "conservative" means "the only right way to think about anything." But the very word "conservative" comes from the root word "conserve," which means to *save that which already is*, to protect the status quo. Technically-speaking, conservatives are not interested in seeking change or modifications, even those for the better; we are interested in keeping everything the way it is. Another way of saying this is: we are afraid of change, simply because it *is* change. Change, to those of us indoctrinated on conservatism, seems equivalent to opening the door to *abuse*.[54]

Jesus: Conservative or Liberal?

Someone reading this might be thinking, "Well, then, what does he want us to do? Become a bunch of 'liberals'?" We (conservatives) have been thoroughly conditioned to believe that not only are "liberals" inherently bad people, but everything *about* the word "liberal" is inherently bad as well. There's nothing sinful with being a free thinker—one who is not afraid to embrace change and is open to different perspectives. The world—and the church—has always benefited from those who can "see" more, better, and further than others are willing to look.

Liberal-*ism*, on the other hand, is a serious problem, especially in the context of religion. This mindset seeks to liberate itself from the very thing that establishes and keeps us in fellowship with God in the first place: His doctrine. Liberal-*ists* (in religion) have a very different view of "sound doctrine," because they look upon "doctrine" as more of a guideline, divine suggestion, or "fluid" concept, not something timeless, universally-applied, unchangeable, and having a singular conclusion—i.e., the very attributes of *truth*.[55] The problem with those steeped in liberal-*ism* is that they seek change just for the sake of change, and show disregard (or even contempt) for all traditional practices and long-held beliefs just because they are traditional and/or long-held. The liberal's mantra is, essentially, "That was then, but this is now": *then*, sitting down with friends over a few beers was unacceptable; *now*, it's different. *Then*, homosexuality was condemned by God (Rom. 1:24–27); *now*, we applaud one's sexual self-expression. *Then*, same-sex marriages were condemned as being deviant, immoral, and abominable to God; *now*, we are a "progressive," "tolerant," and "open-minded" society that feels comfortable critiquing God and His position. There is nothing holy or acceptable about this kind of reasoning; it is the doctrine of demons

(1 Tim. 4:1). And, this is no better approach than that of staunch conservativ-*ism*—especially when it comes to Christianity. The gospel of grace will not and cannot flourish in either environment.

A question I have posed to many seasoned Christians is this: Was Jesus a conservative or a liberal? My fellow believers struggle with how to answer it. By saying "a" conservative or "a" liberal, as I purposely do, forces Jesus into one camp or the other. This immediately exposes the problem at hand: *we* have labeled these camps, not the gospel. Our labeling process is subjective at best and does not conform to God's sound doctrine. Nonetheless, conservatives want to see Jesus as a conservative, and liberals will paint Him as a liberal.

The fact is: Jesus was both conservative *and* liberal. With regard to God's Law, Jesus was most certainly a protectorate of that which God had already decreed. He declared that the Law must *never* be changed—not one word of it—until it had been entirely fulfilled (by Him) (Mat. 5:17–19). (Compare this with Paul's similar language concerning the gospel in Gal. 1:8–9.) Correspondingly, Jesus sharply rebuked the Pharisees who tweaked the Law of Moses to fit their pet theology and leverage their political advantage (Mat. 15:1–9). He called them hypocrites when they made themselves out to be law-*keepers* when instead they acted as law *changers*. He said of them, "But in vain do they worship [God], teaching as doctrines the precepts of men" (quoting from Isa. 29:13). Jesus' conservative view of law was set in sharp contrast to that of the liberal-minded Pharisees who were willing to adapt the law to accommodate their traditions.[56]

But in other cases, Jesus was indeed liberal in His thinking. Consider how He dealt with the narrow-minded Pharisees in regard to the Sabbath.[57] The Pharisees were intolerant of anyone doing *anything* on the Sabbath, even *good* things (Luke 13:14). Yet, they would lead their own donkey or sheep to water, or rescue that animal from having fallen into a well, on the Sabbath (Mat. 12:11–12, Luke 13:15). Thus, they would show mercy and kindness to an animal but would be unmerciful and uncompassionate to their fellow countryman. When Jesus healed on the Sabbath those who were

suffering with various afflictions, the Pharisees condemned both
Jesus and His actions (Luke 6:1–11). Jesus turned on them, exposing
their heartlessness. "But if you had known what this means, 'I desire
compassion and not a sacrifice,' you would not have condemned
the innocent" (Mat. 12:7). Jesus was *very liberal*—as in, generous,
unbounded, and unconstrained by human fear—when it came to
showing mercy, compassion, and forgiveness to those who needed
it and sought it from Him. Yet, as far as those law-binding Jews were
concerned, His liberal approach to helping people made Him a
dangerous free-thinker who had to be suppressed, silenced, and even
killed, since they could not control Him otherwise.

It should be noted, however, that Jesus *never* violated a single
law of God while practicing His liberal kindness and compassion
to others. This is the balance that must be struck: being *liberal* with
good works must never *compromise* or *violate* the very standard
of what defines such works as "good" in God's sight. To put this
another way: showing compassion to others must never be made
at the expense of honoring God's law. Divine law is just that—it is
of *divine origin* and it is *law*—and laws are meant to be kept, not set
aside in order to gratify someone's personal interpretation of a given
situation. Jesus understood this balance perfectly.

We need to understand this balance as well. We must be *very
conservative* in keeping God's law, because this is what it means to
"honor" law as well as the Giver of law. All authority has been given
to Christ (Mat. 28:18); we cannot violate that authority and still be in
good standing with the One who possesses it. We are never allowed
to modify God's law in order to accommodate personal agendas,
social change, or popular approval; His law is to be kept exactly
as it is. How *Christ* handled God's law should be the same as how
Christians (Christ-followers) do so. Since God's grace is defined by
His law, we have no business modifying grace one bit, no matter how
"progressive" or "forward-thinking" or "tolerant" such modifications
may seem in the eyes of those who think otherwise.

Yet, while being fierce defenders of truth, Christians should
also be very liberal with their good works (Mat. 5:16), mercy (Luke

10:30–37), compassion (Mat. 25:34–40), and servitude (Mat. 20:26–28). This is because Christ was very liberal (as in, *generous*) with these same things. He also had no limit ("no law") on how much love, kindness, patience, gentleness, and self-control needed to be shown (Gal. 5:22–23). While He staunchly resisted any change of God's law, He just as staunchly *advocated* giving good gifts to those in need of them: "Freely you received, freely give" (Mat. 10:8). He was both conservative in the things that needed to be left alone *and* liberal in those things which needed to be openly, freely, and benevolently shared. If this is what Christ the Master did, then this must be what His followers do.

A Risky Proposition

Of course, this balanced conservative-liberal approach is filled with potential risks and dangers. When being protective of God's doctrine, we are accused of being "legalists," "bigots," and "fundamentalist right-wingers." When being liberal with our compassion, kindness, and mercy toward those in need of such things, we risk accusations of being enablers, careless with the gospel, or opening the door to all kinds of abuse. We run the risk of not being *safe*. What if someone abuses what we speak of so freely? What if someone actually misconstrues what we have said, takes our words out of context, or misquotes us altogether? What if, by teaching freely and openly about the wonderful grace of Jesus, we are accidentally associated with those religious groups whose doctrines we cannot embrace?

What are we going to do about all that?

The ideal answer is unexpectedly simple: *nothing*. It is not up to us to monitor or police who does what with the gospel message we preach. The most important thing is that we preach it accurately to begin with. We do not see God fretting over how everyone is misconstruing His love, taking His mercy out of context, or misquoting His Scripture. Instead, we see Him in serene repose, happy to provide salvation to all who seek it (Rev. 4:2–11). We do not see Him being tight-fisted with forgiveness simply because so many abuse this subject in the religious world. He knows all the risks

involved; He knows some will exploit His message for their own
selfish benefit; He knows some take selfish advantage of that which
was meant for a selfless expression of His love (Phil. 1:15–18). These
things are inevitable; He expects them; *we* should expect them.
In fact, these will happen despite our most stringent measures to
prevent them.

Jesus was not executed for being a righteous man, healing people,
or going about "doing good" (Acts 10:38). He was executed because
the powers-that-be saw Him as a dangerous man who preached
a dangerous gospel—one that endangered those who heard it as
well as those who preached it. His revolutionary exposition of the
Law of Moses threatened the Jewish leaders' religious status and
their control of the people. Jesus' preaching demanded a spiritual
transformation in those who heard it and held them accountable to
God rather than to the rabbinic leaders. Paradoxically, His message
of love, grace, and mercy made Him (and later, His followers)
vulnerable to all kinds of abuse.

Today, Jesus Christ remains one of the most well-known and
most misrepresented historical figures in the world. His gospel still
remains open to abuse, misuse, and misrepresentation. The subject
of God's grace—the core of Christ's gospel—will always be abused
by someone, somewhere. Despite your best efforts and mine, we
are never going to remove the possibility for this to happen. Some
will do this out of ignorance; others, out of opportunity (for profit,
popularity, or self-promotion); still others, out of spite. Most, if
not all, will claim to have good intentions in their "interpretation"
of grace, even when such interpretations flatly contradict biblical
teaching. Even my own understanding of the gospel may be imperfect
or immature in some way of which I have not yet been made aware.

Yet, the potential for abuse should never limit our discussions
on grace among fellow Christians or our teaching of it to those who
remain outside of covenant with God. We must not be so afraid of
what someone might *do* with the gospel that we never *share* it. It is
not "safe" to limit the subject of grace to closed-room, members-

only discussions. In fact, it is sheer cowardice to do so. It does not imply that we have something to defend, but that we have something to hide. Children of God are to have a spirit of power, love, and discipline—not timidity, fear, and paranoia (2 Tim. 1:7–9).

"But," someone gasps, "we don't want God's gifts to be given to those who don't deserve them!" We might not say these words out loud, but we might agree with the point. This assumes that *conservatives* deserve God's gifts, but not those whom the conservatives do not endorse. This assumes that *anyone* deserves God's gifts, when in fact *no one* does. No one *deserves* to be forgiven; deservedness is not even part of the equation. Grace is not about what is deserved, but what is absolutely needed in order to save a soul from ruin. So then, what we in conservative circles are afraid of is this: someone is going to be *saved* without our approval—in essence, outside of our control.

God has defined what grace is; based on this, we can know who ought to receive it. The trouble is: we confuse God's terms of fellowship with our own litmus test of fellowship. Therefore, the possibility remains that someone can actually be saved without our consent, even though no one can be saved outside of *God's* consent. We must rise above our doubts and fears and focus on this: whoever is genuinely in fellowship with God should also be received as being in fellowship with us (1 John 1:1–3).

There is a lot going on in the background of these thoughts, and it is not my intention to speak to all of that right now. The point is: central to our (conservative-minded) fear over the abuse of grace is the fear of our lack of control of the gospel itself. We have been led to believe (by others who have also been led to believe the same thing) that we are the gatekeepers for the gospel truth. No one can understand it as well as we can; no one teaches it like we do; and no one can practice it as purely as we practice it. I realize how arrogant this sounds to the uninitiated, but this is a real mentality—and it creates a real problem. Basically, *we* have tended to avoid the subject of grace because we cannot control what *God* does with it.

But therein is the rub: grace is God's business, not mine, not yours, and not ours. God is fully capable of dispensing it correctly; He is fully capable of regulating it within the context of His covenant with believers. No one is accidentally going to receive His grace; no one is going to be justified, forgiven, or saved due to some blind luck or careless oversight on God's part. No one can stumble into heaven any more than he can mistakenly be cast into hell. Men may *try* to force their way into God's kingdom, but they are simply not capable of doing this (Luke 16:16). Every person enters into covenant the same way: through the application of the blood of Christ (an act of God) and his obedience to the word of God (an act of human faith).

Summary Thoughts

God gives saving grace to those who sincerely ask for it and are willing to be transformed by it. He refuses to give saving grace to anyone who is unwilling to obey His Son. He is able to oversee the distribution of His divine gifts; this is not something with which we need to concern ourselves. If we are Christians indeed, then we are the recipients and preachers of God's grace. We are not, however, its policemen or regulators. Those who abuse His grace—especially the preachers and teachers who ought to know better—will have to answer to Him for doing so, not to us. There is one Lawgiver and Judge, and it is not me, you, or us (Jas. 4:12).

Jesus was conservative in regard to God's law, but very liberal in regard to showing mercy and kindness to those in need. Jesus never pursued one at the expense of the other: He was never compassionate at the expense of God's law, and He never used God's law as a club to coerce people into submission. Jesus understood the necessary balance and relationship between law and love. At the same time, He knew that others would not exercise this same discretion, and yet this did not stop Him from doing what He came to do. The question is: will we follow His lead? More specifically, will *you*?

We cannot be afraid of teaching the gospel of grace. This subject is too great and this gift is too priceless to be hiding it under topics we feel more comfortable (or "safer") talking about. God is not going to violate His own doctrine; He is not going to save someone—*anyone*—in contradiction to how we have been saved. Do not worry about this; this is His business, not mine or yours. Your job, and mine, is to preach His truth to anyone and everyone who is willing to listen to it.

Chapter Eleven
⪻ *The Problem of Pride* ⪼

*. . . [A]ll of you, clothe yourselves with humility toward one another,
for God is opposed to the proud, but gives grace to the humble.
Therefore humble yourselves under the mighty hand of God,
that He may exalt you at the proper time, casting all your anxiety
upon Him, because He cares for you.* (1 Pet. 5:5–7)

An article in the Minneapolis Star Tribune (September, 1994), entitled, "If God Is Dead, Then the Late 20th Century Buried Him," boldly stated:

> There are some who naively cling to the nostalgic memory of God. The average churchgoer takes a few hours out of the week to experience the sacred. . . . But the rest of the time, he is immersed in a society that no longer acknowledges God as an omniscient and omnipotent force to be loved and worshipped. . . . Today we are too sophisticated for God. We can stand on our own; we are prepared and ready to choose and define our own existence.

If the situation was bad in 1994, then it is far worse today. Our country has been bewitched by satanic forces, hijacked by false religion, and deceived into thinking that we (people) are smarter than God, do not need Him, and thus have dispensed with Him without formality. We have sunk into a level of moral depravity, moral ignorance, and disregard for anything lawful or holy that would make people in 1994 blush with shock and shame.

Christians are quick to say "Amen!" to all of this, but many of us are not far behind the rest of the country's insatiable craving for entertainment, sensuality, or materialism. Someone has said that we all have a God-shaped hole in our lives that only God can fill, but many try to fill this chasm with gods of our own making. Instead of drinking from God's "living water," many people—including Christians—dig their own wells in a vain attempt to quench an irrepressible thirst (Jer. 2:13). Others are virtually sleepwalking through life as if in a spiritual coma, numb to God's kindness, Christ's sacrifice, or the call of His gospel. Only when some personal or national tragedy rattles their souls do they wake from slumber.

Jesus talked about a man whose greed for wealth and a "merry" life blinded him to his moral responsibility to God (Luke 12:15–21). Paul warned Christians against thinking that they could not fall like Israel did (1 Cor. 10:12), or thinking that they were something when they were nothing (Gal. 6:3). James talked about Christians who put confidence in their plans but made little preparation for the end of their lives (Jas. 4:13–15). He said that they boasted in their arrogance (4:16)—in other words, they bragged about how boastful they were.

Boasting, arrogance, hubris, cockiness, feelings of immortality or invincibility—however you want to characterize it—all boil down to human pride. Today's person has been conditioned to believe that he (or she) is truly "prepared and ready to choose and define my own existence." Never mind that our existence is, according to Evolution, the result of millions of years of inexplicable change, random accidents, and genetic miracles in the first place. Apparently, we have mutated and evolved to the point where we are able to deify ourselves.

The paradox of human pride, however, is that it demands to be worshiped at the same time that it seeks to be validated. Pride craves the attention, applause, and praise of others, while it longs to bow to whatever god will gratify its thirst for fulfillment, contentment, and completion. The typical modern American, therefore, longs to parade his (or her) wisdom, wealth, and accomplishments on social media. He thrives on showing you how talented his children are, how beautiful his grandchildren are, all the places he has gone, and all the celebrities (real and imagined) with whom he has taken selfies. He finds a measure of gratification in his iPhone, his gaming skills, the concerts he attends, the restaurants and bars he frequents, and his dog.

While vaunting the highlights of his wonderful life to others, he simultaneously longs to be validated by some authority, presence, or deity greater than himself. He has an enormous ego, but he also has an enormous inferiority complex that no mere mortal can remove. He seeks validation from someone greater than his equal, and assumes that this greater being will somehow justify his existence. (Have you ever noticed, for example, that aliens in movies are always *more intelligent* and *advanced* than we are? Hollywood consistently portrays them as having an almost god-like power.) He makes himself a slave to celebrities because these people can (he thinks) give him a greater sense of importance than he can find in himself or those of equal status to him. He worships singers, musicians, actors, and sports figures as though they were divine beings strutting through his own little artificially-constructed universe.

This desperate attempt—because it *is* desperate, and it is *only* an attempt—to fill that God-shaped hole with something inferior to God always takes its toll. The desire to flaunt, parade, promote, and brag about his seemingly wonderful life never diminishes. It either intensifies or it morphs into other ways of expressing itself. Human pride is always looking for new paths of self-exaltation, just as it is always seeking some new (or better) god to worship. Pride craves wealth and material things, and is terrified of poverty and destitution. It will do nearly *anything* to be accepted and loved, even sacrifice friends, families, children, or marriages. When it comes to self-preservation, anything and anyone is expendable. It will even choose suicide as a way to "show others" that it is daring, brave, independent, and "in control of my own existence."

Trusting in False Gods

Inexplicably, while God offers exactly what the human soul is looking for, most souls refuse to seek Him. What better way to "boast" than to say that you have spiritual fellowship and holy communion with the most powerful Being that exists! And, what better way to be validated than to have this most powerful Being say that He knows who you are, shows you His love, and calls you His child (1 John 3:1)! You cannot do better than this. No god of your imagination, human origin, or this world can hold a candle to this kind of affirmation.

But human pride, being deceived by its own reasoning, often scoffs at the idea of a divine Creator who has given us life and who sustains our existence. Human pride likes the idea of such a Being giving it attention, approval, and affirmation; it does not like the idea of having to fully *surrender* to this Being in order for this to happen. We want a god to worship, but we want to worship him on our terms, not his. We want a god to boast *to*, not a god that determines how we are to live and love. We want to have a god *in* our lives, but we still want to retain god-like control *of* our lives.

Unhappy with what the God of heaven offers, we go looking for another god (or gods) that will give us everything we want: completion, validation, and approval *without* requiring us to relinquish our pride. Any other god we choose, however, fails to provide the completion and validation we seek. We worship science, technology, and computers, but we still feel a gaping, yawning, God-shaped hole in our being. We worship medicine, pharmacology, and prescriptions, but these do not fill that empty spiritual chasm within us. Many turn to alcohol, illicit drugs, and marijuana, but all these do is temporarily make us forget about the God-shaped hole; they cannot fill it. Others turn to sexual fetishes, pornography, steamy affairs, but these are only temporary and often unsatisfying fixes; the aching emptiness remains. Some even turn to motivational speakers, celebrities, spiritual gurus, and self-proclaimed mystics, but these do nothing for the soul. They are just as lost and empty as we are—they just do not want to believe it, do not know it, or do not want you and me to know it.

We read self-help books, hoping to find the keys to empowerment, control, independence, and spiritual completion. These books often promise to: unlock the secrets of life, happiness, and success; make people like us; make us millionaires; help us find our inner self (but then what?); enable us to attract women (or men); have sex with strangers we pick up at bars; teach us to cook like prize-winning chefs; think like mind-blowing philosophers; and empower us to overcome virtually any obstacle that is set before us—all without any need for God or the Bible. But these books are all written by people who, unless they are redeemed by the blood of Christ, are just as lost as everyone else—they just do not want to believe it, do not know it, or do not want you and me to know it.

God mocked the ancients who took a tree and fashioned it into an idol, then fell down and worshiped it saying, "Deliver me, for you are my god" (Isa. 44:12–17). Yet, looking at what so many of us do today, little has changed. We have traded the wooden idol for a cell phone, or the stone statuette for a laptop, or the obelisk for a prescription vial or bottle of vodka, but the problem remains the same. We want to think of ourselves as a Christian nation, especially in the wake of tragedy and the senseless loss of life, yet we are far more like ancient Athens which Paul visited—a "city full of idols." We will prostrate before whatever idol or image or solace is set before us while the "unknown god" goes virtually unrecognized and unheeded (see Acts 17:16–31). We are so intoxicated with pride that we are unaware of how ridiculous we sound and how arrogant we have become. We unconsciously brag about how boastful we are.

A Spiritual Sickness

Pride is an incredibly powerful and insidious force. It is also far more common than we would like to admit—among believers as well as unbelievers. It is like germs, bacteria, and other microscopic bugs: they *are* everywhere but we are typically oblivious to them. The more we learn about them, however, the more cognizant we are of their existence. So it is with pride—and to liken it to a "germ" seems altogether appropriate. Wherever there are people, it is virtually guaranteed that pride will be there too, raising its ugly head, clucking its self-confident dogma, exalting itself at the expense of other people, boasting of its amazing insight and accomplishments. Listen closely, and you will hear it oozing out of conversations, seeping out of good works, and slithering out of seemingly pious endeavors. Or, it will be so incredibly loud and screeching you simply cannot avoid hearing it. Many conversation threads on social media are nothing more than vehicles for those drunk with pride to rant about their self-proclaimed wisdom.

We have all encountered unashamedly arrogant people at some time or other. But pride does not always manifest itself with such blatancy. When we think of a "proud person" we tend to picture one who is haughty, narcissistic, self-righteous, condescending to others, and who walks around with his (or her) nose in the air. Or, we might think of someone who simply refuses to allow anyone else the same respect, deference, and/or recognition that he (or she) allows himself. The fact is, even those whom we would deem "good people" can be arrogant—maybe not always toward you and me, but toward God.

Consider the elderly lady who bakes cookies for her neighbors, retrieves their mail for them while they are on vacation, and calls everyone "sweetie" or "honey." You know the one I'm talking about. You would hardly think her to be a "proud and arrogant" person, right? Actually, it's quite possible. Not outwardly, mind you, but where it counts the most: in her resistance of God, which is also a denial of His grace. If she has access to Christ's gospel and yet has refused—for any reason—to obey it and to give her heart to Him, it is her pride that stands in the way. We can say the same of that refined and crisply-dressed man who is always so polite and courteous to everyone, dresses impeccably, and smells clean and fresh with a perfect hint of fine aftershave. If his heart is filled with pride and thus refuses to obey the Lord, then his soul is *dead* to Him and stinks to high heaven with the rottenness of self-exaltation. God does not find favor with people who bake cookies for others or who dress well and smell good. He finds favor with those who humble themselves, repent of their sins, and revere Him and His word (Isa. 66:2b). We are not to draw conclusions about people "according to appearance," but we are to exercise "righteous judgment" (John 7:24), for this is the way God judges us.

Proud people may be found in any church on any given Sunday. We would like to think our Christian status makes us impervious to pride, but we are hardly immune to this. Having a songbook in one's hand or a Bible on one's lap does not automatically eradicate pride from one's heart; bowing one's head in prayer does not guarantee that he has bowed his heart in humility. Human pride among Christians is what gave the apostle Paul a great deal of grief and suffering. His infamous "thorn in the flesh" (2 Cor. 12:7–10) may well have been the constant assault of *other people's pride,* in one form or another. Jesus had to strongly rebuke the Christians in Laodicea because they were self-sufficient, self-absorbed, and "lukewarm" in their devotion to Him. In other words, they were a proud people who talked about Christ and the grace of God but felt like they really did not *need* either one (Rev. 3:14–22). The Laodiceans, like so many churchgoers today, confused social or material success with spiritual success. They were intoxicated with pride, and Jesus said that that made Him literally sick to His stomach.[58]

The Reality of the Human Condition

If we could see ourselves (or our church) as the Lord does, we might be very surprised—and possibly *repulsed*—by what we would find. Director John Carpenter came out with an intriguing film in the 1980s called *They Live!* It was a preposterous story about a construction worker who stumbles upon some special sunglasses which, when one looks through them, reveal an alien race disguised as humans living amongst the general population of New York City. (Some New Yorkers reading this are probably thinking, "Yeah, and what's so unusual about that?") These "sunglasses" exposed normal-looking humans as freakish monsters. Yet these alien-monsters were *everywhere,* even posing as people who were trusted and respected in society. Imagine how horrifying this would be if it were real! Imagine if we could look out over a crowd of people and see past the façades, beyond the false pretenses, and through all the hypocrisy, so that we could see them for *who they really are.* We would likely be shocked to find out the truth. Those whom we deem insignificant may be more righteous than we ever suspected, while those whom we deem pious and holy may look like misshapen ghouls.

God *does* see people for who and what they really are. He does it all the time, and He is doing it right now with *you.* He knows who you really are, not who you think you are, or how you want others to see you. He knows what you have given to Him and what you have withheld from Him. He knows how you have tried to serve Him, or how you have refused to try, having put your will ahead of His. He knows when you have humbled your heart, and when you have asserted your arrogance. Lest anyone think I am looking down from an ivory pedestal, I myself have been seduced by my own pride more times than I can count.

When we think we stand is when we ought to be most cautious. When we feel confident, self-assured, and pleased with ourselves is when we ought to sit up, take notice, and recognize that human pride is swelling our heart. Ancient Israel serves as an example of those who failed to recognize their own problem. God gave them abundance, prosperity, and protection, which should have made them a humble and grateful people. Instead, they let their privileged relationship with the Lord go to their head. They became complacent, then self-dependent, and then wanted to be like all the surrounding heathen nations. They became proud in their heart and thus resisted the God who had given life to their nation in the first place (Ezek. 16:1–34). God's severe discipline of them—up to and including their humiliating exile into foreign lands—has been "written for our instruction" so that we would not follow in their own error. "Therefore," Paul wrote, "let him who thinks he stands take heed lest he fall" (1 Cor. 10:6–12).

This same pride which devastated the congregation of Israel also devours and destroys congregations of God's people today, just as it does would-be followers of Christ. Why do fellow believers fail to get along with each other? Because of internal pride and selfish arrogance. Why do Christians fail to accomplish the "good works" that we have been created "in Christ" to perform (Eph. 2:10)? Because we are flush with prosperity and have too much time on our hands, which leads to complacency and self-absorption, which leads to everyone pulling into his (or her) own little world and casually ignoring the fact that people are dying in their sins and need to hear the gospel. Why do congregations split in half or simply disintegrate over petty disagreements, petty issues, and petty reasons? Because pride turns us into ugly, selfish, and petty people who are more concerned with being right and saving face than with "[looking out] for the interests of others" (Phil. 2:3–4).

How much pride does it take to spoil a good heart or a good congregation? Not very much. Years ago, a friend of mine who worked at a wastewater treatment plant invited me on a tour of this facility. (I know, it does not sound very exciting, but it was one of the more fascinating field trips I have ever been on.) At one point, we were standing on an eight foot square metal grate that spanned an open culvert coming into the plant. My friend explained that this culvert carried raw runoff collected from the city's sewers and drains, forming a dirty, brown, and contaminated river. "It's actually 97% pure water," he told me, "with only 3% impurities." In other words, this water is nearly pure but the little bit of filth makes it unusable for any human use or consumption. This, with only 3% impurities!

So it is with the human heart: it can be mostly pure, but a little bit of pride makes it unusable to God for the work He needs us to do. You would never bathe in the water coming in through that culvert, or cook your food with it, or drink it. Similarly, God will never use anyone whose heart is polluted with pride to be in fellowship with Him or involved in His holy work. Jesus confronted a church in Sardis that portrayed themselves as a congregation that was very much "alive," but He said, "you are dead" (Rev. 3:1). You can be certain it was *pride*, in one form or another, that was killing them.

An Insatiable Appetite

Pride is an appetite, a craving that can only be filled when it gets what it wants—and what it wants is *always* contrary to what God wants since it always exalts itself against Him. Paul talked about divisive people whose "appetite [lit., belly]" seeks something very different than what Christ offers them (Rom. 16:17–18); these people make themselves "enemies of the cross of Christ" (Phil. 3:18–19). This is because pride finds its satisfaction in *self*, whereas the believer finds his satisfaction in *Christ*. The proud person will never be fulfilled with the business of heaven: he hungers and thirsts for things of this world, but is never satisfied by them (Mat. 5:6). Since he seeks to be satisfied in himself rather than in God, he believes in himself more than he believes in God. Since he turns to the world in a vain attempt to gratify his worldly appetite, he turns away from God and seeks those who will "tickle" his ear (2 Tim. 4:3–4).

Jesus said that no one can serve two masters (Mat. 6:24), so the proud Christian—an oxymoron if ever there was one—finds himself in an irresolvable dilemma. He cannot serve Christ *and* his own ego, so he will choose one over the other, or he will deny one or the other. Instead of sanctifying *Christ* as Lord of his heart (1 Pet. 3:15), he enthrones his own *pride* and bows in allegiance to it. This turning away from God to seek satisfaction elsewhere manifests itself in different ways. As I said earlier, we often do not even recognize pride when we see (or experience) it. Consider the following examples:

- **Covetousness.** This is the act of seeking satisfaction in the things of this world instead of Christ. Covetousness equates to idolatry (Eph. 5:5, Col. 3:5)—an unholy, misplaced worship—for which people make costly sacrifices, including their own souls (Mat. 16:26).

- **Sexual lust.** This refers to seeking satisfaction in physical, sensual pleasure and eroticism rather than in spiritual fellowship with the Lord. Sex is not a bad thing in itself, but the proud person makes sex his god, and he worships the creature and not the Creator (Rom. 1:25). The homosexual community, for example, trumpets its sexual lifestyle with celebrations of "pride." (Talk about irony.) Rather than the "lustful passion" of "those who do not know God," the faithful believer maintains his body "in sanctification and honor" (1 Thess. 4:4–5).

- **Bitterness or resentment.** This seeks satisfaction in personal revenge or any form of sustained anger or hatred. A bitter person simply refuses to let go of past hurts or injuries inflicted against him; his grudges give him (he believes) a certain amount of control over that situation. Resentment involves condemning a person repeatedly for whatever injuries (real or imagined) that person has caused. The believer, on the other hand, seeks satisfaction not in maintaining hurts and injuries but in forgiving them and entrusting himself to the One who judges all things righteously (1 Pet. 2:23).

- **Gossiping.** Pride is always a control issue, and gossip is the illicit control of information about another person. Paul characterized it as "devil talk."[59] The child of God, however, finds his satisfaction in speaking the truth and maintaining holiness in all his conversations (Eph. 4:25).

- **Explosions or outbursts of anger, in all their forms.** In this case, the proud person seeks satisfaction through intimidation, physical strength, and/or verbal bullying. He lives his life on his terms, but always at the expense of someone else's fear. When someone (or something) interferes with those terms, he reacts with anger since his ego has been challenged or threatened. The faithful Christian, however, is a peacemaker who seeks peace whenever it is possible to do so (Mat. 5:9, Rom. 12:18), and never at the expense of others or Christ's gospel.

- **Impatience.** As with explosions of anger, one's pride believes that its own schedule, plans, mode of operation, etc. are superior to everyone else's. The proud person seeks satisfaction in having everything and everyone comply with his supreme view of himself. Those who do not comply will experience his disappointment, contempt, and/or wrath. In contrast, the believer waits upon the Lord and is patient for His will to be accomplished in him. He is "patient with all men" (1 Thess. 5:14) and does not seek to impose his schedule or plans upon everyone else.

- **Self-pity.** This is a more subtle and unsuspecting form of pride. The self-pitying person finds great satisfaction in being recognized as a sort of backward hero. He has ironically "succeeded" at self-martyrdom and simply views himself as a "survivor" because he has lived through some difficult experience. John Piper explains:

  > Boasting is the response of pride to success. Self-pity is the response of pride to suffering. Boasting says, "I deserve admiration because I have achieved so

much." Self-pity says, "I deserve admiration because
I have sacrificed [or suffered—MY WORDS] so much."
Boasting is the voice of pride in the heart of the strong.
Self-pity is the voice of pride in the heart of the weak.
Boasting sounds self-sufficient; self-pity sounds self-
sacrificing.[60]

> The one who trusts in the Lord does not need to boast in
> himself, nor does he need to draw attention to his suffering.
> He rests assured that God will remember his sufferings and
> will compensate him fully in the life to come (Jas. 1:12).

Anytime a person seeks to justify, vindicate, establish, exalt, or gratify
himself—and this will almost always be at someone else's expense—
he is exercising his pride. On the other hand, when a person allows
God to justify, vindicate, establish, exalt, or gratify him, he exercises
humility. When proud people are weak or threatened, they become
fearful, stressed, anxious, and (in some cases) abusive. Humble
people, on the other hand, allow God to use *their own* weaknesses
to His advantage (2 Cor. 12:9–10) because they set their minds well
beyond this life (Col. 3:1–4).

Pride and Grace Are Incompatible

What does this have to do with the grace of God? *Everything,*
inasmuch as grace and pride cannot coexist: "God is opposed to
the proud, but gives grace to the humble" (1 Pet. 5:5). Grace cannot
operate in an environment hostile to His Spirit and His Son. The
proud heart has not prepared itself to receive God's grace because it
does not think it really *needs* it. Human pride does not mind if God is
in the picture, but it certainly does not want to hand over the reins to
Him. The proud person may nominally "accept" the gospel because
of what it offers him (i.e., a salve for his guilty conscience, a showcase
for his piety, a church family to hang out with, etc.), but he does not
devote his heart to it. He certainly will not stake his soul on it. He
secretly refuses Christ—and thus His grace—because He represents a
threat to his soul's self-exaltation. The gospel, to the proud Christian
(again, an oxymoron), is too intrusive, too demanding, and too risky.

Pride is, in a nutshell, *any resistance* of God's grace. This is true whether that resistance is in the form of rejecting the offer of salvation altogether, or refusing to cooperate with God once a person has entered into a covenant relationship with Him. The unbeliever who trusts in the "flesh"—that is, in human effort or power—makes himself hostile to God (Rom. 8:6–8). The Christian who *also* trusts in the flesh betrays his commitment to the terms of God's covenant with him. (We are speaking here of a prolonged behavior rather than an isolated incident.) While he portrays himself as a genuine believer, he is an unbeliever in practice. The proud Christian talks differently than the humble Christian.

The proud says of his accomplishments, "Look at me—see what I have done!"; the true believer says, "Look at *God* in me—see what He has done *to* me and *for* me and *through* me!" The proud says of his sins, "I'll take care of these—I will not be defeated!"; the humble believer says, "I am a sinner, am fully responsible for having sinned and am helpless on my own to remove my sins. However, the grace of God has overcome my sins so that I am found innocent in the sight of my Lord!" The proud will look upon the gospel's demands as interfering with his will, his schedule, and his life; the humble will look upon these demands as a protection against drifting away from his Savior—something he does not want and cannot afford to do.

A Matter of Self-Denial

The way to overcome human pride is not found through churchgoing, listening to sermons, and doing (more) good works. Pride is a matter of the heart—really, a control issue—rather than a matter of mere religion (or, the mechanics of religion). When Jesus asks us to "come after" Him, the first thing He requires of us is that we lay our pride at His feet. This is what He meant when He said that every disciple "must deny himself" (Mat. 16:24). The only way to subdue something as powerful as your (or my) human pride is to surrender it to Someone who is able to do what our pride can never do. This is not a conditional surrender, but a full and unconditional one. Jesus does not ask for a little piece of your heart or a few hours a week of your attention; He expects you to lay everything down, to declare yourself fully and completely in subjection to Him. He does not want a small slice of the pie chart of your life; He demands—and *deserves*, for what He has done and what He offers you—the entire pie, so to speak. You are entirely unprepared to receive His gift of saving grace unless and until you have given Him your heart.

You are in full control of your pride. You must not think of your pride as something apart from who you are, as though it were some detachable extension of yourself. Jesus does not ask you to deny an extension of yourself; He asks you to deny *yourself*—who you are, what you believe, how you live, and what you will to do. Your pride, just like mine, seeks to exalt itself against anyone or anything that threatens it. Self-denial allows you to see Jesus *not* as a threat to your ego (which He really is), but instead as a Savior of your eternal soul (which He is also). Pride will want to stiff-arm Jesus at every turn, every decision, and every instruction. Pride will second-guess everything He wants you to do, or think that His commandments are inconvenient, could be improved upon, or are unnecessary. Humility—the voluntary submission of the human will—trusts in the Lord, regards His commandments as "not burdensome" (1 John 5:3), and welcomes His mercy and grace.

This can be illustrated in baptism: in the same way you are fully immersed in water, so you are fully immersed in Christ. Your *entire body* is "buried" with Him in water just as your *entire self* is surrendered to Him in allegiance. In this way, you become *united* with Him—completely, entirely, and absolutely (Rom. 6:5). Just as every part of your physical body is subjected to the watery grave, so every part of your will, your loyalty, and your pride is subjected to the Lordship of Jesus Christ. We cannot pretend to give our "all" to Jesus, when in fact we are withholding some for ourselves.[61] Better to bend the knee *now* in allegiance to Christ than to wait until you are forced to your knees in terrifying expectation of divine punishment (see Phil. 2:9–11).

God will not give His grace to anyone who will not give up his pride. This requires that we lay our entire life, our relationships (with spouses, children, family, friends, and *everybody*), our hobbies, our allegiances—yes, even our very identity—at Christ's feet. We cannot love family more than Christ (Mat. 10:37); we cannot love human praise more than divine approval (Mat. 6:1, 5); we cannot love *ourselves* more than we love God (Luke 14:26). He knows exactly what we have given to Him, as well as anything we have withheld; the human heart is "laid bare" before Him (Heb. 4:12–13). We can fool our friends, fool the church, and even fool ourselves, but we will never fool God; "Do not be deceived, God is not mocked" (Gal. 6:7a).

Self-denial is not merely a temporary or superficial deprivation of some creature comfort or personal pleasure. It is not merely the denial of an opportunity to sin, nor the decision to do something good. Self-denial, as Jesus speaks of it (Mat. 16:24), is an all-encompassing, all-or-nothing, full surrender of your pride to God. It is confessing that your way is not His way, and His way is superior to yours. It is putting this confession into practice by allowing His way to *become* your way, and His thoughts to condition your own. It is taking responsibility for your sins against Him—and realizing that *all* sin is ultimately against Him—rather than blaming circumstances, others, or even God for "what happened." It is realizing that the world is shrouded in spiritual and moral darkness, and that *you also* are shrouded in spiritual and moral darkness unless you walk in the fellowship of God's light (1 John 1:5–7).

Self-denial, cross-bearing, and following Christ translate to a pledge of allegiance to the One whom *you have chosen* to be your Lord and Savior. All other allegiances must pale in comparison; all relationships that insist that you betray Him are expendable. Discipleship to Christ transcends anything with which we are familiar. It is otherworldly, unparalleled, uncomfortable, inconvenient, and uncompromising. And Jesus knows all this. He knows exactly what He is asking of you; He knows the difficulty of what He demands. There are many nominal "Christians" in the world—i.e., churchgoing, men-following, and would-be disciples— but relatively few men and women who actually give Christ *full control* over their hearts, lives, and behavior.

All spiritual blessings come to us through the work of the Holy Spirit. When we receive the Spirit in our baptism (Acts 2:38), we receive the manifold grace that He provides. (Remember: whatever God gives to us that we could not acquire on our own, but is necessary for salvation, is *grace*.) Not only is the very *giving* of the Spirit grace, but so is all that the Spirit brings to the table, so to speak. Likewise, any resistance of the Spirit's divine influence is a resistance of divine grace, inasmuch as grace is the *work* of the Spirit. "[W]alk by the Spirit," Paul wrote, "and you will not carry out the desire of the flesh. For the flesh [i.e., human pride—MY WORDS] sets its desire against the Spirit, and the Spirit against the flesh; for these are in opposition to one another, so that you may not do the things that you please" (Gal. 5:16–17).

Left to ourselves, we naturally gravitate toward the "things that [we] please." This means that our pride, apart from divine influence, will try to retain control whenever it can. The Spirit leads us directly to God; our pride will want to blaze its own trail (but does not know where to go). The Spirit instructs us to "put to death" the proud deeds of the flesh (Rom. 8:12–14); our pride is what gave life to those deeds in the first place, and tenaciously wants to keep them alive and intact. The Spirit transforms us into the image of Christ; our pride wants us to remain conformed to the corrupted world (Rom. 8:29–30, 12:1–2, 2 Pet. 1:2–4, et al). There is no compatibility between human pride and God's Spirit. Thus, we cannot listen to—or follow—both at the same time.

Summary Thoughts

Pride seeks satisfaction *apart* from God, while humility finds satisfaction *in* God. In order for God to apply His grace to the human soul, that person must surrender his pride and seek no other Rescuer, Redeemer, or Lord. Entering into a covenant relationship with God is a cooperation, not a contest; it is a partnership, not push-and-pull competition. The one in need of saving grace cannot be challenging, critiquing, or resisting the One who owns this grace and is the only source of it. Instead, he needs to submit himself—not just in part, not just part of the time, and not just the parts he chooses to submit (while withholding others)—to "the living God, who is the Savior of all men, especially of believers" (1 Tim. 4:10).

The reason for this submission, however, cannot simply be to unlock the gates of heaven and allow the sinner-turned-saint to enter in. Christ is not the Warden whom we must please in order to be paroled from our incarceration; rather, He is the *Living Savior* who has made salvation possible and plentiful through an incomprehensibly amazing sacrifice. He is not asking merely for our token or even begrudging allegiance; He is asking for our love, respect, and gratitude. Humility is not about cowering in fear before the One who can destroy you. In its most noble context, humility is the yielding of our spirit and the suppression of our pride in order to love the Lord with all our heart, soul, and mind. He not only deserves this, but we ought to be happy to give it to Him.

Many today may well think God is dead and that the secularized, humanistic, and shamelessly arrogant world buried Him. But the world speaks in ignorance, is blind to its own folly, and is stumbling headlong into ruin. Those who dwell in spiritual darkness cannot appraise spiritual things because they do not even understand them (1 Cor. 2:12–14). Human pride thinks that it can simply cast God over its shoulder, but it is God who will cast the proud person into the "outer darkness" unless he comes to his senses, repents of his sins, and surrenders his heart to the King of kings and Lord of lords. God is rich with mercy, grace, and patience, but these are all limited-time offers, and He will not wait forever for any person to take advantage of them.

To be with Him in His heaven, God requires that you voluntarily give Him everything you have to offer—your life, your love, your heart, your allegiance, and even your pride. These things are not your *payment* for salvation, since only the blood of Christ can ransom your soul. Rather, these are expressions of your faith and trust in God, by which you have access into God's grace. To human pride, this seems an excessive and even unnecessary imposition. But to the one who longs to be forgiven and longs to dwell with God, this is an excellent, priceless, and most desirable exchange.

Section Three:
The Grace-filled Life

Chapter Twelve
⸻ *Bringing Grace to Life* ⸻

And the Word became flesh, and dwelt among us,
and we saw His glory, glory as of the only begotten from the Father,
full of grace and truth. . . . For of His fullness we have all received,
and grace upon grace. For the Law was given through Moses;
grace and truth were realized through Jesus Christ. No man
has seen God at any time; the only begotten God, who is in the
bosom of the Father, He has explained Him. (John 1:14, 16–18)

Early in my Christian life, I always referred to the Holy Spirit as an "It." I never really thought anything unusual about this until I noticed that Jesus *never* referred to God's Spirit as an "It" but always as "He" or "Him." This intrigued me, and I suddenly realized I had been speaking of the Holy Spirit of God—the intercessor for my prayers, the guiding light in my spiritual walk, the power and influence for the church on earth—as an impersonal, euphemistical, non-living "Thing" instead of the Divine Personage that He is. I had unwittingly and unintentionally reduced a member of the Godhead to an abstract concept or an ambiguous ghost-like emanation from heaven.

My shallow depiction of the Holy Spirit said a lot about me, and it was not very flattering. Granted, mine may have been a typical habit of most people who are young in the faith. Even so, I was robbing the Spirit of His rightful identity and denying Him the honor that He rightly deserved. But the harm was not just against God's Spirit; it was against me as well. I treated the Spirit as though He were a mere conceptual idea—a surreal, uninvolved, detached Force which mysteriously directed my life through some almost magical means. I never *said* all this, but in hindsight, this is how I *saw* Him. My very treatment of Him as an "It" said it all.

Part of the reason for all of this was because the Holy Spirit was so foreign to me. Part of it, too, was that I remained disrespectful of Him, in that I was not following Him as I ought to have been. As long as I *kept* Him an "It"—an abstract concept, an indistinct, generic "life force"—He would never have the close, personal, and influential effect on my spiritual life that I needed Him to have, and that Jesus *wanted* Him to have. Jesus once told those who had gathered to listen to Him, "If you then, being evil [i.e., in comparison to God—MY WORDS], know how to give good gifts to your children, how much more will your heavenly Father give the Holy Spirit to those who ask Him?" (Luke 11:13). Does the Father give me a divine "It" when I ask Him to dwell in my heart, or does He give me a part of *Himself* to direct my thoughts and my footsteps? Can I have fellowship with an "It" (2 Cor. 13:14)? Does an "It" intercede for my prayers (Rom. 8:26–27)? Does an impersonal, non-identifiable "It" lead me to God (Gal. 5:16)? Clearly, I had to recalibrate my understanding of how God worked in my life.

Now I no longer refer to the Holy Spirit as "It" but always as He or Him. While the Holy Spirit has not changed at all, my *perception* of Him has. I no longer regard Him as a "something" to help me, but a "Someone" that speaks to my heart. Now I understand, too, how our terminology reflects our level of growth and maturity. We all begin our spiritual journey with God as children, yet as we grow in knowledge and increase in faith, our language changes to reflect our better grasp of the heavenly wisdom God has revealed in His word. This process is natural and expected.

Fleshing Out the Concept of Grace

I would like to draw a parallel between my misunderstanding of the Holy Spirit's identity and the personification of grace in Jesus Christ. I have been purposely referring to grace as "it" throughout this book in anticipation of making the point we are now considering. And, in future chapters I will continue to refer to grace as "it" with regard to the package of gifts that God gives to believers (i.e., forgiveness, intercession, spiritual blessings, providence, a "way of escape," etc.). Grace, as it is nearly always used in the New Testament, *is* an "it," not a person or a "he." At the same time, we need to appreciate the One (Christ) who embodies divine grace in Himself, and who is responsible for providing grace to those in covenant with God.

The apostle John tells us that Jesus was, in His human form, "full of grace and truth" (John 1:14). In the same way that we understand Christ to be the embodiment of truth, we can see Him to be the embodiment of grace. Jesus was not merely graceful in His actions or to those whom He met; He *is* saving grace to us—grace that is holy, heavenly, divine, and supernatural. While being "full of grace," He also is the full manifestation or representation of God's kindness and benevolence to us. We could not understand God's grace without ultimately or even immediately involving God's Son. We could not define saving grace without defining the Savior who lived with the fullness *of* this grace. Whenever we refer to a "man (or woman) of grace" among the brethren, we actually refer to a man (or woman) who emulates Christ. One who embraces the gospel of grace is one and the same as one who lives with Christ in his (or her) heart.

To illustrate this thought, we can insert "Christ" where the word "grace" (as a doctrinal, theological concept) is used in Scripture. For example, in Eph. 2:8 Paul wrote, "For by grace you have been saved through faith; and that not of yourselves, it is the gift of God." Here, "it" refers to the doctrinal application of God's salvation and all that accompanies this. But you can see Christ written all over this. If we read this as, "By **Christ** you have been saved through faith; and that not of yourselves, but **He** is the gift of God," the doctrine of God has not been altered or compromised in the least (compare with Rom. 3:23–24). This is not an attempt to reduce Christ to a concept, but just the opposite: to realize that the concept means nothing apart from Christ.

We can also view this in a negative sense. In Gal. 5:4, Paul declared to those seeking to justify themselves through human effort, "You have been severed from Christ, you who are seeking to be justified by law; you have fallen from grace." In this statement, Paul used a Jewish literary device (called a Hebraism) which unites two thoughts by expressing them in parallel form. The conclusion is the same regardless of which expression one chooses. Thus, to be "severed from Christ" is equal to having "fallen from grace." Transitively, "Christ" here is equal to "grace": if one has a right relationship with Christ then he has access to God's saving grace because Christ is the personification *of* His grace. A Christian who speaks and sings about Christ but rests upon his personal piety, good works, or biblical knowledge to justify his good standing before God is a modern example of what Paul said to the Galatians.

In either case—i.e., positively or negatively—we are forced to recognize the ultimate and inseparable connection between Christ and God's saving grace. All those who are "in Christ" are in a covenant relationship with God *through* Christ. These people are not only striving to keep God's commandments, but they are living the grace-touched and grace-filled life of those who walk with God ("under grace"—Rom. 6:14). All those who are disciples *of* Christ (on His terms, not theirs) are also recipients of the grace of God made possible *through* Christ.

The Summation of All Things

Christ is not just an important character in God's plan of redemption; He is, in a very real sense, the *only* character. While we credit Noah, Abraham, Moses, Samuel, the prophets, the apostles, and an untold number of faithful men and women for their part in supporting the great plan of salvation, all of these are like mere candle flames while Christ is the brilliant Sun, the Light of the world (John 1:9–10, 8:12). Without Christ, all of these men and women together could not help us; they would be just as helpless and lost as everyone else. Without Christ, there is *no redemption* from divine condemnation for our sins, regardless of how faithful one has been or how hard one has tried to compensate for this. Without Christ, the entire gospel of salvation implodes, having nothing to offer.

It has been observed that all of the world's major religions (outside of Christianity) began with some religious, charismatic, or cultic leader, but no longer need that leader in order to survive. Such religions will still honor their leaders in one way or another, but they are able to carry on without them. Buddhism began with Buddha, but survives without him; Islam began with Mohammed, but he is dead and Islam is still alive; Mormonism began with Joseph Smith, but this religion has since superseded even his own teachings; etc. This is not true with Christianity: without Christ there is no Christianity—not then, not now, not ever. We cannot survive (spiritually) without Him; if He had remained dead in His tomb, our faith is worthless (1 Cor. 15:12–19); if we attempt to supersede His teachings, we forfeit our identity with Him (1 Tim. 6:3–4a); etc.

Without Christ existing *now* in heaven and ruling *now* on His throne at the right hand of God, Christians have no good news (gospel) to preach and nothing to sing about. Without Christ, there is no grace; without grace, there is no redemption; without redemption, there is no salvation; and without any hope of salvation, there is no peace from spiritual torment and the awful judgment to come. Christ is not a mere figurehead of the Christian religion who once got things rolling and to whom we posthumously continue to honor. Rather, He is the source of saving grace, the personification of saving grace, and—in a very real sense—*our saving grace*. We cannot have a relationship with God apart from Christ any more than we can be alive on earth apart from breathing and blood flowing through our veins.

The apostle Paul wrote, "He [God] made known to us the mystery of His will, according to His kind intention which He purposed in Him with a view to an administration suitable to the fullness of the times, that is, the summing up of all things in Christ, things in the heavens and things on the earth" (Eph. 1:9–10a). The "mystery" here refers to the offering of a covenant of salvation to all humankind, rather than the limited covenant He made with Israel (Eph. 3:1–11). Christ being "the summing up of all things" both in heaven and on earth means that He provides everything we need for "life and godliness" (2 Pet. 1:3) here on earth *and* secures a heavenly home for us in the future (John 14:1–3). Another way to look at this is: He is the source of our faith while we remain on this earth *and* He is the source of our salvation that rests with God in heaven. Yet another way is: He did everything that needed to be done on earth (John 17:3–4) *and* everything that needed to be done in heaven (Heb. 9:11–14) in order to secure the salvation of all those who believe in Him.

Christ is not just one big link in a "great chain of being." Rather, *He is the chain* that binds all things together, binds all believers together, and binds all believers to God. The offering of salvation by grace and through faith is God's "eternal purpose which He carried out in Christ Jesus our Lord" (Eph. 3:11), since there was no angel and no other man who could have possibly done this. God's response to our sin is His divine grace, but this grace could never come to realization apart from the mediatory work of Jesus Christ—His life, death, burial, resurrection, ascension, and all that He did that remains unknown to us until God reveals the full picture to the glorified church in heaven. While Christ certainly entrusted responsibilities and delegated authority to men on earth to carry out His will, nonetheless it remains true that these men owe everything they have to Him—and so do we.

Christ's role in God's "eternal purpose" is not limited to the salvation of men. He (Christ) is also the Creator of the physical world, the One who gives life and authority to angels and men, and the One who maintains the stability and balance of "all things" in the physical universe. This might be hard for some to believe, if we limit our understanding of Him to a relatively young Prophet in the ancient world who was born to a peasant girl, taught people on mountainsides and in the country, and ate dinner with a bunch of fishermen at a campfire by the sea. But we must remember that this Prophet had also "emptied Himself" of the privileges and glory due Him as the Son of God (Phil. 2:5–8) in order to dwell among men and give His life as "a ransom for many" (Mark 10:45). Remember, too, that even in this subdued, limited, and earthly state of being, Jesus *still* performed numerous miracles, healed people of all kinds of diseases, cast out all kinds of demons (Mat. 4:23–25, Mark, 1:34, Luke 4:40, 7:21, et al), exercised authority over the physical elements (Luke 8:22–25), walked on water (Mat. 14:22–27), and *walked out of His own grave* (Mat. 28:5–7).

Christ's earthly ministry is not the full extent of who He was and what He has done (and continues to do). His supremacy over all things is not an exaggeration; the full extent of His reign far exceeds what our limited earthly existence is even able to comprehend. The Holy Spirit has revealed (all bracketed words added):

- "All things came into being by Him, and apart from Him nothing came into being that has come into being" (John 1:3).
- "For by Him [Christ] all things were created, both in the heavens and on earth, visible and invisible, whether thrones or dominions or rulers or authorities—all things have been created by Him and for Him. And He is before all things, and in Him all things hold together" (Col. 1:16–17).
- Christ reigns "above all rule and authority and power and dominion, and every name that is named, not only in this age, but also in the one to come. And He [God] put all things in subjection under His feet, and gave Him [Christ] as head over all things to the church, which is His body, the fullness of Him who fills all in all" (Eph. 1:21–23).
- "[God's Son is the] appointed heir of all things, through whom also He made the world. And He is the radiance of His glory and the exact representation of His nature, and upholds all things by the word of His power" (Heb. 1:2–3).
- God the Father has ordained that His Son "will come to have first place in everything. For it was the Father's good pleasure for all the fullness to dwell in Him" (Col. 1:18–19).

The purpose for citing these verses is to give evidence for Christ's power and authority to make grace come alive to *us* through *Him*. "Power" has to do with the ability to act; "authority" has to do with the right to act. Christ has both: He has the ability to impart saving grace, and He also has the right to do so.

God has gone to great lengths to make Christ real to us (by bringing Him into the world and demonstrating His power and authority to us), and so He has gone to great lengths to make *grace* real to us. He does not want us thinking about grace as a mere theological concept. Rather, He wants us to see the Lord Jesus as the very essence of grace—the same Lord who sits at the right hand of

God and who oversees *all that occurs* in *everything that exists!* Is His grace able to reach you? He knows exactly who you are, *where* you are, and what you need from Him. Is His grace able to help you? The same Jesus who walked out of His own grave, having overcome this world, death, and Satan, is the One who promises to help you. You have no reason to doubt Him; He has proven Himself to be infinitely more reliable to you than you will ever be to Him.

But in order to enjoy the Lord's salvation, you cannot view Him as a cutout version of who He really is. He wants fellowship with your soul, not merely the intellectual agreement of your mind. He desires your worship of Him, not your theological assessment of Him. He wants to be your Savior—this is true whether or not you are presently a Christian—not simply a religious figure to whom you give obligatory nods of respect.

The One Who Brings Grace to Life

God is the God of the living, not of the dead (see Luke 20:27–38). This means not only is He perpetually alive, but He also gives life to our spiritual being as well as our physical bodies.[62] Just as the Living God had a powerful influence on Abraham, Isaac, and Jacob, so He has a powerful influence on believers today. Just as the Holy Spirit breathes earthly life into every living person (Gen. 2:7), so He breathes spiritual life into the "new creature" in Christ (2 Cor. 5:17). And just as the power of God brought Jesus out of His grave, so that same power will resurrect believers from *their* graves (John 5:28–29, Rom. 8:11).

The immediate application of all these things is limited to this life, but it also carries us into the life to come. Just as marriage and procreation are limited to our earthly existence, so is saving grace. Once we are in heaven, we will not need the grace of God any more than we will need spouses or children.[63] Grace is for those whose sins must be covered in order for fellowship with God to exist; in heaven, sin—and all the ravages of sin—will be no longer. Once we are in heaven, the covenant we have with God now *through* Christ will have been fulfilled *by* Christ—i.e., His work in us will have reached its fruition, inasmuch as we will be with Him forever.

Even before Christ appeared in the flesh, there was still a need for forgiveness of human sins if God was going to have fellowship with anyone. The sacrificial system of the Law of Moses revealed a need for divine grace and atonement through blood, even though the ultimate sacrifice had yet to be given. The Law was given "because of transgressions," as a kind of measurement to define just how devastating and pervasive sin is. The Law *itself* was not a means of perfect justification, but just the opposite: it proved how it was impossible for a sinner to be justified *by* law once that law had been transgressed (Gal. 3:19–21). Thus, even during the period of the Old Testament, people had to be saved by God's grace through the demonstration of their human faith in Him. And if men are saved by grace, their salvation "is no longer on the basis of works, otherwise grace is no longer grace" (Rom. 11:6).

As covered in earlier chapters, Christ ultimately had to step out of His world and into ours in order to provide the once-for-all sacrifice that a myriad of animal sacrifices could never accomplish (Heb. 10:1–10). In other words, grace had to be more than a lamb offering, more than the pouring out of animal blood, more than a prophetic oracle, and more than the anticipation of a coming Messiah. Grace had to come alive—it had to become a Living Being—in order to *give* life to those who needed it (Him). Sins committed by humans required the worthy sacrifice of Someone who bore the image of the human problem but was Himself *more than human*. Sins committed in the earthly context required a heavenly response. Men who sold themselves into the power of darkness required "the Light of the world" (John 8:12) to save them.

Throughout all of human history, *every* sinner that has ever been saved has been saved the same way: by grace and through faith. And, as we demonstrated earlier, this means that every sinner that has ever been saved—regardless of time, ethnicity, nationality, or individual covenants—has been saved by Christ and through faith in God's "eternal purpose which He carried out in Christ Jesus our Lord" (Eph. 3:11). When Christ was revealed from heaven, grace was revealed from heaven. Just as Christ has always been, grace has always been. The absolute surety of Christ's obedience to God in carrying out everything necessary to serve as the world's Redeemer allowed God to forgive the ancient Israelites (and others) of their sins in anticipation of this offering. "But when the fullness of the time came, God sent His Son" (Gal. 4:4): when it was made abundantly clear just how desperate we are without God and how hopeless we are without grace, "Christ Jesus came into the world to save sinners" (1 Tim. 1:15).

Summary Thoughts

Given all that has been said, it is impossible for one to be saved by grace apart from having a genuine, obedient faith in Christ. No one should expect to receive divine forgiveness for his sins who has not first given his full allegiance to the divine Son of God. On the other hand, *all* who entrust their souls to the Savior of the world will indeed be saved by Him: His grace is His response to such faith. Sin separates us from God; saving grace reconciles us to Him. Your decision to sin caused your separation from God, just as my decision to sin caused mine; but your faith in God's system of salvation through grace is what draws you near to God, just as my faith draws me to Him. We have all fallen the same way, and we are all saved the same way: we all hear the same gospel, obey the same commandments, believe in the same Savior, and are forgiven by the same blood—*Christ's* blood.

Grace is not a personal feeling, spiritual wish, or magical experience. Just as Christ is real, so His grace is real; just as Christ now lives in those who have been saved by grace (Gal. 2:20), so grace must bear fruit in the lives of those who have been saved by Him. Wherever we see the grace of God at work, we know Christ is at work, since it is impossible for grace *to* work apart from His active intercession. When we beg God to forgive our sins, this is carried out by His remembering the sacrifice His Son made *to* forgive us. Just as Christ has first place in everything in God's world, so He must be given first place in the life of those who claim to be His disciples.

We who are faithful Christians serve a Living Savior, not a man-made religion, a wooden cross, or biblical doctrine. Doctrine is necessary to know what grace is (and how, when, and to whom God applies it), but doctrine cannot reconcile our souls to God.

Our sinful condition cannot be rectified by the keeping of laws and commandments; if it could, we would not need a Savior or grace. It is impossible to have a deep, spiritual relationship with a concept, but it is entirely appropriate for us to have a deep, spiritual relationship with Jesus Christ. All this is made possible, not because we are such wonderful people, but because Christ is most certainly a wonderful Savior, and He stepped into our world, allowed Himself to be nailed to a cross, and "[tasted] death for everyone" (Heb. 2:9) in order to invite us into fellowship with His Father.

Just as Christ is real, so His grace is real. Just as His grace is real, so one's submission to Him must be real in order for His grace to be imparted to him. In other words, it is not enough to know about grace, or to even know Him who *is* grace; it is necessary that we live a grace-filled life—thus, a Christ-filled life. This life is the "narrow" way that leads to eternal life, and it is the way that leads us to the very presence of God Himself. Our next several chapters will begin exploring what this grace-filled life looks like and why it is so beneficial to us.

Chapter Thirteen
⟫ *Approaching the Throne of Grace* ⟪

Therefore, since we have a great high priest who has passed
through the heavens, Jesus the Son of God, let us hold fast our confession.
For we do not have a high priest who cannot sympathize with our
weaknesses, but One who has been tempted in all things as we are,
yet without sin. Therefore let us draw near with confidence to the
throne of grace, so that we may receive mercy and find grace to
help in time of need.
(Heb. 4:14–16)

I use a word processing program to write the manuscripts for my books. This program is capable of far more than I will ever know—not because I *could not* know, but because I am unwilling to take the time to learn it. My needs are very basic; therefore, my working knowledge of the program remains purposely limited. If my needs were greater, then I would look into what else it could do for me. As it is, pretty much all I do is type, and apply some simple formatting, so a great deal of the capabilities of this program go unused. (Someone is already thinking, "But if you knew more, then it could make your manuscript preparation so much more efficient!" Yet, you underestimate my disdain for this kind of thing. But I digress . . .)

Unfortunately, many Christians apply my same logic concerning word processing toward learning the word of God. In other words, they only tap Scripture for what they need at the moment, but fail to realize its full potential. It is one thing to forego the many features of a man-made computer program; it is quite another to forego the spiritual instruction of our Creator. Not everyone who owns a Bible takes the time to learn the great treasure of its spiritual truths, much less apply them to practical living. I am always amazed by how *little* factual information some Christians know of the Bible, even when they have been Christians for decades.

Thankfully, there are other Christians who have immersed themselves in the study of God's word. When they do discover yet another one of its treasures, their eyes are opened to entirely new dimensions of the mind of God, so that everything they had previously learned about Him is now seen in a new and enlightened way. Passages they have read and re-read many times over suddenly take on new meaning and challenge their present perspective. This has certainly happened to me; perhaps it has happened to you as well. Maybe it was a sermon you heard, a study you engaged in, a period of acute mental clarity—any or all of these can bring to your attention what you had overlooked for years.

One particular passage that has had this kind of profound effect upon me personally is this one: "Therefore let us draw near with confidence to the throne of grace, so that we may receive mercy and find grace to help in time of need" (Heb. 4:16). Several years ago, while engaged in a study on the priesthood of Christ, this verse stuck out like a single giant oak tree on an endless field of grass. Despite my familiarity with it, I suddenly saw something I had not seen before. This discovery powerfully affected my entire understanding of the gospel, allowing me to appreciate Christ's role in my salvation even more than I had previously.

A Manifold Grace

First, some context is in order. The book of Hebrews focuses upon the superiority of Christ over all things: angels, Moses, the Levitical priesthood (described in the Law of Moses), and the high priest *of* that priesthood.[64] Hebrews also explains what Christ did that no man or angel could ever do: sit at the right hand of God (1:3); "taste death for everyone" (2:9); become a high priest according to God's divine oath (7:20–22); enter the heavenly tabernacle with His own blood (9:11–12); mediate a new covenant *in* His blood (9:15); offer Himself as a "once for all" sacrifice for the sins of the entire world (10:5–10); etc. Christ's work is better than and superior to all the work of anyone and everyone else—men, angels, or any other created being.

Hebrews gives prominent attention to the high priesthood of Christ.[65] The role of priests in the Old Testament (and the ancient world in general) was to intercede between God and His people. This intercession required: educating the people as to who God is and how to draw near to Him; offering ritual sacrifices prescribed by the Law; offering blood sacrifices for the atonement for sin (of individuals as well as the nation); ministering to God by way of the tabernacle and its services[66]; and transmitting revelations from God to His people. The Levitical high priest represented the highest level of religious authority within the nation of Israel, and his role (because of his proximity to God) even transcended that of Israel's kings. It was imperative that the high priest be a man of high character and completely devoted to his ministry, since the moral fitness and well-being of Israel depended upon his intercession and the atonement for sins that came through the sacrifices that he alone was allowed to offer.[67] If the people's sins were not mediated through sacrifices, and if Israel's sins were not mediated through the ministry of the high priest, then the Israelites could not have fellowship with God. The high priest's role was critical to establishing and maintaining this fellowship.

However, the Levitical priesthood was not perfect, and could not serve the needs of God's people perpetually. It had three major limitations. First, the high priest was a man, and thus he could (and did) sin like any other man. In fact, before serving as a mediator for Israel, he had to offer sin offerings for himself (Heb. 5:1–3). Second, the priesthood, since it was filled by men who could sin, was susceptible to corruption. We see this, for example, in the case of Eli's sons (1 Sam. 2:12–17), and in the high priests in the time of Jesus (John 11:47–53). Third, the high priests, no matter how well they may have served, eventually died. This necessarily implies that they were always succeeded by other men, who may or may not be of the same moral caliber as the one that died.

The author of Hebrews makes it clear that Christ has risen above the Levitical high priesthood. First of all, He could not *be* a Levitical high priest because He was from the tribe of Judah, not Levi. Thus, He was prevented *by* Law to serve in this capacity *under* Law. God ordained Him as a high priest, not according to Law, but through a divine oath; He was not ordained by men (and a Law that was meant to govern men), but by God Himself (through a heavenly decree that transcended all human authority). A new priesthood necessarily required a new "law"—a new means of intercession between God and men—and the obsoletion of whatever existed prior to it (Heb. 7:11–22, 8:1–13). Thus, Christ's becoming the new high priest of God meant that the old (Levitical) priesthood *and* the Law of Moses had to have been fulfilled by Him, for God will not have two laws, two priesthoods, and two covenants of salvation operating concurrently.[68]

This also means that Christ, our high priest, rose above all the weaknesses of the Levitical priesthood. He never sinned, so there was no need for Him to make atonement for Himself before serving the people. (We might ask: if He *had* sinned, by whose blood could His atonement ever be secured?—and other mind-numbing questions.) Also, His priesthood could not possibly be corrupted by men, since it is transcendent *of* men and His office is not filled *by* a mere man. If His kingdom is not of this world (John 18:36), then it stands to reason that His priesthood is also otherworldly, and therefore is immune to human corruption or defilement. And finally, He cannot die—"since it was impossible for Him to be held in its [death's] power" (Acts 2:24, bracketed word added)—and therefore He serves as an ever-living, never-dying, eternal high priest who offers not redemption for a given day or year, but in view of eternity (Heb. 9:12).

An Eternal High Priest

What does all of this mean to Christians? And, specifically, what does all of this have to do with grace? More than we might realize on both counts. Christ has "passed through the heavens," which means He has entered into that absolutely holy tabernacle wherein God dwells *in order to intercede for us* as a high priest of the highest order. This heavenly tabernacle is not a physical place or building, but refers to the very Presence of God Himself—in essence, His throne room, His celestial-like palace (as John describes in his vision in Rev. 4). No sinner can stand before God; we are not worthy to do so. No angel can stand before God on our behalf, since no angel has ever been a human being and therefore cannot adequately represent one. It was necessary—and *ingenious*—for One who was both a human *and* divine being to enter into God's presence and present to Him the greatest sin offering that could ever exist: *Himself.* Apart from such intercession, forgiveness of sins—and thus fellowship with God—is not just unlikely, or difficult, but *literally impossible.* We are made holy not through our own works of human effort, but through the divine intercession that Christ provides through His own blood (Heb. 9:13–14). God receives *us* because He has received His Son's offering on our behalf.

But there is more to consider, especially with regard to the verse cited earlier (Heb. 4:16): "Therefore let us draw near with confidence to the throne of grace, so that we may receive mercy and find grace to help in time of need." High priests do not sit on thrones, but they minister as servants. Kings do not minister as servants, but reign with great authority. High priests offer mercy, intercession, and gifts (offerings) on behalf of the one who wishes to draw near to God. Kings rule, offer stability, and provide justice on behalf of all those within their realm. High priests deal with atonement and consecration; kings deal with administration and law. High priests (in ancient times) worked standing up, ministering to the altar and temple; kings reigned while sitting upon a throne, giving commands and rendering decisions.

Kings do not really have anything to do with grace, but do exercise justice. Thus, a king cannot seek atonement for a person's sins, but he does have the legal right to declare a person guilty who has violated his laws. Or, he can declare a person innocent if he has not committed a crime, or if a sufficient penalty has been fulfilled in the case of one who *did* commit a crime. A high priest does not oversee justice and law, but he does have the ability to offer mercy and grace to the law-breaker. Ideally, then, the high priest and king work toward the same objective: perfect justice. One seeks it through making laws, enforcing laws, and punishing law-breakers; the other seeks it through re-establishing the status (and *life*) of the law-breaker who seeks forgiveness and reconciliation with the king.

The picture here is not absolute, for kings *can* offer forgiveness of sins against *them* (as in Mat. 18:23–35), and high priests *are* required to observe, enforce, and punish those who defy *religious* laws (as in Deut. 17:12). In some cases, the two work together (as in 2 Kings 23:4). But the two offices are not interchangeable: priests do not sit on thrones to rule, and kings are not allowed to carry out the ministry of the high priest (see 2 Chron. 26:16–21 for the tragic result when King Uzziah tried to do this). The only legitimate exception to this is when the two offices are both held by one man. Such is the case of the ancient king-priest Melchizedek (Gen. 14:17–20), whose dual capacity became the type (or, foreshadow) of the Messiah—a subject to which the Hebrews writer gives a great deal of attention (Heb. 5:8–10, 7:1–17).[69]

When Christ ascended to heaven, He sat down at the right hand of the Father (Acts 2:33, Col. 3:1) to serve as King over the Father's kingdom. But He also intercedes for us as the high priest of the believer's confession in Him (Rom. 8:34, Heb. 3:1). Thus, Christ serves in the office of the High Priest *and* as King of kings and Lord of Lords (Rev. 19:16). He is the epitome of spiritual intercession *and* spiritual justice; He is our compassionate Chief Shepherd *and* legal Advocate (Heb. 13:20, 1 Pet. 5:4, and 1 John 2:1–2); He provides the propitiatory offering for our sin (i.e., His own blood) *and* declares us innocent after we have been cleansed. He sits upon the throne of grace to do for us everything we cannot do for ourselves with regard to securing our salvation.

A good king will not ignore justice for any subject in his kingdom who has violated any of his laws (or simply, violated *the* law). Even when he does extend forgiveness, there must still be a payment made for the crime committed. Every crime creates a debt, and every debt must be paid by *someone*. (Remember from an earlier chapter: a law that has no penalty is not a real law at all; it is simply an idea that is not or cannot be enforced.) Christ has the ability to forgive us of our debts, but He cannot do so without a proper *payment* for those debts having been made. What He did was absorb the payment (or, the justice) for our sins in Himself through His sacrificial death on the cross: "and He Himself bore our sins in His body on the cross, so that we might die to sin and live to righteousness; for by His wounds you were healed" (1 Pet. 2:24).

This means: Christ's pronouncement of our innocence has been secured by nothing less than His own blood sacrifice for our sins. The King who declares us justified to the Father is also the High Priest who has provided the sacrifice *in Himself* necessary for this justification. Both the pronouncement of innocence *and* the offering that makes the innocence possible are summed up in one Savior. Both of these are acts of grace, since they are what He does for us that we cannot do for ourselves. Not even God the Father can absolve us of sins apart from His Son, and therefore not even God the Father can provide *saving grace* without directly and necessarily involving His Son in the process.[70] Without Christ and all that He has done for us—and continues to do for us—there is no "process." Without Him, there is no grace.

Access to the Father

All things belong to the Father, but He has given authority over all things to His Son (Mat. 28:18, Eph. 1:18–23). The kingdom of heaven, throne of heaven, and life itself belong to the Father, but these have been put under the Son's control. (Only the Father Himself is exempt from being under the Son's authority; see 1 Cor. 15:27–28.) The "throne" does not have to be a literal sitting place at all, but symbolizes a position of power and authority. The one who wishes to have access to the Father must be cleansed, justified, and approved by the Son, since "no one comes to the Father but through Me [Jesus]" (John 14:6*b*).

Christ's position as our eternal King *and* is all about gaining *access* to God the Father. The Father *owns* salvation; therefore, we need access to Him in order to obtain this. It does not matter how wonderful life with the Father is if *we cannot reach Him.* With such access, however, salvation is not only possible but is made real and cannot be taken away from us by anyone (John 10:27–29).[71] The apostle Paul wrote, "This [i.e., the revealed gospel] was in accordance with the eternal purpose which He [God] carried out in Christ Jesus our Lord, in whom we have boldness and confident access through faith in Him" (Eph. 3:11–12, bracketed words added). In Christ— meaning: in our covenant relationship with God *through* Christ—we are given confident access to the Father, which is the entire purpose of the gospel.

"Therefore let us draw near with confidence to the throne of grace, so that we may receive mercy and find grace to help in time of need" (Heb. 4:16). Christ can sympathize with our weaknesses even though we cannot fathom His infinite power and glory. We have no clue what it means to be a Divine Personage, but He knows intimately what it means to be human. Christ has endured and overcome every kind of temptation known to man, whereas we have succumbed to these and thus have brought about our own spiritual ruin (Jas. 1:13–15). Christ now judges in favor of those who turn to Him, rather than in condemnation of them. He listens to believers with the compassion of an eternal High Priest, yet He will judge the ungodly with the power and authority of a great King. He listens to those who belong to Him, and is patient with those who seek His truth, yet He will ultimately destroy all "those who do not know God and . . . those who do not obey" His gospel (2 Thess. 1:8).

In order to gain access to the Father, you must first be "in Christ"—in a covenant relationship with God *through* Christ. You cannot hope to gain access to the Father apart from your humble submission to His Son (Eph. 2:18). Even after you have entered into a covenant of salvation with God, you still must present yourself before the throne of grace, where Christ sits in all His majesty. The means by which you approach this throne is important, for neither Christ nor God will extend favor in the case of impropriety or irreverence. Thus, you must approach the throne of grace:

- **In faith.** Since you cannot see beyond the visible world, your entire involvement with the spiritual realm is predicated on your *faith* that it—and everything in it—exists. You cannot come to God without believing that He exists *and* is willing and able to help you (Heb. 11:6). All access to the Father will be denied to the one who does not believe in the reality of this access and the method by which it is given.
- **In prayer.** Prayer is a real and visible demonstration of faith. One who does not pray admits that he does not have faith; one who

prays without believing violates what his faith claims to be true
(Jas. 1:5–8). One cannot approach Christ's throne through any
means other than prayer. No earthly temple, sanctuary, religious
organization, ordained priest, or sacred object can do what
the humble prayer of the contrite believer will accomplish in
approaching the throne of grace.

- **Bearing gifts.** Under the Law of Moses, men were commanded to
  approach the Lord three times a year, "and they shall not appear
  before the Lord empty-handed" (Deut. 16:16). Jehovah—the
  God of Israel—deserved to be recognized and properly honored
  by those in covenant with Him. Similarly, you must recognize
  Christ as your Lord and Savior, and He deserves the same kind of
  respect and honor. You must have something to *bring* to Him, for
  you must not appear before the throne of grace empty-handed.

The gifts you bring to the throne of grace are not to be viewed as a
payment (or penance). Christ has already paid the price for grace;
there is no way your gifts could ever equal or supersede His. You are
not *purchasing* anything; rather, you are demonstrating your deep
appreciation for the honor of entering into the King's presence.
To prove this, your presentation before the throne must cost you
something. In 2 Sam. 24:24, we read of Araunah, a God-fearing man
who was willing to give King David his threshing floor for free in
order for him (David) to make sacrifices to God. Yet, David replied,
"No, but I will surely buy it from you for a price, for I will not offer
burnt offerings to the Lord my God which cost me nothing" (2 Sam.
24:24). Likewise, even though your gifts to Christ cannot be at all
comparable with the worth of His gifts to you, He still *wants* your
gifts and He still *deserves* the honor you bring to Him.

It is not left up to you to determine what gifts to bring before the
throne of grace. God is "a great King," and "from the rising of the sun
even to its setting, My name will be great among the nations" (Mal.
1:11, 14). Now that God the Father has handed over everything to His
Son, He (Christ) deserves this same level of honor and deference.
Who are you or I, small and powerless as we are, to tell the King of all
that exists what will please Him? It is His place to tell us, not ours to

tell Him. Thus, the revealed word of God describes four types of gifts
He seeks from us:

- **Praise.** The entire fifth chapter of Revelation is a doxology—a
  hymn of praise—to Christ, the Lamb of God. The entire host
  of heaven renders praise and seven-fold blessings to Him; all of
  creation joins in the rhapsodic chorus of worship. If angels of
  God, who are much higher, stronger, and more capable than us,
  offer glorious praise to the Lord Jesus, then so should we. This is
  especially true because of all that He has done *for* us. "Through
  Him [Christ] then, let us continually offer up a sacrifice of praise
  to God, that is, the fruit of lips that give thanks to His name"
  (Heb. 13:15). No one can truly praise the Father without giving
  praise also to His Son; "He who does not honor the Son does not
  honor the Father who sent Him" (John 5:23b). The Son deserves
  our highest praise; no one less than Him is worthy of it.
- **Gratitude:** Grace is everything that God does for us *through Christ*
  that we cannot do for ourselves. Allowing us to approach His
  throne of grace is itself an act of grace, since we do not deserve
  this privilege but cannot be saved otherwise. Christians are
  supposed to be "overflowing with gratitude" (Col. 2:6–7) in their
  walk with Christ; this is not a casual request, but an expectation
  of those who have been saved by His blood. "Therefore, since we
  receive a kingdom which cannot be shaken, let us show gratitude,
  by which we may offer to God an acceptable service with
  reverence and awe" (Heb. 12:28). God has appointed Christ to be
  the King and High Priest of His kingdom; He (God) also demands
  that we approach Him (His Son) with "reverence and awe." It is
  irreverent to come before the King without a sincere expression
  of thankfulness and gratitude (Eph. 5:20, Col. 3:17).
- **Petitions and requests:** I have heard Christians say, in so many
  words, "I know I should ask God for His help on [whatever],
  but I didn't want to bother Him." Yet, since Christ has *asked* for
  our petitions, we are not bothering Him to provide them (John
  14:14). In fact, we bother Him in another way when we do *not*
  provide them! The King has requested *your* petitions; do not deny

Him this request. When you and I ask Him for things—blessings, help, answers, providence, or whatever we believe is needed—according to His will, He is happy to give them to us. "Be anxious for nothing," Paul instructs us, "but in everything by prayer and supplication with thanksgiving let your requests be made known to God" (Phil. 4:6).

- **Private burdens:** These first three categories of things to bring to the throne of grace—praise, gratitude, and petitions—are appropriate to bring before a Great King. These are *kingly* gifts, in a sense; they are fitting expressions of honor from the citizens (of the kingdom) to their King. But the king of any domain, in his official capacity *as* king, does not want to hear the confessions, private troubles, and personal groanings of each individual citizen. If it is something the king can deal with in his benevolence—petitions, requests, supplications, etc.—then that is one thing; our private, internal, and spiritual turmoil goes beyond the context of an earthly king's concern.

  ▫ But Christ is not only our King, He is also our High Priest. And as such, He *is* willing to "deal gently with the ignorant and misguided" (Heb. 5:2); He *can* identify with our troubles and sorrows; He is *able* to relate to our human condition. "For we do not have a high priest who cannot sympathize with our weaknesses, but One who has been tempted in all things as we are, yet without sin" (Heb. 4:15). In other words, He is willing to receive even our most private, intimate hurts and struggles, *and* He is capable of responding to them with perfect wisdom. If He were *only* a King, we would be denied this critical need. Since He is both King *and* High Priest, we have *everything* we need in order for our souls to be made complete in Him (Col. 1:28).

  ▫ As our High Priest, Christ wants to hear our confessions of sin and pleas for forgiveness. He is not asking us to handle these on our own—which is impossible—so He wants us to bring these things to Him. "If we confess our sins, He is faithful and righteous to forgive us our sins and to cleanse us from all unrighteousness" (1 John 1:9). We may have to confess our sins to others (Jas. 5:16), and especially to those whom we personally offend (Luke 17:3–4), but *all* sin is against Christ and therefore all confessions of sin must also be brought to Him. Doing this also tests our faith, since we are being asked to trust that He will take care of us in whatever way serves our best interests, even when we have not performed well.

◦ Furthermore, it is an honor to Christ when we entrust to Him our faith, our hope, and our souls (2 Tim. 1:12)—and even our heaviest burdens. "Come to Me, all who are weary and heavy-laden," He has said, "and I will give you rest. Take My yoke upon you and learn from Me, for I am gentle and humble in heart, and you will find rest for your souls" (Mat. 11:28–29). These are not the words of a king, but are the compassionate invitations of a benevolent high priest.

〜

Grace is not a "thing" we need every once in a while. The throne of grace is not a "place" we go to a few times a year, like some go to a church building or cathedral on Christmas and Easter. The more we appreciate the need for grace, the more we will find ourselves bowing reverently at Christ's feet. Grace is critical in the three main areas of our spiritual walk: dealing with our sins; walking in fellowship (with God and His people); and overcoming the struggles of this life. In each of these areas are things for which *we* are responsible and things which are *too much* for us to handle. Grace never removes our own responsibilities, but does cover all other areas that must be addressed in order for us to be saved. We have been granted access to God through His Son's throne of grace, but it is our responsibility to appear before that throne according to how we have been instructed, and bearing those gifts which He has requested.

Laying Your Gifts at His Feet

Until now, you may have been in full agreement with all that has been said in this chapter. Yet, someone may take issue with the idea of approaching *Christ* in prayer rather than the *Father*. The fact is: it is impossible for us to approach the Father *except* through Christ

(John 14:6), and any time we pray directly to the Father, Christ is interceding for us (Rom. 8:34, 1 Tim. 2:5, 1 John 2:1–2, et al). While it is common practice to address all prayers to God, there is nothing unbiblical or inappropriate in addressing prayers to God *through Christ*. This is not referring to the "in Jesus' name" formality that many Christians tag on the end of their prayers; rather, *all* prayers must be in Jesus' name and go through Him personally. This is what the throne of grace is all about; He is our only access to the Father.

Even though we are speaking of a spiritual communion with Christ here, visualize this entire scenario in a physical perspective. Imagine lifting up your gift to the Lord with your own two hands. (Wrap up the gift in something, if you choose, that you feel would be appropriate.) Now picture a glorious throne, gleaming with brilliant light and surrounded by fantastic guardian angels ("living creatures"), in the midst of the most beautiful celestial palace your imagination can produce. On the throne sits the Son of God in all His glory—glory far too wonderful for human words—bathed in colorful, serenaded with ethereal music, and emanating the greatest peace your soul has ever experienced—and you approach Him with your humble gift. I suggest that you picture the actual Personage of Christ in human form (because we cannot even imagine what a Divine Being looks like otherwise), but without distinct details.

Imagine that you are standing in the spirit, so to speak, in this indescribably beautiful throne room at the center of all that exists, and the Lord Jesus welcomes your approach and bids you to draw near to Him. You do so fearfully and reverently—not with fear of being destroyed, but in awe of His incomprehensible presence—and lay your gifts at His feet. *Visualize this in your heart.* See yourself laying your praise, your gratitude, your petitions, and even your burdens at the feet of Christ. Lay before Him your earthly fears—He wants you to *let go* of these, since He can deal with them and you cannot. Lay your heartache and grief at His feet—release them from your hand. Lay before Him all your earthly disappointments, the sting of those who have betrayed you, and the gnawing pain of the loss of loved ones—*relinquish control* of them, for they will destroy you, but

He can deal with all of them. Lay at the Lord's feet your bitterness, your addiction, your anger, your emptiness, your loneliness, your every weakness—lay all of these at the feet of the King and High Priest of your salvation.

This is your "gift" to the Lord—this is what He has requested of you. While you might think these things to be hardly fit for the King of the entire universe, it is exactly what He wants *if* it is offered in genuine faith. God's gifts to us are those which we could not have received without Him. Yet, our offerings of praise, gratitude, petitions, and burdens are gifts from *us* that He could not have received otherwise. God cannot force these from our hands; He cannot extract these from our hearts against our will. When we freely and completely *give* these things to Him, they are precious in His sight. He regards such tribute as a high honor; the sacrificial, freewill offerings of His people bring Him great pleasure.

"Therefore humble yourselves under the mighty hand of God, that He may exalt you at the proper time, casting all your anxiety on Him, because He cares for you" (1 Pet. 5:6–7). The offering of your praise, gratitude, and petitions are acts of humility, faith, and respect. Relinquishing control of your struggles is also an act of humility, since this demonstrates greater faith in Christ's ability to deal with these things than in your own feeble ability. In doing so, you are saying, in so many words, "Lord, I cannot bear this burden without You. My soul is being tormented and/or overwhelmed with this burden, but You are infinitely stronger than I am. I freely give You this burden because You are willing and capable of dealing with it in such a way that serves Your best interest, which will always be in *my* best interest." Such is the spiritual attitude of one who has truly placed full confidence in the One who sits upon the throne of grace.

To clarify: "relinquishing control" of your burdens does not mean you give up all *earthly responsibility* toward those things. For example, if you are in a loveless marriage (through no fault of your own), laying this burden before the Lord does not mean you no longer have to make any effort in that relationship, or that you can just walk away from it altogether. Laying your burden at Christ's feet does not absolve you of what is still required of you; it only gives to Christ what is *too much* for you. If Christ chooses to remove your burden from you entirely, then that must be His decision, not yours. But in every case, you are expected to fulfill your earthly responsibilities and trust that He will not allow you to be overwhelmed in the process (1 Cor. 10:13, in principle).

The burdens you lay at Christ's feet should be those which you are *unable* to endure, not what you do not *like* enduring—or think you *cannot* endure. (However, there is nothing wrong with telling Him what you do not like, or do not want to endure, as long as your "venting" to Him ends with, in so many words, "Not my will, but Your will be done.") Christ will not allow you to be overcome with this world, but only if you put your trust and confidence in Him. His promise to you—namely, that you can overcome through Him (John 16:33)—is conditioned upon your belief that He will spare you from whatever would destroy your soul.[72] In faith, you give to Him what you cannot bear, cope with, or overcome *on your own*. The objective here is the salvation of your soul, not necessarily your physical comfort, convenience, or preference. Saving grace is not intended to make your physical life less troublesome or more comfortable by removing all your difficulties. Rather, it is to bridge that huge chasm between where you are *now* and where you *need* to be in your fellowship with God the Father.

The reason for all this explanation, beyond its immediate practical value, is because someone will inevitably respond with, "Yes, I gave all my burdens to the Lord, but I'm still suffering!" Suppose someone was drowning in the ocean, but suddenly he receives a life preserver thrown to him from a nearby ship. Now suppose that, while he clings to this ring that has spared him from certain death, he complains to the ship's captain, "I appreciate the gesture of you having thrown me this life preserver, but I'm still very wet!" The purpose of the life preserver is not to remove him from the ocean, but to keep him from drowning *in* it. This is parallel to the complaint of a Christian whose soul God has spared from certain ruin: "I appreciate the 'way of escape,' but I'm still *suffering*!" Of *course* he is still suffering: this sin-

corrupted world is *filled* with suffering. In fact, the more conformed
one becomes to Christ, the more he (or she) may suffer—just as
Christ Himself suffered. In fact, it is for this purpose—that we would
suffer for His name's sake—that He called us in the first place (Mat.
5:10–12, 1 Pet. 2:21). The purpose of grace is not to take us out of this
world, but to save us *from* it.

You should never make the removal of all suffering your primary
objective. It may well be that God wants you to suffer for reasons
He does not have to explain to you. Or, it may be that He needs
you to suffer for what He has *revealed* to you in His word—namely,
for the sake of righteousness. You should never put your personal
comfort or preferences ahead of God's will. What you are to seek
first is the advancement of His kingdom and the noble virtue of His
righteousness (Mat. 6:33), not the alleviation of every discomfort,
regardless of the level of severity. You should, however, pray that
Christ will remove from you what is unbearable—i.e., what is
insufferable—and not merely what exceeds your comfort zone or
affects your life as you have come to enjoy it.[73]

Leaving the Throne of Grace

Bringing your gifts to the throne of grace is not the full extent of
what is asked of you, however. While you have gifts to offer the King,
He has gifts to give to *you*. While you have poured out *your* heart to
the High Priest who sits on the throne of grace, it is necessary for you
to receive "the kind intention of *His* will" (Eph. 1:5, emphasis added).
Believers must never leave the throne of grace empty-handed; this
contradicts our dependence upon the One who occupies that throne.
Christ's intention is for you to "be filled up to all the fullness of God"
(Eph. 3:19), not merely for Him to receive the comparatively small
gifts of the human heart.

In keeping with the visualization of your presentation before the
throne of grace, picture yourself having knelt at Christ's feet with
your gifts and burdens. Once you have released your gifts to the King,
your hands are now empty—and you need to let Him *fill* them. Before
you leave His presence, you are to receive from Him the help that
you so desperately seek. His gift is not a mere "care package" that

will tide you over until you get back on your feet; it is the means to your spiritual survival. His gift is not a trinket or memento for you to put on your dresser or store in your curio cabinet; it is a priceless endowment that only a Divine Being is capable of providing you. His gift is not another burden for you to lug around in your heart; it is weightless, completely bearable, and *liberating*. His gift is whatever your soul needs in order to overcome this day, this week, this year, and this life in order to be with Him in the end. His gift is exactly what you need—no more, but never any less. This gift is *His grace*.

Christ wants to hear your concerns, but He is not just a Divine Listener. He wants to receive your concerns, but He is not just a Divine Receiver. He also wants to *help* you with your concerns because He is (among many, many things) a Divine Help in your time of need. That is what being an Advocate is all about (1 John 2:1–2). He is the only One who truly can help any of us; that is why we pray to Him.[74] "[L]et us draw near with confidence to the throne of grace, so that we may receive mercy and find grace to help in time of need" (Heb. 4:16). Mercy spares us from what we deserve: condemnation and punishment. Grace gives to us what we do not deserve, but what we desperately need in order to overcome this world.

In preparing to receive your gift from the eternal High Priest who sits at the right hand of the Father, do not merely cup your hands, expecting only a small token of consolation. Instead, open wide your arms to receive His grace, for it is a tremendous gift and a "living hope" (1 Pet. 1:3). His grace—like a beautiful, priceless, and magnificent present wrapped in light and the finest adornment imaginable—is given to you *without cost*. You could never have afforded it on your own, and you will never have to pay it back. It is also given to you *without limit*. Whatever needs to be done to preserve your soul *will* be done, no matter how big the problem, how long it has been going on, how insurmountable it seems to you, or how impossible it appears to those who refuse to believe in the One who provides it.

It is not necessary—and, likely, not even humanly possible—to always know what this gift is that Christ imparts to you. He knows what you need far better than you will ever know. He responds precisely *to* that need, not your limited understanding of it. You may not even recognize His gift at first, even after receiving it; you may have no idea why He gave you *that* gift (instead of something you expected), or when it should be used. But be absolutely confident of this: His gift of grace—which is really a bundle of many gifts—is *exactly* what you need in order to deal with whatever it is you are facing. His grace is *exactly* what you need in order to endure, overcome, grow, mature and *flourish* as a child of God. Christ the Savior knows your needs perfectly and comprehensively; the grace He gives is custom-tailored to each believer's needs so that he "will never stumble." His gift will be "abundantly supplied" to whomever humbly approaches His throne of grace (2 Pet. 1:8–11). Again, it is not necessary for you to know all the details of His gifts. It *is* necessary that you believe: His gifts are real; they are powerful beyond human comprehension; you cannot duplicate or exceed them anywhere else or by anyone else's power—including your own. Finally, it *is* necessary that you receive His gifts in humble faith and overflowing gratitude.

Summary Thoughts

God's revealed word is not something to which we give cursory attention, or use only for things we deem necessary. Unlike a manual explaining a word processing program—most of which will be entirely useless to whatever you are doing—God's word is the only information we have to get us successfully from this life to the next. The less we pay attention to it, the more damage that is done and the more our soul suffers. The more we pay attention to it, the better we understand the will of the Lord and how to draw closer to Him.

The throne of grace is not a mere fixture in the spiritual realm meant to impress us, along with crystal mansions, streets of gold, harp-playing angels, and whatever else people envision when they think about heaven. Rather, it denotes the "place" to which every believer is to come, bearing gifts for the King and High Priest who sits upon that throne. The Holy Spirit has disclosed to us (in the gospel of

Christ) what these gifts are to be; offerings of such great importance for such a great King are not to be left to our own imagination. He wants our praise, gratitude, and petitions, but He also wants our private burdens, fears, doubts, sufferings, and grief. In humble faith, we are to lay all of these at His feet.

But Christ does not just receive prayers; He also responds to them. *How* He responds is His business; it is enough that we believe He *does* so. He always has something to give to those who approach His great throne: a gift of inestimable value and perfectly conformed to whatever needs we may have. This gift is really many gifts, all designed by the Creator Himself; they are always good and profitable, will do exactly what serves our best interest, and will never fail to work. We are not receiving a mere thimbleful of help from an all-powerful Divine Being; we are receiving an abundance of help from the only One in the entire universe—the visible *and* invisible world—who truly *can* help us.

Someone may respond to all this by saying, "But *I* overcame [insert: problem] without Christ's help. Therefore, I do not *always* need Him; some things I can handle by myself." We do not approach the throne of grace because we are unable to do anything at all; we approach it (Him) because Christ's way is always *superior* to ours. In coming before His throne, we defer to Him in every way: we ask Him to resolve our dilemmas in His way, on His schedule, according to His will, and all for His glory. In deferring to Him, we also admit that His way is not just "a" workable solution, possibly on par with our own; rather, it is *the best* solution and the only *acceptable* solution. While anyone may enjoy a small measure of success on his (or her) own power, no one will be *saved* by his own strength. Those who try to save themselves will lose everything in the end—and this is exactly what Christ wants us to avoid.

Hopefully, you have found what has been expounded upon in this chapter to be very valuable to you. But now that the explanation is given, it is up to you to put what you have learned into practice. In other words, it is up to you to draw before the King of glory and

High Priest of your confession, bearing gifts of faith and humility, and receiving from Him what no one else is capable of giving you. He longs to see you, because He loves you more than you can possibly understand.

Chapter Fourteen
═ *Touched by Grace* ═

*For the grace of God has appeared, bringing salvation to all men,
instructing us to deny ungodliness and worldly desires and to live
sensibly, righteously and godly in the present age, looking
for the blessed hope and the appearing of the glory of our
great God and Savior, Christ Jesus . . .* (Titus 2:11–13)

It would seem, on the surface, that God's saving grace would be
something that *every person* would want for himself (or herself).
We are all in such great need, and His grace has so much to offer—
more than we can even comprehend. Despite this, there are several
reasons—no *good* reasons, but reasons nonetheless—why Christians
may resist the grace of God. As previously discussed, these include:

- Confusion, whether self-inflicted or as a result of deliberate
  ignorance.
- Lack of doctrinal understanding (of grace, and related subjects).
- Failure to believe in grace.
- Guilt (or, feeling "*too* guilty" to deserve grace).
- Improper reaction to other people's (or religions') abuse of grace.
- Pride, in all its forms, exaltations, and delusions.
- Seeing grace only as an "it" rather than appreciating the
  embodiment of saving grace in Jesus Christ. (However, I will
  continue to refer to grace as an "it" in this book to avoid confusion
  between talking about Christ Himself and the doctrinal teaching
  of God's saving grace.)

From this list alone, it becomes clear why people who *want* saving
grace may be unwilling to get past their personal hang-ups over it. Or,
they may talk a lot about grace, but may be hard-pressed to define,
teach, or doctrinally defend it.

Not only do people struggle to accept the biblical teaching
on grace, they also struggle to embrace the grace-filled *life*. This
refers to the Christian life that is supposed to be both defined and

refined by grace. Christians are not merely supposed to learn about grace as a concept—that is, as a topic of Bible classes or spiritual conversations—but we are also expected to put what we receive from God into action. This is easier said than done, because:

- **the grace-filled life is hard—not impossible, but certainly difficult.** We are all naturally inclined to take the path of least resistance; grace calls us to a higher path, a nobler life, and a transcendent love. Someone says, "But I live a grace-filled life, and *my* life isn't difficult!" Such a person may not really understand what is required of him (or her). Living by grace is not a different life than discipleship to Christ (as if we get to choose between the two), but they are one and the same. Jesus likened discipleship to bearing one's cross on the way to his *death* (Mat. 16:24). Yet, despite its demands, the life that is defined by grace provides a superior means of dealing with this life, and provides the most realistic, practical, and rewarding life there is.

- **the grace-filled life requires discipline and effort, which is, of course, why it is difficult.** It is not hard to default to one's self-will or gratify one's self-interest. Even animals do the same! When animals want to sleep, they sleep; when they want to eat, they eat; when they want to mate, they mate; when they want to growl or purr or attack or kill, they do so. This is also how carnal-minded people live. They have no moral guide to adhere to, no spiritual principles to live by, and no heaven or hell to think about. There are no consequences for their crimes (so they think), as long as they do not get caught. Christians, however, are to "keep seeking the things above, where Christ is, seated at the right hand of God" and set their minds "on the things above, not on the things that are on earth" (Col. 3:1–2). They abide by a heavenly standard, which means they live on a different plane than the typical "man of the world." This higher plane—the grace-filled life—demands their discipline and allegiance to Jesus Christ, not their personal gratification.

- **the grace-filled life requires transcendent sacrifice, which pits it squarely against everything this world seeks.** The unbeliever does not make sacrifices for a better life to come; his earthly life is his only concern. He serves himself by believing and doing whatever brings him the greatest personal joy, and this limited, temporary, and very superficial joy is all he will ever know. The faithful Christian, on the other hand, serves God *first* and is rewarded later. Inspired by the grace that God has extended to him, he also extends mercy, grace, and forgiveness to others—all at his own expense. He suffers loss for God in this life in order to gain something he could never have acquired otherwise: *eternal* life. He relinquishes his heart, his will, and his own identity in order to live with Christ in his heart (Gal. 2:20), follow Christ's will, and be identified with Him. All of this is a most difficult thing to do (which is why most people simply will not do it), but discipleship to Christ leads us to nothing less than this.

- **the grace-filled life denies external, worldly influences as a means of determining how one should live.** Specifically, this refers to the human craving for acceptance and approval, and the peer pressure that often inflames this craving. People who are *of* the world listen to (and seek the approval of) those whom the world highly esteems: "They are from the world; therefore they speak as from the world, and the world listens to them" (1 John 4:5). However, those who are "born of God" (John 1:12–13) seek to worship God, just as God seeks their worship (John 4:23–24). Those who are inspired by heavenly grace are not concerned with what the world thinks of them; they know "that which is highly esteemed among men is detestable in the sight of God" (Luke 16:15). The world *hates* Christians since we call attention to the world's sins and spiritual irresponsibility by our very association with Christ (John 15:18–22). "In all this, they are surprised that you do not run with them into the same excess of dissipation, and they malign you; but they shall give account to Him who is ready to judge the living and the dead" (1 Pet. 4:4–5).

⌒

"And who is adequate for these things?" (2 Cor. 2:16*b*), for this all seems a bit overwhelming. Left to ourselves, *no one* would be "adequate" to live the life of a child of God. But this is what divine grace is all about: making us *fit* and *able* to serve Him despite our fallibility, inadequacy, and human weaknesses. Being "fit" has to do with our worthiness to serve our King (i.e., atonement for sins, sanctification of the Spirit, transformation of the mind, etc.). Being "able" refers to having what is necessary to carry out our individual ministry to God (i.e., being strengthened by Him, being prepared for "good works" [Eph. 2:10], being equipped to do His will [Heb. 13:20–21], etc.). Christ does for us what we cannot do for ourselves, in the context of our service to Him. While fulfilling our Christian responsibilities would be literally impossible apart from His grace, "with God all things are possible" (Mat. 19:26).

Hollywood Christianity?

People love the idea of being rescued by God—especially through some angelic or miraculous means. We want to believe that God is in the background of every difficult or perilous situation, just waiting to part our Red Sea, take down our Goliath, or stop the sun in the sky for us so we can continue to fight our battles. Many see God as a kind of "triple-A" rescuer—like the guy who offers roadside assistance to stranded motorists, happy to replace a battery, provide a gallon of gas, or give us a tow. Many people pray for divine deliverance from their own self-inflicted messes, with no real intention of preventing a repeat of those messes in the future. And, many think that God is there to *perform* against all odds, simply because we are hurting so badly. I have listened many times to families gathered around the deathbed of a loved one, holding out for "a miracle" healing, cure, or resuscitation.

"Calling All Angels" (2003) is a song by the pop-rock group *Train* which articulates this yearning for some kind of otherworldly intervention. The song expresses the fear, disappointment, and despair of this life, and how we all "need a sign" that God is nearby, waiting to deliver us from all the badness of this world. (There seems to be the implication, too, that if God does not actually send His angels, then He has only contributed to our disillusionment.) In typical fashion, however, the song mentions no sense of allegiance, moral responsibility, or obedience to God on *our* part—we just want God to do *His* part. God needs to provide a reason to believe; God needs to build hope inside of us; God needs to do this or that; but what do we need to do for God?

There have also been a few TV shows in the last number of years that camp on this same idea ("Touched by an Angel," "Highway to Heaven," etc.). The general strategy of each episode involved someone going through a crisis in his (or her) life who was not dealing with it very well. Enter an alleged angel of God, who becomes personally involved in the protagonist's life and thus in his crisis. As the episode continued, the "angel" teaches this troubled soul some moral lesson which he would have to implement before the credits rolled. This, of course, was infallibly successful and afterward the "angel" goes on his heavenly way looking for another distraught or troubled soul to help, console, and enlighten.

Many otherwise irreligious people will welcome God (or, at least, the idea of God) on this most superficial, unobtrusive level. In their minds, it is perfectly acceptable for God to send an angel, work a miracle, exorcise a personal demon, alter circumstances, or do whatever else people think God is sitting around waiting to do for people today. But you notice in these Hollywood dramas that people are *never* told to deny themselves, take up their crosses, and follow the Lord Jesus (Mat. 16:24). The "angels" never tell them to give up *all* the things, practices, or relationships in their lives which are offensive to God or destructive to their souls. The protagonists are never encouraged to actively participate in a congregation of believers wherein they can share in collective worship to God and contribute to the work of His kingdom.

Instead, the "angel" drops into their lives, educates them in some moral lesson which they likely knew all along but were too stubborn or proud or angry or hurt to have implemented on their own, and solves their dilemma for them. This is what people want: a God to solve their problems—just the individual, incidental, and crippling *problems*—that's all. "Then You can leave, God, until my next crisis. But be ready to act on my behalf the next time I run into trouble!" is the unstated but very obvious response of such people.

This is the preferred "God" of the twenty-first century, the ideal, non-interfering, non-demanding "God" that is custom-tailored for a postmodern, pro-choice, "me first" America. This "God" is convenient, completely tolerant of every lifestyle, absolutely non-judgmental, and always there when you need Him. He does not ask questions; He only dispenses answers—usually the miraculous kind, since everyone wants a "sign" in which to believe. After His job is done, the crisis is over, and the storm has passed, He conveniently disappears into the celestial palaces of heaven, waiting for another time when He can rescue some hapless person from his (or her) troubles.

A Very Limited Surrender

While many people would not mind being "Touched By An Angel," they would certainly not want to be "Slapped Upside the Head By a Demon" or "Bushwhacked by Beelzebul." Many people openly confess there is a good force in the world—especially when that good force brings them blessings, advancement, or some personal advantage. Yet, few take Satan and demonic forces very seriously. It is acceptable to have helpful (but non-interfering) angels swooping in to rescue us every now and then, but the idea of losing one's soul in the "outer darkness" (Mat. 8:12) makes everyone very uncomfortable. The idea of an eternal heaven is received with open arms; the idea of an eternal hell is offensive, repulsive, and socially unacceptable.

But the gospel of saving grace is not about rescuing people from minor scrapes, traumas of life, or even physical suffering. Saving grace is about saving our *souls*, not saving our necks, saving face, or saving the comfortable way of life that we have come to enjoy. God's love—the love that compelled His Son to come into this world and bear an unspeakably awful death on the cross—focuses not on the incidental problems that we will inevitably face, but on rescuing us from "the domain of darkness" (Col. 1:13–14). He knows that if we are *not* rescued, then we will experience a horrifying, extremely painful, and never-ending existence in the world to come. People say things like, "How can a loving God send people to hell?" But whatever awaits the fallen, impenitent soul is what that soul has brought upon itself. God never made anyone sin; He only gave us the *freedom* to sin. We used that freedom as a means of self-exaltation or self-gratification, but it was never meant to be this way.

One of the most well-known passages in the Bible is John 3:16: "For God so loved the world, that He gave His only begotten Son, that whoever believes in Him shall not perish, but have eternal life." Many people read this as: "For God so loved the world, that He gave His beloved Son so that *no one should perish*, but *all* will have eternal life (no matter what)." But this is not what it says, and no amount of creative customizing will change what it *does* say. What it actually says is this: *we are all perishing*—not only physically, but spiritually—unless and until we take responsibility for what we have done (in having sinned against God) and seek His only solution for our demise: His Son. Thus, we are *all* losing our souls to the outer darkness if we do not take full advantage of God's gospel of saving grace. This grace is not made available to us because God has it in for us and wants us to suffer, but just the opposite: He wants to *save* us from ourselves and wants us *with Him* for eternity.

The kind of decision, however, that calls upon God for salvation is not something that can be limited to the span of a TV episode, a euphoric worship service, a week at Bible camp, or even a month of solid commitment. It is a decision that demands one's heart and soul—a *full* surrender, not a limited or temporary one. Christ did not give His innocent life on the cross so you or I could give Him a nod of thanks now and then, or a frantic 9-1-1 call for deliverance from our crisis-of-the-moment. He died to put an end to the sin in our lives, transform us into what we never could have been otherwise, and prepare us to enter into the very presence of God in a very *good way*. Rather than face the "wrath of God"—as all unrighteous people will do, whether or not they choose to believe it (Rom. 1:18–20)—we are able, through Christ, to walk in fellowship with God *now* and *forever*.

Returning to the fanciful premise of an angel being dispatched to rescue someone from their moral crisis, we could ask: why would an angel that worships Christ as Lord render help to anyone who proudly refuses to do the same? A *fallen* angel may readily respond to a person's call for help—not to offer benevolent assistance, but rather to convince him (or her) that he does not need to turn his heart to Christ. A fallen angel would do its best to convince a person that he only needs God to deliver him from his present suffering so that he can resume the life that he has chosen to live otherwise. A real angel would never advise this; a fallen angel will enthusiastically do so. A real angel would direct us to the gospel of Christ; a fallen angel will deceptively lead us away from that gospel toward a *different* gospel—one that caters to the self-serving, self-indulgent, and self-defined man of the world. Just because this "man of the world" calls himself religious, spiritual-minded, or even "Christian," does not mean his heart has been truly converted *to* the truth or transformed *by* the truth.

When we invoke "the truth," we are not talking about *your* truth, *my* truth, or a *church's* truth. "The truth" is that which sets us free from our spiritual demise, rather than perpetuating false conclusions (including: delusions about angelic rescues; Band-Aid "fixes" to human souls; believing in a "God" that only wants to help relieve earthly suffering, not teach us how to live as morally responsible people; etc.). "The truth" is what comes from God, not from mere angels. Even if an angel *did* tell us of a "truth" (or, gospel) that contradicted that which God has already revealed in the New Testament, we are *strictly forbidden to listen to him* (Gal. 1:8–9). Jesus said: "If you continue in My word, then you are truly disciples of Mine; and you will know the truth, and the truth will make you free" (John 8:31–32). This is an "if–then" proposition: *if* you continue in His word, *then* you will know "the truth" *and only then* will His truth "make you free." But if you do not know His word, believe in His word, or continue in His word, then you will never be "free" and no other so-called truth in the world will ever make you "free."

The question we should be asking here is: "free" from *what?* This takes us back to John 3:16: free from "perishing." The word "perish" (in this context) has no reference to physical death, because this happens to everyone, regardless of their moral standing. Rather, it has to do with the present condition of one's soul which will be made *permanent* upon his physical death, unless something is done to change this situation.[75] More graphically, knowledge of the truth and following after Christ gives us freedom from the *wrath of God* that will be visited upon every soul in the hereafter that refuses to accept God's generous offer of salvation through His Son. It is bad enough when one sins against God in the first place; that person's condemnation is only compounded when he deliberately resists His love, His Son, His gospel of salvation, and His free gift of divine grace in order to address that sin responsibly.

The man of the world is content to let God or His angels touch his life now and then, but he will not give his *heart* to Him. In dramatic contrast, the one who hears "the truth," responds to it with humble obedience, and chooses to follow Christ from that point forward, will be touched by the grace of God. Such a believer is deeply grateful for all that God has done to rescue his soul from its awful future, and looks forward in faith and great anticipation to "share in the inheritance of the saints in Light" (Col 1:12). His gratitude is not displayed with a simple "Thanks, God, for getting me out of that scrape!" but with a lifetime of service and devotion to Him who came down from heaven out of love and compassion for His creation. The child of God—being *made* a child of God through a spiritual adoption by the Father (Rom. 8:15–16)—gladly allows God's Spirit to guide his steps and guard his heart, since he has already proved to be incapable of doing this on his own. This believer, being first convinced of the truth and then converted *by* the truth, willfully and gladly allows God to transform his heart into whatever serves His best interest (Rom. 12:1–2, Eph. 2:10). Having entrusted his soul to God in this life, he is fully convinced that He will take care of his soul in the life to come (2 Tim. 1:12).

Conversion and Transformation

Conversion is a lifelong process, not a one-time event. One's baptism marks the *beginning* of one's lifelong conversion process but is certainly not the *entirety* of it. Shortly after talking about dying to the world and being united with Christ in baptism (Rom. 6:3–7), Paul goes on to talk about the ongoing need for "putting to death the deeds of the body" (Rom. 8:13) *after* baptism. Thus, it is a common mistake to minimize one's conversion to a symbolic ritual rather than seeing this ritual as a commitment to a lifelong and continuous action.

The original Greek word often translated "converted" in the New Testament means to be turned around, to cease going in one direction and take up a different direction.[76] This is how Jesus uses it in Mat. 18:3, for example, when He said, "[U]nless you are converted and become like children, you shall not enter the kingdom of heaven." This means: unless you *change the direction of your heart and your life*, you cannot *be* a child of God. What is really being talked about here is repentance; unfortunately, many people (including Christians) equate "repentance" only with stopping some specific wicked behavior. In fact, repentance (as a kind of perpetual conversion) has to do with changing your *life*, not just changing one particular *behavior*.

Human nature resists change, especially the older you get, but change is necessary if you are going to draw near to God. In order to turn toward God, you must turn away from whatever opposes Him. But change by itself is not the answer. Change must be made for the right reason, and in the right direction. The wrong reason indicates that the heart is not where it should be; the wrong direction means a lot of energy will be expended without the desired results. Stephen Covey (*7 Habits of Highly Effective People*) warns against putting your ladder on the wrong wall: you will spend a lot of time and energy climbing it, but it will lead you further and further in the wrong direction.[77]

Conversion has an objective: transformation.[78] Conversion begins the process of change and creates a fertile heart and humble attitude for the change; transformation *is* the change. In a sense, conversion and transformation are two concepts that work together, and never independently, in the heart of the ever-growing and ever-maturing Christian. One cannot be transformed (actually changed) before he is converted (turned around and re-positioned *for* change); likewise, one cannot claim to be converted (turned in the right direction) if indeed he refuses to be transformed (actually *going* in that right direction). You might look at this like going up a switchback stairwell in a parking garage or high-rise building. You have to keep changing direction (in following the stairs) in order to re-position yourself to climb higher, but then you need to *climb higher*. Each floor or level you reach is higher than where you were before—and brings you increasingly closer to your destination.

This process of conversion and transformation cannot be limited to a one-time occurrence. Genuine Christians are *ever* being converted and thus *ever* being transformed through their relationship with God through Christ. This is what Paul meant in Romans 12:1–2 (emphases added):

> Therefore I urge you, brethren, by the mercies of God, to present your bodies a living and holy sacrifice, acceptable to God, which is your spiritual service of worship. And do not be conformed to this world, but be **transformed** by the **renewing of your mind**, that you may prove what the will of God is, that which is good and acceptable and perfect.

Your mind cannot be renewed until it is in the right "place" for the renewal process to occur. Christ cannot renew a mind that resists Him, or that clings to whatever opposes Him while claiming to "draw near." First, you must "[lay] aside the old self with its evil practices," and then you will be able to "put on the new self who is being renewed to a true knowledge according to the image of the One who created him" (Col. 3:9–10). This "new self" is something you are responsible for "putting on," but it is not something that you created on your own. (If you could create your own spiritual transformation, then you would not need Christ.) The Lord gives you what to wear (Rom. 13:14, Eph. 4:24, 6:10–17, et al), but it remains your responsibility to put it *on*. You cannot effectively or realistically carry out the Lord's work in the world unless you wear the spiritual attire that He has provided you.[79] In effect, you must wear the King's clothes. This begins upon your baptism (Gal. 3:27), but it continues throughout your spiritual walk with Christ. Put another way: this begins with your initial conversion to the gospel, but your ongoing transformation that brings you ever closer to the image of Christ (Rom. 8:29) will take the rest of your life. For every stage of your transformation, a new conversion (or, change of mind and behavior) is required. If the conversion stops, then so does the transformation; if the transformation stops, it is because the conversion stopped.

God's saving grace is involved in every step of the process just described. Grace provides the reason for your conversion, the direction to which you should turn, and the strength *to* turn. You did not come up with these things on your own; you cannot find your way to heaven based upon your own skill, cleverness, resources, or merit. Grace also provides the power and dynamics necessary for your transformation. When you become a more mature, more spiritually-minded, and more Christ-like person, this is not something you did on your own but is what Christ performed *in* you (Eph. 3:14–19). You positioned yourself for the change, but Christ made the actual change real. Returning to our stairwell analogy: He provided the steps for you to climb; He gave you the opportunity to climb them; He provided the strength to climb them; and He is the One toward whom you are climbing.

We are converted by grace and transformed by grace. Instead of being "touched by an angel," we are touched by grace—and our lives are never the same because of this. The grace-saved life is also the grace-inspired life. Grace does not just save us, but it (He) also changes us into heaven-thinking and heaven-bound people. We think, speak, and act with grace when we submit to the One who provides this grace—in essence, when we internalize grace (Christ) in our hearts. The grace of God is far greater and does far more than an angelic encounter could ever do (if indeed such encounters ever even occur). Angels did not die for us, do not reign over us, and cannot confer saving grace upon us. But we who are made in God's image are brought to the very threshold of heaven itself, to the throne room of God Himself, through the abundant grace which He has lavished upon us. This is something we do not deserve and never could have done on our own. It takes an *act of God* to transform a human soul.

The Grace-filled Life

The grace-transformed heart will be manifested in a grace-filled life. If one is truly touched by grace, the fruit of this heavenly effect cannot be suppressed or hidden. (The same is true of one who is *not* transformed: this cannot be hidden, either.) The only way a person can become Christ-like is to be transformed by His grace; the only way he can be led by the Spirit (Gal. 5:16–17) is to be transformed by the grace of God that comes *through* His Spirit.[80] One who rejects God's grace also rejects His Son *and* His Spirit; likewise, one who rejects God's Son also rejects His grace. This is an all-or-nothing proposition; it cannot be otherwise.

God wants us to be transformed people, not mere churchgoers. Grace is not only involved in every aspect of the transformation; it is the transformer. Transformation—real spiritual change that manifests itself in holy behavior—is not just a good idea, but it is absolutely necessary in order to walk in the light and be forgiven of our sins (1 John 1:7). Christians cannot derive spiritual energy from the world's system—it is incompatible with heavenly objectives. Likewise, a worldly-minded person cannot appraise spiritual things, since his mind operates on a completely different level (1 Cor. 2:11–14). However, a transformer—grace—will allow the believer to think and learn on a different level than was ever possible without it. Grace re-trains, re-programs, and re-configures the mind (heart) to live on a different plane than one who remains outside of Christ.

The unconverted person cannot be transformed by grace as long as he resists the *source* of that grace—Jesus Christ. This person has been led to believe that he does not need saving grace, does not need saving at all, or will try to save himself. He does not see things as they really are, but only as he has been conditioned (by the world, his peers, family, friends, or self-delusion) to believe. This can all change,

of course, but he must be the one to *initiate* that change. If he allows
the gospel message of God's love and grace to penetrate his heart,
then he can "come to the knowledge of the truth," come to his senses,
and "escape from the snare of the devil" (1 Tim. 2:4, 2 Tim. 2:25–26).

"For the grace of God has appeared, bringing salvation to all men,
instructing us to deny ungodliness and worldly desires and to live
sensibly, righteously and godly in the present age" (Titus 2:11–12).
Christ is the One who "has appeared," manifesting Himself to the
world in the form of a perfect human being. His blood sacrifice
"[brings] salvation to all men," calling us to Himself through His
gospel (2 Thess. 2:14). All this speaks to what has been done—
particularly, what *He* has done—for us. Christ did not "appear" in
order to start a new religion, construct church buildings, or give us
rituals of worship to re-enact week after week. He manifested Himself
to the world in order to save us *from* the world—and, in a very real
sense, to save us from ourselves.

The rest of Paul's statement to Titus (2:11–12) concerns what
we are to do for Him. We are to "deny ungodliness and worldly
desires"—the very things that corrupted our souls in the first place.
We have no right to continue in the sins and sinful lifestyles that
required Christ's *death on the cross* to remove. Just as there is no
sin in Him, sin must not be allowed in ourselves (1 John 3:5). Many
Christians, having been desensitized by the daily assault of an
ungodly world, carelessly allow unholiness, irreverence, and sinful
behaviors to find a comfortable and familiar place in their lives. This
creates a numbing effect upon their conscience and their faith. It is
not hard to find Christians whose daily lives (apart from Sunday)
are nearly indistinguishable from the lifestyles of those who remain
outside of covenant with the Lord. But this is a shameful thing to
say of those who ought to be "a people for His own possession"; we
should be "zealous for good deeds," not seeking to identify with the
world (Titus 2:14). Ungodliness in all its forms must be sacrificed for
the sake of our allegiance to Christ. There is simply no compatibility
between worldliness and godliness (2 Cor. 6:14–18).

We are also to "live sensibly, righteously, and godly" (Titus 2:12)—that is, "in a manner worthy of the calling with which [we] have been called" (Eph. 4:1). In order to do these things, we must "cleanse ourselves from all defilement of flesh and spirit, perfecting holiness in the fear of God" (2 Cor. 7:1). In order to walk in light, truth, holiness, righteousness, and humility, we have to put to death the sinful "deeds of the body" that have no place in a Christian's life (Rom. 8:12–14). We are to imitate whatever attitude Christ demonstrated in His walk upon this earth (Phil. 2:5). Being conformed to His image—which means internalizing His virtues— serves His best interest, which always serves our best interest, as well as the best interest of all those within our circle of influence. It truly is a win-win-win situation.

The grace-filled life is one that is completely dependent upon God. At the same time, the believer is morally responsible for all those things that God has instructed him to do. The believer trusts in God's ability to perform where he cannot, but God expects him (or her) to perform in whatever ways he is most certainly capable of doing. The believer cannot perform acts of divine grace, nor will God perform acts of human faith; each participant in the covenant relationship has a specific role to play, and these roles never interchange or overlap. Together, God and the believer seek the same spiritual objective: the salvation of the believer's soul. "God is faithful" to His part of the covenant (1 Cor. 1:9); the believer is expected to be faithful to *his* part as well.

All of this sounds good, and—because it comes to us from God—it *is* good. But, realistically, it takes *time* to master it. It takes time for the Light of the gospel to expose all the ungodliness and worldly desires that we have hidden in our hearts. It takes time for us to come to terms with our moral responsibility and walk in an appropriate manner. It also takes time for us "to live sensibly, righteously, and godly in the present age," especially when we are relentlessly bombarded by Satan and all the residual evil that is in the world. Living a grace-filled life is not something that comes natural to us; it

226 ~ *The Gospel of Saving Grace*

is a life that needs to be learned, practiced, and consciously pursued. The current of the world is swift and strong; we cannot underestimate its power and influence. This means that we must aggressively and diligently strain to overcome it, for nothing less than this will work. Those who listen to Christ's instruction will draw near to Him and find a "way of escape" from the world (1 Cor. 10:13); those who do not are just fooling themselves into thinking that they can overcome the world *differently* than this. Satan loves to dupe people into thinking they are walking the narrow road to life when in fact they are simply following the world's broad path of destruction.

Furthermore, the rejection of wickedness and the pursuit of godliness must be happening simultaneously. When I was a young Christian (in my teens), it was pounded into my head all the things that young people should avoid: drugs, drinking, dancing, gambling, smoking, promiscuity, immodest apparel, etc. While the intention behind all this teaching was good, it was generally reactive, not proactive. Sermons confronted (or reacted to) one worldly behavior after another, but seldom taught me (proactively) how to live by faith, walk in truth, or develop a personal relationship with the Savior. Grace was barely mentioned, because few understood it beyond "unmerited favor." Many churches today still pursue this lopsided approach: they focus on all the things to reject (which *is* necessary), but not necessarily those things that must be pursued (which is *also* necessary).

On the other end of the spectrum are churches that dwell heavily on all the good things—love, faith, fellowship, grace (or, at least, a version of it), forgiveness, worship, etc.—but are unwilling to confront the sinful temptations and behaviors of their members. Thus, these members are led to believe that if they *are* members, engage in worship, feel spiritual, and experience "awesomeness," then all is well. On the side, they can watch R-rated movies, secretly view pornography, play many hours of video games that glorify murder and mayhem, smoke marijuana, carouse and drink with their worldly friends, attend music concerts that promote all kinds of unholiness, and think nothing of the glaring contradiction.

Living by grace means sacrificing all those things that *will destroy our souls* if we continue in them. Christ's blood is fully capable of removing our guilt and condemnation, but only if we are honest about who we are, what we have done, and our allegiance to Him. Living by grace also means being receptive to and fully embracing all those things that draw us closer to Him because we want to *be* with Him. Christ's blood does not cleanse us so that we will continue in sin, or find new sins to dabble in, but so that we can walk in the good works He has prepared for us (Eph. 2:10). We cannot focus on the one instruction ("perfecting holiness in the fear of God") without also focusing on the other ("let us cleanse ourselves from all defilement of flesh and spirit"). Lopsided Christianity is really not Christianity at all; it did not come from Christ, but is a perversion of the revealed truth.

Summary Thoughts

There are many people who would love nothing more than to be "touched by an angel," so to speak. Christians, however, ought to be touched by *grace*, and the fruit of this encounter ought to be evident in our everyday lives. If God does send angels to help us, so be it, but angels cannot save your soul. On the other hand, one who has never been touched by grace has no hope of a favorable presentation before Him in the hereafter. Instead of looking for encounters with angels, we should be "looking for the blessed hope and the appearing of the glory of our great God and Savior, Christ Jesus" (Titus 2:13). When Christ does return, the only ones He will bring home with Him are those who have been saved by His grace through their faith in Him.

Unless we know, believe in, and obey God's truth, we are "perishing" (John 3:16). God's truth tells us what we need to do, what God does, what will happen to us when we listen to Him, and what will happen if we do not. Knowledge by itself has never saved anyone, but we do need heavenly knowledge and wisdom in order to *be* saved. Your truth will not save you, just as my truth will not save me, but God's truth will save us both. His truth shows us how we can overcome this world and be with Him in His world. Jesus Christ *is* the way, the truth, and the life, and no one can or ever will come to God the Father except through Him (paraphrase of John 14:6).

When we are convinced of divine truth and enter into a holy covenant relationship with God, we will be transformed by Christ. While we initiate all of these actions, we do not have the power to carry them out on our own. Our conversion is dependent upon information that God has revealed; our covenant with Him is one He has offered to us, not the other way around; and our spiritual transformation is dependent upon Christ doing for us things we cannot see, do not know, and do not fully understand. In the ever-continuous process of conversion and transformation, we ascend upward toward a higher plane of thinking, serving, and living than we ever could have achieved otherwise.

The grace-filled life is not just a "clean" life, as though merely abstaining from wicked things will be sufficient. The one who is saved by grace must also be increasingly conformed to Christ, which requires keeping His commandments and living according to His will. Abstaining from ungodliness and pursuing righteousness must happen simultaneously, as neither action by itself is sufficient in bringing us to our goal. We are never asked to do what is humanly impossible, or even *personally* impossible. Whatever God asks us to do in faith is no more or less than what you and I are capable of doing. All this takes time to master, but time must be viewed as a gift of God, not as a crutch that allows us to put off until tomorrow what needs to be done today.

The one who says he has been touched by grace must believe in the real and effective presence of Christ in his life. Just as there was power in Jesus' physical touch to heal people of their sicknesses, paralyses, and blindness, so there is power in His "touch" of our souls to bring healing, regeneration, and restoration. Spiritual healing is infinitely more important than physical healing, as our souls will infinitely outlast our bodies. Christ's healing touch of grace is so powerful that it will leave an impression upon us that will remain throughout all eternity.

Chapter Fifteen
⇒ *The All-sufficiency of Grace* ⇐

And He has said to me, "My grace is sufficient for you, for power
is perfected in weakness." Most gladly, therefore, I will rather boast
about my weaknesses, so that the power of Christ may dwell in me.
Therefore I am well content with weaknesses, with insults,
with distresses, with persecutions, with difficulties, for Christ's sake;
for when I am weak, then I am strong.
(2 Cor. 12:9–10)

The above quotation is profound, just as it stands. The more you dwell upon it, the more you see; the more you see, the more you understand the dynamic relationship between God's grace and human faith. Its approach is counterintuitive—in other words, it goes against the grain of human thinking, human expectations, and human perspective. No one typically boasts about his weaknesses; no one typically is "content" with being insulted, distressed, and persecuted; and no one typically welcomes personal suffering as a route to spiritual greatness. Most people are, in fact, completely *unconcerned* with spiritual greatness.

The world teaches us to boast, brag, project ourselves, talk about ourselves, magnify our accomplishments, and step on other people in order to advance. Christ teaches us just the opposite: boast in *Him*, promote *Him*, magnify *Him* and *His* accomplishments, serve others in *His* name, etc. This is confounding to the world, but then again, the world stumbles in moral darkness and ignorance. It is the world, not Christ, that is backward.

The above quotation is even more impressive because of the one who wrote it: the apostle Paul. He literally suffered those things he mentioned—weaknesses, insults, distresses, persecutions, and difficulties (2 Cor. 11:23–31)—and yet he never lost sight of his living hope in Christ. Most of us have not endured much actual suffering for the sake of the gospel, yet Paul risked his life and well-being everywhere he went to preach it. While we may have been spared all this (so far), there are Christians throughout the world today who live under threat of persecution, confiscation of property, loss of freedoms, and even death itself—all because of their faith in Christ. No doubt these Christians can readily identify with what Paul said about himself.

Even so, God allowed Paul to see visions of heaven that the rest of us have been denied (2 Cor. 12:1–4). No doubt He did so in order to support his faith while he endured a career of suffering that would have otherwise destroyed him. These visions were of such privilege that God needed also to give Paul a "thorn in the flesh" to keep him from "exalting" himself (12:7). Imagine that: a man who has already suffered so much for Christ, and now he is given a "thorn" to keep him from gloating. God knew that any man who has seen such wondrous, otherworldly things would have reason to boast about them, and He did not want Paul to succumb to this. Thus, He provided Paul with a constant reminder of his earthly ministry, to keep him focused on *this* rather than on *himself.* Three times Paul entreated God to have this "thorn" removed, but his petition was denied. In fact, God responded in such a way that may seem unconcerned for Paul's suffering: "My grace is sufficient for you, for power is perfected in weakness." It appears, at first glance, that God was punishing Paul for something that He had invited him to see! But things are not always as they seem, and Paul's case proves to be no exception to this.

God was not punishing Paul for something for which he was not responsible. Christ stated earlier that Paul was "a chosen instrument of Mine, to bear My name before the Gentiles and kings and the sons of Israel; for I will show him how much he must suffer for My name's sake" (Acts 9:15–16). This suffering was not to punish Paul, but to exalt Christ; it was necessary to keep Paul humble, refine his character, and set a precedent for other believers. Paul's "thorn in the flesh" was not the full extent of this suffering, but did serve as a real-life example of it. (Whether this "thorn" was literal or figurative is not necessary to pursue at this point. Suffice it to say that, whatever it was, it caused him such great pain that he begged to have it removed.)

"My grace is sufficient for you"—this is the only explanation that God provided Paul (or, possibly, it is the only *part* of a fuller explanation that Paul revealed to the Corinthians). God's grace was all Paul needed in order to overcome the world, endure his suffering for the gospel, and fulfill his apostolic ministry. Paul thought that the removal of this "thorn in the flesh" would expedite carrying out these objectives; God not only disagreed, but He pointed His servant in a completely different direction. In doing so, He provided him with one of the most profound perspectives that has been revealed to us in the New Testament: when all is said and done, God's grace is *all that we need* in order to be with Him.

What "All-sufficiency" Means (and Does Not Mean)

"Sufficient" means: that which suffices (for whatever is necessary); or, that which suitably serves a known purpose. Since God is a purpose-driven God, and we are to live purpose-driven lives in obedience to Him, it stands to reason that whatever is "sufficient" for us will serve *His* purpose, not gratify *our* wishes. Whatever serves *His* purpose always serves our *own* purpose, when we live in agreement with Him. Yet, the all-sufficiency of God's grace is often misunderstood to mean that God will give us whatever we want whenever we think we need it. Such thinking puts us in the driver's seat, not God.[81] This also treats Him like a vending machine, dispensing gifts and blessings whenever we call upon Him to do so, rather than honoring Him as the all-powerful and all-knowing Creator that He is.

God's all-sufficiency is intended for a specific application. It is not intended to improve your driving, enhance your cooking abilities, land you a great job, make you physically attractive, help you lose weight, or give you washboard abs. Now, if any of these things happen and you wish to attribute this to God, so be it. But the gift of His grace is not given so that we can enjoy such mundane successes or improvements. God is not uncaring about our day-to-day lives, but is primarily concerned with our life-to-eternity journey. Thus, when we talk about the all-sufficiency of grace, we mean this in respect to one's spiritual relationship with God. All human souls share common objectives, including:

- **Love.** We all want to love and be loved. To be loved by *God* is the essential desire of every soul; to *love* God is the highest aspiration of the human existence.

- **Stability.** The human soul cannot function in chaos and instability. An unstable person is filled with fear; dysfunctional relationships, marriages, and homes are filled with tension and unrest, and are always on the verge of collapse.

- **Control.** This is similar to stability except that "control" has more of a personal aspect to it. We want to have a say in what we do, how we live, and where our lives are heading. We do not have to make all the decisions but we certainly want to make the really important ones.

- **Possessions.** Having something to call our own gives us a sense of power and control outside of ourselves. This creates, in a sense, an extension of ourselves over a larger domain than our physical person. Possessions also provide the soul with something to trust in—something to save us from unhappiness, despair, or death.

- **Redemption.** Not everyone desires to be "saved" as Christians understand the phrase, but the soul *does* want to be rescued from fear (of judgment, harm, or punishment), inadequacy, and sins. Everyone seeks some form of absolution (divine or otherwise) from poor decisions and personal blunders. Redemption comes in many forms: divine forgiveness, praise from others, a successful career, noble deeds, a lifetime of service to some worthy cause, material wealth, an impressive education, good works, or even self-martyrdom.

- **Peace.** Just as the human soul cannot function without stability, so it cannot function without peace. Internal peace is the absence of spiritual conflict, but for some this requires (they believe) the absence of external conflict as well. The human mind abhors conflict, as when two dominant forces are vying for supremacy (e.g., pride vs. humility, self vs. God, unrighteousness vs. righteousness, etc.), and will do everything in its power to resolve this dilemma. This resolution does not have to meet God's approval; it just has to *work*, which means it must remove the conflict. Even a decision that is delusional, irrational, or based on false information is acceptable, if indeed it achieves "peace of mind," however temporary, fragile, or artificial that peace might be.

• **Contentment.** Above all else, and really as the *sum* of all these other needs, people want to be content (or satisfied, or "happy"). The human soul is not merely fond of contentment; it *craves* it passionately, and will go to great lengths to obtain it. People can live in difficult circumstances, and endure all kinds of abuses, poverty, and hostility, but if they can learn to *be content within themselves*, then all is bearable. Being discontented (or, unhappy) is the most miserable of all conditions; the soul will accept lies, worship idols, betray friends, sabotage marriages, and even kill in order to obtain contentment. To experience unhappiness without any perceived hope of that situation ever changing drives people to extraordinary measures, including suicide.

〜

Is God's grace able to fulfill all these needs? The same Creator who gave life to your soul also knows how to *keep* it alive—not just in a barely-hanging-on-by-the-skin-of-your-teeth survival mode, but in an existence that is rewarding, flourishing, and fully functional. Jesus did not die on the cross just so you could experience a different kind of misery in following Him than you would have had otherwise. Rather, "[He] came that they [His sheep] may have life, and have it abundantly" (John 10:10b, bracketed words added). God's saving grace imparts *abundant* life to you—something you are unable to obtain on your own. In application, His grace provides your soul with:

• **Love.** While God loves *all* people—and unconditionally—He loves those who belong to Him *specially*, just as a mother who loves all children loves *her own* children with a special love. "See how great a love the Father has bestowed on us, that we would be called children of God" (1 John 3:1)—this is not the common love that God bestows upon all people, but is a special love reserved for those who have loved Him in return. Your soul desperately wants to love and be loved, and God gives you the highest expression of His love *and* is the highest object of your love that exists.

- **Stability.** Jesus likens the soul that trusts in God to one who "dug deep and laid a foundation on the rock" (Luke 6:47). His divine power provides a stability that is unmatched anywhere in the universe, since nothing can threaten, dethrone, or destroy God, and no one is able to snatch those who depend upon Him out of His hand (John 10:27–29).

- **Control.** This is paradoxical, since the very *best* form of control the human soul can ever achieve is by surrendering all control to the Father. Since He has unlimited power and authority, and since He is in control of all that exists, to put one's soul under His control serves that person's very best interest. All other controls (i.e., people, powers, authorities, kingdoms, and dominions) will ultimately fail, but God's kingdom will last forever—and so will those who are citizens of His kingdom.

- **Possessions.** While God is capable of giving you all the earthly possessions you could ever want, this is not His objective. However, it *is* true that the believer will inherit all things that the world has been seeking (and continues to seek) in vain (Mat. 5:3–10). Christ is the heir of all that exists (Heb. 1:2), and He promises to share His inheritance with all who believe in Him (i.e., His church, or "bride"). Whatever gifts God gives to His children will be all-sufficient; you will not be lacking in anything—not now and especially not in the life to come.

- **Redemption.** This speaks to the very heart of divine grace. Forgiveness of sins is one of the crowning glories of God's gifts to us, for if the soul is forgiven, then all is well. The idea of "redemption" necessarily implies a purchase: if the blood of Christ has *purchased* your soul, this means He now *owns* you as His own possession (1 Cor. 6:19–20). This serves your soul's best interest, for whoever is God's possession will live with Him forever: "The world is passing away, and also its lusts; but the one who does the will of God lives forever" (1 John 2:17).

- **Peace.** The only way you can be at peace with God is if you have believed in His Son and been redeemed by His Son's blood. Peace with God and unity with God rise or fall together; one is at peace with God only when he is reconciled to Him through Christ. This is not something any of us can do for ourselves, but literally requires an act of God and (thus) an act of divine grace.

- **Contentment.** We are content with God when our sense of self-worth, fulfillment, and completion are found in Him, without seeking these elsewhere. Human pride seeks contentment in itself, or its own form of contentment; the humble child of God is happy to be *with* Him, and does not need anything more than who He is and what He provides. Since this world is incapable of providing contentment for the human soul, we must seek "the things above, where Christ is, seated at the right hand of God" (Col. 3:1). Again, this is not something we are able to do on our own; only God's grace allows us to do this.

"We proclaim Him, admonishing every man and teaching every man with all wisdom, so that we may present every man complete in Christ" (Col. 1:28). Christ is the One who completes us, not ourselves, not the church, and not Bible reading, hymn singing, or churchgoing. Whatever comes from Christ for the salvation of our soul is a gift of God—the very definition of saving grace. To be complete means to be brought to an ideal standard, a mature end, or a perfected state of being. It is His power that is able to bring perfection out of something (i.e., our human condition) that is inherently weak, flawed, inadequate, and prone to failure. You and I cannot do this— we have proven this over and over through the many times we have sinned—"but with God all things are possible" (Mat. 19:26). After all, "God is able to make all grace abound to you, that always having all sufficiency in everything, you may have an abundance for every good deed" (2 Cor. 9:8).

To illustrate this, look at what God did with regard to His Son. Jesus' generation found Him to be somewhat of an embarrassment,

especially with all the attention that He received. He was born
to a peasant family in very humble circumstances and raised in
an unimpressive town (Nazareth); He lacked formal religious
education; and He freely associated with "sinners" and other people
of disrepute. He was arrested—a shameful ordeal in itself—and was
accused of all kinds of wrongdoing in what the people believed (or,
wanted to believe) was an honorable, God-fearing court of law (Mat.
26:59–60a). He was beaten, spit upon, ridiculed, and humiliated.
Then He was nailed to a cross—the Roman government's way of
getting rid of those who do not deserve to live—along with sinful
men, even though He Himself was never legitimately charged with
an actual crime. And there He suffered—painfully, shamefully, and
horrifically—for six hours while His countrymen leered and jeered at
Him with mocking taunts and awful insults.

What we see in all of this is (what appears to be) *tremendous
weakness*. But remember what God told Paul: "[My] power is
perfected in weakness" (2 Cor. 12:9). Through the "weakness"
of Jesus' humble life, and the incomprehensible reproach of His
torturous death, God demonstrated His *tremendous power*. He
raised His Son from the grave and presented Him alive before many
witnesses (1 Cor. 15:3–8); He continued to provide miraculous signs
even after His resurrection (Acts 1:3); He raised Him into heaven in
the presence of His own disciples (Acts 1:9–11); and He exalted Him
to His own right hand in heaven (Acts 2:33). In due time, He will
summon all of humanity before His Son to honor and vindicate Him
forever.

Many people today think God (and believing in God) is "foolish,"
but this is the conclusion of those who are spiritually ignorant,
morally depraved, and "perishing" in their own sins (1 Cor. 1:18–24).
Many regard Jesus' crucifixion as a sign of weakness, but in fact it
takes an all-powerful and *genius* God to bring about the otherworldly
salvation of millions of souls through a humiliating, seemingly
hopeless, and yet perfectly orchestrated act of human sacrifice. While
the smug, impenitent, and helpless world scoffs at God and treats His
Son with great contempt, God continues to bring about life, light,

salvation, and *hope* for all those who call upon His name for salvation (Rom. 10:11–13). His power is most certainly perfected in weakness.

But What about That "Thorn"?

God's divine power is stronger than you or I will ever know or can even comprehend. Christians are quick to *say* this (in our songs, prayers, sermons, and amens), but the real test of our belief in Him is not measured in our liturgies (worship services), but in our discipleship (service worship). We cannot be praising God's saving grace while languishing in our fears, our everyday troubles, our disappointments with people, and our manifestations of unbelief. We cannot be exulting in God's power, strength, and ability to deliver us, while we are allowing ourselves to be overcome with personal weaknesses or second-guessing His leadership.

We—and when I say "we," I include myself—tend to focus on the "thorn" in our side rather than the God of our faith. This is very *human* to do so, but it is not very *Christian* of us. We live in a society that has been conditioned to believe that all suffering is bad, and thus we are not to suffer—not even for a moment. Drugstores are filled with "pain relievers"; pharmacies are filled with narcotics designed to remove all perception of pain; therapists promise to remove the pain of some childhood trauma or difficult experience; we are not supposed to question any person's belief system so as not to cause them the pain of being "offended." Having a "thorn" in our side—and then God choosing not to *remove* this thorn—grates against everything we have been led to believe in our fragile, thin-skinned, and hyper-sensitive world. Given this, it is no wonder that so many Christians find themselves "upset," "disillusioned," or even "angry" with God for not alleviating their suffering, no matter what degree they experience it. God's *refusal* to remove our "thorn" (wrongly) translates to an *inability* on His part to do so. Our weakness magnifies His weakness (or so we imagine), since a truly all-powerful God would (should!) have removed whatever bothers us.

I do not know what Paul's "thorn" was. Some think it was malaria; others, his eyesight (see Gal. 4:14–15); still others, an individual person who tormented him (see 2 Tim. 4:14); or, it may have been the unrelenting assault of the Judaizing teachers. In the end, it really does not matter; whatever it was, it did not prevent him from fulfilling his service to Christ. I know this because: 1) if it *had*, God would have removed it; 2) since God did *not* remove it, it did not *have* to be removed; and 3) Paul was told to focus on God's *grace*, not the thorn in his side.

What is *your* "thorn"? It is likely that you have one (or several). Maybe you have a serious health issue, or some kind of physical impairment or disability. Or, maybe there is someone in your life who is constantly causing you grief. Or, perhaps you are trapped in a miserable job, poor living conditions, or a loveless marriage. In any case, is God's grace sufficient for you? Is His grace—all that He does for your spiritual well-being and your soul's disposition in the afterlife—*enough* for you? Can you—*will* you—find contentment and peace in this life despite that thorn(s) in your side? Have you entreated Him multiple times to remove this thorn, and He has said "no"?

Have you accepted this answer? Or have you been made bitter by it?

Often, when Christians get what they want from God, they say things like, "God be praised!" or, "God is faithful!" or, "God answers prayers!" Our atheist friends say of this that we are quick to credit God when things go our way, but we fall altogether silent when they do not. They call this "counting the hits, but not the misses"—a baseball batting analogy. Their understanding of "hits" and "misses" is messed up, but they do have a valid point: we do not like God to deny our prayerful, tearful, and often passionate pleas to *pull the thorn out of our side.*

Yet, God said "no" to Jesus when He asked to remove the "cup" of His crucifixion (Mat. 26:39; see Heb. 5:7–8). And He said "no" to Paul when he asked to be relieved of the thorn in his side. If God will deny them, might He also deny you? And if He does, has He done you any injustice? Is it necessary for God to *take away* your weakness, or is it sufficient that He magnifies His divine strength *through* your weakness? Is it necessary for *you* to feel powerful, victorious, and exalted, or is it sufficient that *He* be powerful, victorious, and exalted through the great faith that you entrust to Him to deliver you *regardless* of your weakness?

God does not *personally* need to impress you or me with any great show of power. Many people want Him to work miracles for them, and when He does not, they become disappointed and disillusioned. But God never promised to work miracles for you; He promised to impart His *grace* to you. If you wish to know what miracle-working power He is capable of performing, read your Bible—especially the gospel accounts (Matthew, Mark, Luke, and John). Jesus has demonstrated all that is necessary in order to convince the sincere and open-minded person that He is in charge, He is more than qualified to lead us, and He is not going to be hindered by our human inadequacies. "God . . . is at work in you," Paul said, "both to will and to work for His good pleasure" (Phil. 2:13). He does not need to remove all of the thorns in our sides in order for His grace to prevail and provide for all that needs to be done.

Do you believe all of this?

Many people—including Christians—believe that God's grace and human suffering are incompatible realities: if one exists, the other must not. To deal rightly with the subject of suffering would take us far beyond the scope of our present study; others have already written well on it.[82] But the bottom line is twofold: First, **God's saving grace is not nullified by human suffering.** Grace deals with spiritual salvation, whereas human suffering is a manifestation of the corrupted human condition. Grace is not intended to remove all human suffering, but gives us the means to deal with it rightly and according to a heavenly perspective.

Second, **human suffering is not an insurmountable problem for God's grace.** We can know this because Jesus overcame every form of human suffering in His earthly ministry. Through His divine power, He showed divine mastery over sickness, disease, blindness, deafness, lack of food, lack of money (Mat. 17:24–27), demon possession, and even death itself. It was not His purpose to put an end to all these things, but merely to show His power *over* them. In demonstrating

His power to heal—and tying this directly to His power of *spiritual* healing (as in Mark 2:1–12)—Jesus proved that nothing in our world or the spiritual world is too great of an obstacle for His grace to overcome in order to save the human soul.

Some Christians want to believe that their association with God ought to exempt them from human suffering or earthly injustice. And yet, faithful Christians get in terrible car accidents, endure the loss of loved ones, and are harassed by corrupt governments. Christians are victims of terminal illnesses, are killed in occupational and transportation accidents, and continue to be innocent victims of crime, terrorism, wars, and random acts of violence and hatred. The question comes down to this: Is it fair that God *allows* His children to suffer? The answer is: *since* God is a Supreme Being who has power and authority over all that exists, and *since* His children do indeed suffer in this life, *therefore* it is fair that His children do indeed suffer here. You do not have to like this answer, but in the end, there is no better answer without accusing God of failing His people or intentionally inflicting malicious harm against the righteous—and you really do not want to go there.

Not only will Christians suffer the same things that other people suffer, regardless of their beliefs, but we will suffer *for* our beliefs. In fact, Jesus promised this (Mat. 16:24), as did Paul (Rom. 8:16–17, 2 Tim. 3:12, et al) and Peter (1 Pet. 1:6–9). We should not be surprised by this when it happens. If Jesus accepted His own suffering as a human being *and* as a martyr for God (1 Pet. 2:21–24), then we should accept the fact of our suffering for His name's sake. "Yes," someone will say, "but Jesus accepted that suffering before He ever came to this world." But every believer, upon accepting the name of Christ as the source of his salvation (Acts 4:12), also accepts the sacrifices and hardships that accompany that decision. We must not expect a cross-less life while walking in the footsteps of our Savior. This calls to mind the words of Job: "Shall we indeed accept good from God and not adversity?" (Job 2:10). If God allows us to suffer, we should know that His grace will prevent us from being *overwhelmed* with suffering, and will deliver us from it if that is what

He deems necessary. His grace *can* remove every thorn from the side of every believer, *if* this serves His divine purpose.

Sometimes people create their own "thorn in the flesh" by making poor decisions repeatedly over the course of time. This results in self-inflicted problems that they may claim are "coincidental" or "circumstantial," but are in fact, consciously or not, intentional. A famous talk radio host/counselor once said: "What you allow, will continue." This is so true. When we *allow* ourselves to be irresponsible, we should not be surprised when our lives are embroiled in constant trouble, turmoil, and pain. Not only this, but we bring all kinds of grief and heartache to those who love us and want what is best for us.

When people consistently reject biblical teaching, wise Christian counsel, and responsible behavior *and at the same time* cater to their own desires, listen to the counsel of irresponsible people, and choose the path of least resistance, it is no wonder that they suffer "thorns." These thorns are "messengers of Satan," as Paul described them, but they have been invited into one's life rather than having been purposely *given* to us to keep us from boasting in ourselves. God's grace will *not* be sufficient for irresponsible people, since they are intentionally seeking something different than His grace to complete them. His power will *not* work through their weakness, simply because they are choosing to be weak rather than seeking God's strength in place of their own.

We have all seen Christians who suffer from one spiritual ailment or another, who are always "sick," and who have turned being "weak" into a career rather than a temporary phase. These people do not (yet) understand the power offered by the Great Physician. They want healing, but for reasons other than what God wants. What they really want is someone to get them out of the scrape they are in (through the process described above) so they can resume where they left off before that all started. They do not believe in the power of divine grace; they trust in themselves more than they trust in God. They do not want spiritual transformation; they want a pain reliever. Someone else has said: "Before we lead anyone to the source of healing, we must ask them if they are willing to turn away from what made them sick in the first place." This is incredibly insightful.

Christians with self-inflicted thorns usually present a heavy burden to their congregations and demand an unnecessarily disproportionate amount of care and attention. They are always "struggling" or holding onto their faith "by the skin of my teeth," as they put it. The fact is, they are simply not allowing grace to be all-sufficient for them and are seeking fulfillment, completion, and sufficiency elsewhere, or nowhere at all. Often, they are addicted to the attention and sympathy heaped upon them by those who feel sorry for them but have not yet realized that this is all a giant charade. Their actions speak louder than their words: they are untouched by God's love, unmoved by His mercy, and unchanged by His grace. And, until they come to their senses and choose a radically different course, their insensitivity to God's kindness will remain. I once came across a greeting card that said on the front, "There is a reason for everything." Inside, it read: "And sometimes that reason is that you continue to make stupid decisions that lead to disastrous results"—or something to that effect. While the message was painfully blunt, it may well be the truth.

Contrast such people with those who are truly spiritual giants in Christ's church: hard-working, diligent, and heavenward-looking disciples. While in need of personal encouragement and moral support from time to time, they ultimately find their strength and support in the grace of God. They are by no means marginal Christians, for they have forsaken and sacrificed everything—even their own pride—in order to serve the Lord with all their heart, soul, and mind. Such people truly appreciate the all-sufficiency of saving grace, for without it (Him) they would have no hope and would be unable to serve Christ in the least. These people are not flawless, but their faith has been tested, refined, and matured by God's activity in their lives. They have been through the fire, and have proved to be faithful. These, like Noah, are "blameless" in their character and "walk with God" (Gen. 6:9).

Somewhere between these two extremes is where we might find ourselves. Most of us (Christians) are sincerely striving to serve our Lord but are still in the process of being perfected by Him. We trust in the grace of God, to be sure, but are still learning how to implement that grace in every facet of our lives. In a sense, we are like explorers, searching excitedly through the mind of God, finding new troves of spiritual wealth all the time, and sharing our treasures with those who will appreciate them. But we are not like the explorers of old who vainly sought a fabled Fountain of Youth or a non-existent Northwest Passage. Our search is never fruitless or disappointing, but is always filled with expectant hope and lucid endeavor. In our faith and through His grace we find in Christ what does not exist here upon this earth. In fact, we find what so many others are seeking but who refuse the means by which to search for it. Paul understood this, and prayed on behalf of the Christians at Ephesus

> . . . that He would grant you, according to the riches of His glory, to be strengthened with power through His Spirit in the inner man; so that Christ may dwell in your hearts through faith; and that you, being rooted and grounded in love, may be able to comprehend with all the saints what is the breadth and length and height and depth, and to know the love of Christ which surpasses knowledge, that you may be filled up to all the fullness of God. (Eph. 3:16–19)

Paul prayed that they and "all the saints"—which is *all Christians*—would reach the highest expression of spiritual existence possible—not in heaven, but *here upon this earth*. He told them they could know that which surpasses knowledge, that is, they could know that which was impossible for any person to know apart from divine intercession. This knowledge is more valuable than any worldly wealth, since it takes us beyond anything that money can buy. Our feet remain upon this earth just like everyone else's, but our heart and mind are kept in God's heaven, in the very dwelling place of our Father and Savior. We toil and sweat and grapple with life's challenges here on earth just like everyone else, but we have the means by which to deal with life's triumphs and tragedies in ways the world simply cannot understand. We have a very real and viable connection to the Lord through prayer and He has a very real and viable effect on our earthly life by His grace. Through our faith in Him, He "is able to do far more abundantly beyond all that we ask or think, according to the power that works within us" (Eph. 3:20). He promises us not merely an adequate life but a *super-abundant* life! The gospel of grace says that we *can* and *should* have such a life.

Summary Thoughts

"My grace is sufficient for you, for power is perfected in weakness." Perhaps we now have a better understanding of what God meant by this statement. He does not need us to be powerful before we come to Him. Instead, His power will work *through* the weakness of our human condition—our inadequacies, lack of understanding, infirmities, doubts, and fears. In fact, God wants us to acknowledge our weaknesses and surrender our control to Him so that we will approach Him with an attitude of humility. "God is opposed to the proud," Peter says, "but gives grace to the humble" (1 Pet. 5:5).

Is God's grace all-sufficient for the believer? After all that has been said, this really is no longer the question. The real question is: do you believe that God's grace is all-sufficient for *you*? The answer to that question depends not upon what God has revealed in His word, since this is true regardless of your answer, but upon your own faith. If you believe in His authority, His power, and His ability to save you *no matter what* you face in this life, then yes, His grace is more than sufficient for you. If you choose to believe otherwise, then you are depending upon something stronger than His grace to save you. Yet, the fact remains: there *is* nothing stronger, and *anything* else will only disappoint you—if not now, then most certainly in the hereafter.

James wrote, "Consider it all joy, my brethren, when you encounter various trials, knowing that the testing of your faith produces endurance. And let endurance have its perfect result, that you may be perfect and complete, lacking in nothing" (Jas. 1:2–4). *Lacking in nothing.* This is true, of course, before the trials as well as in the middle of them, but your confidence grows increasingly stronger as you overcome each trial through the strength that God alone supplies.

Regardless of what is lacking in your physical existence—friends, creature comforts, financial security, optimal health, or ideal circumstances—God's grace will bring about your soul's perfection. And if you remain faithful until death, then you will enjoy all eternity with Him, forever *lacking in nothing.*

Chapter Sixteen
⟹ *The Effect of Saving Grace on Believers* ⟸

*". . . lay aside the old self, which is being corrupted in accordance with
the lusts of deceit, and . . . be renewed in the spirit of your mind,
and put on the new self, which in the likeness of God has been created
in righteousness and holiness of the truth." (Eph. 4:22–24)*

O ur country is in such a mess.

Our cities are overwhelmed with social problems;
our highways are clogged with cars; our infrastructure—roads,
interstates, bridges, piping, etc.—is falling apart. Our national
economy is being crushed by trillions of dollars of debt, and every
year this just gets worse. Our country is being overwhelmed with
homelessness, garbage, pollution, mental illness, drugs, alcohol, and
vice.

Present-day America is as polarized as I have ever seen it.
Political issues, social issues, and hot topics (e.g., race, gender,
sexuality, and immigration) cannot be discussed with facts, dignity, or
even common sense. We cannot talk anymore: the days of dialogue,
gentlemanly debate, and a willingness to listen to our opponents
have all been carelessly abandoned. Where once we were courteous,
respectful, dignified, and even God-fearing, we have descended—
with dizzying speed—into an ugly, unholy, profanity-spewing, and
disrespectful society. Where once we were a civilized nation, we
have become barbaric, unwholesome, and very uncivilized. We are
purposely rude, hateful, combative, and malicious.

Despite our awful physical and economic problems, it is the moral
state of our nation that has me the most concerned. We have lost
our moral compass, leaving us to grope in moral darkness. We have
sold the soul of our country to appease a relatively small percentage
of godless people who care only for themselves and their wicked
agenda. Dysfunctional and broken homes have contributed to the
unraveling of our social fabric. Substance abuse—including the abuse

of *prescribed* medications—is rampant, preventing many people from being objective, rational, and self-sustaining. Ethics are deemed expendable; lying, cheating, stealing, and fraud are at epidemic levels. Sexual deviancy is applauded as "virtuous," "progressive," and "admirable," even as it accelerates our social demise and moral deterioration.

It is difficult to speak positively about the gospel message when the light of divine truth seems to be swallowed up by the darkness of an increasingly wicked world. Atheists and secularists are enjoying swelling popularity; meanwhile, church attendance is falling and many congregations are closing their doors. It seems that evil is actually winning and goodness is being stomped out of existence. It seems that God's truth has failed to prevail, false religion is threatening the survival of Christ's church, and every Christian is just waiting to be destroyed (in one way or another) by a very wicked generation. It seems that Satan is more powerful than Christ, and that his awful presence in the world has belittled the work of our Redeemer on the cross. Or so it seems.

The condition of the world—particularly *our* world, in America— is unquestionably dismal. However, things are not always as they seem. We cannot measure the effectiveness of God's "eternal purpose" (Eph. 3:11) with the failure of human effort. The gospel remains far more powerful than we will ever know in this life. Christ has already defeated Satan, and nothing has changed; Christ remains in full control of the entire universe. Truth may be assaulted, twisted, perverted, and ignored, but it will not die and it cannot be killed. Wicked people, perverted behavior, and false religion may enjoy a small measure of success for now, but all such things will run their course and be destroyed by an indestructible God.

Let the wicked world think that it is winning if it wants to, but it is terribly mistaken. We who have been saved by grace ought to know this and live accordingly. Meanwhile, we cannot sit back and allow everyone who is in this wicked world to die in their sins. We also were once part of this wicked world, but now we belong to "the kingdom of His [God's] beloved Son." The saving grace which has redeemed our souls from spiritual ruin ought to have a profound effect on how we regard, influence, and desire to teach those who remain in "the domain of darkness" (Col. 1:13–14).

Lights in a Very Dark World

The effect of saving grace on a human soul is something that remains mysterious to us. There are things God is doing to us, for us, and through us, that we simply cannot fully understand. Even so, we must be careful not to undervalue what we do not understand, and we must not allow the fear of what is happening in the *world* to interfere with God's work in *us*. Our job, as faithful believers, is to produce fruit for God, not be overwhelmed by the actions of unbelievers. "Fruit of the Spirit" (Gal. 5:22–23) is the outward and measurable evidence of that which begins inwardly and, by human calculations, imperceptibly within the soul of one who is in a covenant relationship with God. One who truly walks with God cannot help but be deeply and visibly affected by such privileged fellowship.

What this means is: we who have been saved by grace ought to stand out *distinctly* and *brightly* to those who remain lost in moral darkness. We are not just different from the world; we represent light, salvation, and hope *to* the world. We are not the source of these priceless gifts, but are mere recipients of them. Even so, we are to prove ourselves "to be blameless and innocent, children of God above reproach in the midst of a crooked and perverse generation, among whom you appear as lights in the world, holding fast the word of life" (Phil. 2:15–16). The Greek word for "lights" in this passage can also be translated "luminaries," and has direct reference to heavenly bodies in the night sky.[83] Against the backdrop of the blackness of space, the lights of the planets, stars, and constellations are easily seen. So it is with us: against the backdrop of a morally darkened world, the spiritual light of God's people is magnified and easy to see.

When Jesus came into the world, He was a brilliant Light that stood in great contrast with the rest of humanity that was lost in sin. This was foretold by Isaiah (9:1–2) and fulfilled in Jesus' ministry: "'The people who were sitting in darkness saw a great light, and those who were sitting in the land and shadow of death, upon them a light dawned'" (Mat. 4:16). When the Son of God came into our fallen world, those who were desperate for hope sat up and took notice. Similarly, while we in whom Christ dwells must still coexist with a world of darkness, we provide *heavenly light* to all who see us. And those who are desperate for hope will sit up and take notice—not so much of *us*, but of what has *gotten into* us, so to speak. Jesus said to those who believed in and followed Him, "You are the light of the world" (Mat. 5:14)—in other words, "If I, the Light of the world, am in *you*, then people cannot help but see this, and will be *benefited* by this!"

We who have been saved by grace have experienced God's mercy, forgiveness, and love in ways that those in darkness cannot understand. But this does not mean that they could *never* understand or *never* have what we have. We have no exclusive lock on salvation; we are not more special than these others; in fact, we once belonged to the same darkness that now owns them! But the light of God's kindness that illuminates the hearts and enlightens the minds of believers transforms us from what we *were* into what we never could have *been*. This "light" cannot be reduced to a mere feeling of spirituality, or a spiritual concept; it cannot be confined to a church service or a church building. Rather, it is an outward manifestation of the fruit of an inward transformation. It is the reason *why* God forgave us in the first place, so that He could use us as beacons of light and hope to attract other lost souls to the source of eternal salvation. "For we are His workmanship, created in Christ Jesus for good works, which God prepared beforehand so that we would walk in them" (Eph. 2:10).

God's saving grace is an extension of His perfect love. God loves all people, but not all people love God, and His love *by itself* does not save anyone. If all that was necessary for salvation was to be loved by God, then *no one* would ever be lost, because God loves *all* people.[84] As it is, *all* are "perishing" who do not respond rightly and obediently to His love (John 3:16, 1 Cor. 1:18, 2 Cor. 4:3, et al). Yet, those who reciprocate His love and thus obey His commandments are filled

with His love and will walk accordingly.[85] People who are filled with
genuine godly love are extremely attractive to those who are hurting,
suffering from sin, and longing to be loved. No one has actually seen
God, but when we show to others the kind of love He has shown
to us, people "see" God *in* us (1 John 4:12). When we love like God
loves, people *feel* this—they are magnetically *drawn* to this.

The Fruits of Believers

So far, we have spoken only generally of being touched by God's
grace and illuminated with His love. Yet, the New Testament is filled
with all kinds of specific points to consider on this subject. The gospel
of saving grace must never be left so vague and generalized that
no one really knows what it is or what to do with it. The following
examples provide us with a more concrete view of what is expected of
us.

Proclaim what God has done for you. In Mark 5:1–20, Jesus was
confronted by a man overwhelmed by a "legion" of demons. After
Jesus exorcised all of these demons through His divine authority,
the healed man asked to follow Him. But Jesus had other plans: "Go
home to your people," He told the man, "and report to them what
great things the Lord has done for you, and how He had mercy on
you" (5:19). This is an excellent instruction for all of us who have
received divine mercy and grace. We have a story to tell; we have a
testimony to share; we have a message of hope to spread to a world
that is filled with demons and satanic activity. This means we need
to be *talking* about where we used to be, how God delivered us,
and how blessed we are now for having been rescued. In imparting
divine grace to our souls, God gives each of us a reason to "proclaim
the excellencies of Him who has called you out of darkness into His
marvelous light" (1 Pet. 2:9). Many of us have undervalued or simply
overlooked this simple but profoundly important point.

Live with a heart of forgiveness. God's forgiveness must have a
profound and life-changing effect on our hearts—an effect that carries
into all of our earthly relationships. The forgiveness He has extended
to us is meant to transform us into a forgiving people: "just as the
Lord forgave you, so also should you" (Col. 3:13b). (We can see the

awful consequences of the failure to do this in Mat. 18:21–35.) This does not mean we are to forgive people *unconditionally*, but that we are to have a forgiving heart toward *all* people. Thus, when they ask to be forgiven by us, we are ready and willing to forgive them, just as God is ready and willing to forgive us (Mat. 6:14–15).[86] Our desire to seek forgiveness—and thus, reconciliation and restoration of broken relationships—is foreign to a world that is diseased with retaliation, vengeance, and brooding bitterness over past crimes. Our forgiving heart will appear as a luminary against the black backdrop of the fallen human condition and all of its ugliness.

Be honest, truthful, and authentic. God has been honest and straightforward with us concerning Himself, His revealed message, our soul's sinful condition, and what needs to be done in order for us to be reconciled to Him. This transparent honesty—His ungalvanized, unadulterated, and transcendent *truth*—ought to condition our own dealings with others. We cannot be people who merely claim to believe in the truth, we need to be *walking* in truth and genuinely *speaking* truth (Eph. 4:25, 3 John 1:3–4). This carries with it another responsibility—namely, to speak the truth "in love" (Eph. 4:15) rather than bludgeon people over the head with it. We must not only be honest people, but we must be honest even to our own hurt; we must not only be truthful when we stand to profit from it, but we must be truthful even when it brings us the severest of consequences. We should not forget that when the Jewish leaders adjured Jesus to tell the truth about who He was, His answer sealed their condemnation of Him (Mat. 26:62–66). In like manner, your honesty may seal someone's (or the world's) condemnation of you. Honesty and truthfulness are hard to find in a world saturated with lies, deceptions, and misinformation. When divine truth sets us free from divine condemnation, we become obligated to live by that truth in the presence of all people. This may draw sneers, ridicule, and contempt from some, but it will draw others to God—all because we choose to reflect His truth in our own words.

Live humbly before God and other people. Forgiven people must also be humble people. We do not expect to find humility in a carnal-minded, self-centered, and greedy people; we *do* expect humility in those who have been showered with undeserved saving grace. Not only was humility a necessary condition *for* our forgiveness, it is the virtue that God expects in all whom He has forgiven. Humility is all about deferring to someone *greater* in authority than yourself, or voluntarily choosing to exalt someone *instead* of yourself. The unbeliever does not naturally choose to be humble, and his heart remains defiant—however subtle that defiance may be—against the Lord. But those who are saved by grace have already humbled themselves at Jesus' cross and at His throne of grace. They understand that the route to greatness is *through* humility and servitude, which imitates the Master's own example (Mat. 11:28–30, 20:25–28). We are to "walk in a manner worthy of the calling with which [we] have been called, with all humility" (Eph. 4:1–2), because this is consistent with the attitude and nature of those who have been redeemed. It is very likely that the humble manner in which we demonstrate our faith in Christ will lead someone else to Him.

Exercise moral courage. Doing the right thing, simply because it is right, is a hallmark of the grace-filled life. This does not mean that anyone who does what is right in a given situation is saved by grace, but that moral excellence is what God expects of those who *have* been saved by grace. "Let your light shine before men in such a way that they may see your good works, and glorify your Father who is in heaven" (Mat. 5:16). Our good works and righteous deeds are the fruit of a life that has been transformed by grace. Peter sums this up succinctly: "The one who desires life, to love and see good days, must keep his tongue from evil and his lips from speaking deceit. He must turn away from evil and do good; he must seek peace and pursue it" (1 Pet. 3:10–11). While there are certainly good people in the world whose lives are influenced by God, only those who are *made* good through the blood of Christ will do all that Peter said. Those already in pursuit of life with God will exert a powerful influence on those who also desire to seek life with Him.

Walk with God, not with the world. The distinctive pattern of the Christian lifestyle itself will advertise to all who know us what we believe, who we serve, where our heart lies, and what we believe our future to be. If we are walking in a manner worthy of the Lord, we will not look like the world looks, we will not talk like the world talks, and we will not do what the world does. Our lives will be markedly different and separate from those of unbelievers—or even those who profess to be Christians but remain lukewarm and double-minded. We will abstain from every form of evil and cling tenaciously to that which is good (1 Thess. 5:21–22). On Sunday, we will be in the assembly of fellow believers, partaking of the Lord's Supper, hearing the message of God, singing with joy, and praying with reverent devotion to our Lord. We will forego worldly celebrations, secular events, and even gatherings with unbelieving family members because of our commitment to Christ and His church. We voluntarily give up those things which compromise our faith; we also voluntarily accept the difficult and demanding responsibilities of discipleship to our Savior. We do not do these things out of guilt or compulsion, but out of gratitude and a longing to conform to and ultimately be *with* our Redeemer. Whether or not any unbelievers honor our beliefs, respect our decisions, or even care about our fellowship with God, they cannot help but notice that we are no longer *of* the world, but that our citizenship belongs elsewhere (Phil. 3:20–21).

Summary Thoughts

The world of those who remain outside of Christ is indeed a mess. Meanwhile, we who have entered into a covenant relationship with God *through* Christ are—or ought to be—very much at peace with God, regardless of the moral darkness and confusion swirling all around us. Christ is not just our prominent religious figure, but He is our Savior—He *saves* us from this awful world. He is also our Victor—through His triumph over this world and the grave, He has already destroyed any power that Satan claims to have over us (Heb. 2:14–15).

The apostle John's vision of heaven (Rev. 4:2–11) reveals God in serene repose, fully in control, and completely unthreatened by the realm of darkness or the world of men. His saving grace is infinitely more powerful than all the sin, shame, guilt, and pain we have experienced whenever we have fallen. We are not "just barely" saved; we do not overcome "by the skin of our teeth"; rather, we "overwhelmingly conquer through Him who loved us" (Rom. 8:37). Through the mercy and grace given to us by a benevolent and loving Father, and through the fully capable ministry of our King and High Priest, Jesus Christ, we are forgiven of all debts, cleared of all wrongdoing, and spared eternal punishment. Instead of cowering in fear from the intimidation and ridicule of a godless world, we ought to take courage in the One who has already *overcome* the world (John 16:33).

But we cannot just talk about being saved by grace. We also need to live it out, so to speak. Mere churchgoers just talk about grace and faith; true disciples of the Master actually demonstrate their allegiance to Him in everything they do. Every aspect of our lives, every relationship, and every major decision that must be made is governed by our desire to do the will of the Father (Mat. 7:21). The effect of Christ's mercy, the power of His forgiveness, the purity of His truth, the virtue of His righteousness, the character of His humility, and the swelling hope of being in His heaven cannot help but radiate from us like brilliant sunshine on a summer's day. If we are truly walking in a manner worthy of the gospel of grace, people will not see mere "religion" in us, they will see *Christ* in us.

The grace-filled life is truly the Christ-filled life, since He is the source of our salvation *and* the personification of saving grace. When He fills our hearts and when His word fills our heads, we will share Him with others. First, this will be done passively, through the example of our godly behavior to whomever is paying attention to us. Second, this will be done actively, as we look for opportunities to share His message of love, grace, and hope with those who remain prisoners of Satan, "having been held captive by him to do his will" (2 Tim. 2:26). Our desire is not to be content with our own salvation, but to be busy with the Lord's work until He calls us home. And "home" is wherever Christ is, and will always be.

Chapter Seventeen
⟞Calvinism and Christianity⟝

*Blessed be the God and Father of our Lord Jesus Christ, who has
blessed us with every spiritual blessing in the heavenly places in Christ,
just as He chose us in Him before the foundation of the world,
that we would be holy and blameless before Him* (Eph. 1:3–4).

PREFACE: The following chapter is very different from what you,
dear reader, have encountered previously in this book. So far, I have
not critically examined a particular doctrine involving the doctrine
of saving grace (except only very briefly); I have only focused on the
biblical teaching on this subject. If you wish to skip this chapter, the
rest of the book stands on its own merit. But if you wish to see how
"grace" has been very misunderstood and misapplied in the religious
world, then keep reading. This chapter is not short and simple, but it
is very informative, and it will likely confront you with teachings that
you will seldom (if ever) read about in other books on this subject.

∼

What has been presented in all the preceding chapters is a
biblical definition and exposition of God's saving grace. I have
purposely and conscientiously provided numerous biblical citations
to show the accurateness and genuineness of this teaching. The
underlying message has been: 1) this is not *my* message, but God's;
2) this is not a statement of what my *congregation* believes, but is
a statement of what is true *regardless* of what I or my congregation
believes; 3) the teaching on divine grace is critical to salvation, and
therefore must be treated with great respect, reverence, and diligent
study.

But not everyone who studies the Bible comes to the same
conclusions concerning God's saving grace. This does *not* make the
subject of saving grace a free-for-all—as in, you believe what *you* want
to believe, I believe what *I* want to believe, and it's all good—but that
some people will see things differently. *Why* they see them differently

is often more ignored than the actual differences themselves: it is the "why" that drives these differences, not the other way around. As with other major religious subjects, "grace" is often defined not solely by what the Bible teaches, but in a way that is consistent with a predetermined doctrinal or denominational position. This approach does not seek to understand saving grace objectively, but as a defense (or explanation) of one's chosen religious beliefs.

This is true with Calvinism, which is a doctrinal view of saving grace that differs from what the New Testament teaches. I can say this with confidence, because: 1) no one comes to an understanding of Calvinism by reading Scripture, but Calvinism has to be explained by Calvinists; 2) Jesus, Paul, Peter, and John—the foremost contributors to the content of the New Testament—never said what Calvinism says, but just the opposite; and 3) if Calvinism was Christianity, we would not need to call it "Calvinism," but we would simply refer to it as *Christianity*. The fact that it needs to be separately and distinctively defined exposes it as a *different doctrine* than what the apostles originally preached.

That is strong language, to be sure, but we have to consider what is at stake. If the gospel of Christ says you are saved *one* way, but Calvinism (or any other "-ism") says you are saved a *different* way, we have to choose between the two (Gal. 1:6–7). The Holy Spirit did not reveal two separate, concurrent, and conflicting methods of salvation. Calvinists will argue, of course, that their doctrine—notice, it is *their* doctrine—is completely consistent with Christ's gospel, but under close scrutiny it becomes quite evident that this is not true. The gospel of Christ is God's message from heaven: it was revealed by the Holy Spirit (1 Cor. 2:10, Gal. 1:11–12), inspired [lit., "breathed-out"] by God (2 Tim. 3:16), and proclaimed by Christ's hand-picked apostles (Col. 1:25–28). Calvinism is a man-made doctrine: it was formulated by men (prominently, Augustine, in the 5th century), long after the apostles; it was codified by men (namely, John Calvin, in the 16th century); it has been defended only by man-made councils (or synods); and it continues to be upheld in an unbiblical, man-made system of church organization, namely, denominationalism.

Apostolic teaching was defended not only by a message from heaven, but also by *power* from heaven (1 Cor. 4:20, 2 Cor. 12:12, Heb. 2:3–4, et al). The apostles proved, through the miracles they performed, that they were spokesmen for God. Calvinism comes to us with no apostolic authority, no miracle, and therefore no power. (The same can be said, for example, of denominationalism, Mohammedanism [Islam], and Mormonism.) It is an after-the-fact interpretation of how God saves people that, when pushed to its limits, actually invalidates the written gospel of Christ and the original preaching of it. In other words, if Calvinism is true, then every soul that God has destined to be saved *will* be saved, and every soul that God has *not* destined to be saved *will* be lost, and there is no amount of knowledge, preaching, piety, or prayers that can change either situation. This renders the gospel, the church, Christian living, and all evangelism useless and unnecessary.

What follows is not intended to be a scholarly examination of Calvinism. That is not the intent of this book, nor is this necessary in order to understand "grace." The reason for discussing Calvinism at all is because: 1) it is extremely popular, being the underlying doctrine of several major so-called Protestant denominations; 2) it is often blindly accepted as biblical fact, which means people seldom hold it up to the Bible for examination; and 3) it masquerades as true Christianity, when in reality it is not. (Remember that Calvinism was not codified until nearly 1600 years *after* Christ. The same can be said of the denominations that teach it: they also were not in existence prior to the 16th or 17th century.)

The Roots of Calvinism

Calvinism (a.k.a. Reformed Theology, The Doctrine of Predestination, or The Doctrine of Election and Reprobation) is an interpretation of Scripture, and of salvation in particular, in which the sovereign decision of God determines the salvation (election) or condemnation (reprobation) of every single human soul.[87] This view was popularized by Augustine (354 – 430), and formally articulated by John Calvin (1509 – 1564). It remains the theological backbone of several modern denominations, particularly Presbyterianism.

Augustine was born in ancient Rome, and later became an ordained priest (391), then an ordained bishop (395), at Hippo [modern Anabba], a port city in North Africa.[88] While there, he wrote his two seminal writings, *Confessions* (397) and *City of God* (413–426). In these writings (and others), he laid out his personal view of saving grace that he assumed was the only right way in which to interpret Scripture, based upon the Doctrine of Original Sin (see below).[89] Over time, he developed the doctrine that fallen man was incapable of exercising his own free moral will to bring about his salvation: God not only had to intervene by *His* own will, but unless He did, no one *could* be saved.[90]

Augustine also believed that God predestined (or, foreordained) all who would be saved (by His own choice), and therefore all who would be lost. He claimed that "all human beings in some sense 'sinned in Adam' and share in his guilt; they therefore deserve damnation even if, like unbaptized infants, they have committed no sins of their own."[91] Believing that God *could* save everyone, but chooses *not* to, Augustine assumed that God does not *want* to save everyone. Some, God chooses to save; "in the case of the majority [of those He does *not* choose to save] He simply allows the effect of sin to take its natural course."[92] God apparently has good reason for selecting some but not others, but Augustine never explained this. He simply (and conveniently) deferred to God's "inscrutable mystery" on the matter, which is "hidden in the secret abyss of divine wisdom."[93]

"In the later Catholic tradition Augustine was honoured as the 'theologian of grace' but his teaching on predestination was watered down or simply ignored. It was the reformer [John] Calvin in the sixteenth century . . . who revived the full Augustinian doctrine and brought it back to the centre of theological debate."[94] Calvin "struggled with the great question of how to be right with God" and a "correct understanding of justification."[95] He also wrestled with the question of authority, especially during a time in history when men were challenging the longstanding authority of the Roman (Catholic) Church. The Reformation (16th century), launched officially by Martin Luther's "95 Theses" nailed to the door of the church in Wittenburg in 1517, compelled men to search the New Testament Scriptures for the teachings of God rather than simply accept the teachings of the Roman Church. In his correspondence with Jacopo Sadoleto, one of the cardinals of the Roman Church (1539), Calvin stated that he "was convinced that only through the Bible and the work of the Holy Spirit had he come to know . . . peace in Christ. He was certain that the old church had gravely distorted the truth and needed thorough reform."[96] In 1535, he published (in Latin) his first version of his apology for what he understood the Scriptures to teach (*Institutes of the Christian Religion*) in which he outlined his views on God, the Bible, justification, and Christian living. By the time he completed the final version of this work in 1559, it had grown to an immense theological treatise, and was used as an introduction for the study of theology for students entering into that field.[97]

Calvin believed that man, spiritually fallen and helpless as he is, could never have fellowship with God, righteous and holy as *He* is. The only solution, as Calvin saw it, lay in God's sole decision to save man by imparting Christ's own personal righteousness upon man's soul (what Calvinist's call "imputed righteousness"), so that man would be made holy to God *and*, since Christ's righteousness is perfect and infallible, could never fall from that righteousness.[98] This entire process is what Calvin called "grace." But God's grace, he believed, was not something any person could receive simply by putting his faith in Him and asking Him for it. Instead, the matter was entirely left up to God to decide. Calvin regarded the idea that a person could choose of his own volition to come to God to be "unbiblical and shallow."[99] He believed that "the idea of free will does not take the disastrous effect of sin on human nature seriously enough."[100] Calvin further stated that "such religion takes the glory of salvation away from God and trivializes the work of Christ."[101]

Instead, Calvin believed that "salvation is entirely the work and gift of God and that man contributes nothing at all to it."[102] "Since 'our salvation comes about solely from God's generosity' and 'every part of our salvation rests with Christ that we may glory in the Lord alone,' it must be God who chooses who is to partake of grace."[103] Thus, God alone, apart from the decision of any person, is what determines his spiritual future. This is Calvin's understanding of "predestination" as it is used in the New Testament. "For Calvin, predestination explains the origin of salvation in the eternal will of God. Election removes all human boasting and gives all glory to God in salvation."[104]

Calvin insisted that his conclusions were based entirely upon Scripture. Those who dared challenge him, as he saw it, were trying to know more than what God had actually revealed.[105] The serious flaw in his approach, however, was that he assumed *he was right* in his understanding of Scripture, and therefore any attack on his conclusions concerning justification or predestination was tantamount to an attack on God Himself. Furthermore, Calvin, as well as all Calvinist scholars since him, have been very unclear as to how a person is to know that he is among the "elect" (those whom God has chosen from eternity to save) or the "reprobate" (those whom God has *not* chosen, and therefore are hopelessly damned). Naturally, Calvin numbered himself among the elect; the proof, he would say, lay in the fact that he is a faithful Christian. But if any faithful Christian were to fall from his own faithfulness, then Calvin would say that he was never among the faithful in the first place, but that whatever faith he claimed to have was "temporary" rather than "genuine." All of this is extremely convenient, and is the subjective opinion of one who has already assumed that he is of the "elect." Thus, Calvinists gush about the great election and sovereignty of God because of how they see themselves as recipients of it. Yet, you will never read of a Calvinist who fully agrees with Calvin's take on predestination while recognizing himself to be a "reprobate" that cannot be saved.[106]

Serious Flaws and Contradictions

On the surface, Calvinism appears to be a noble and humble tribute to God's supreme authority. In their own words:

> The Calvinist believes that God is the Lord of life and Sovereign of the universe, whose will is the key to history. The Calvinist believes that He is free and independent of any force outside Himself to accomplish His purposes; that He knows

the end from the beginning; that He creates, sustains, governs, and directs all things; and that His marvelous design will be fully and perfectly manifest at the end of the ages.[107]

Taken at face value, this is true and biblical teaching; God's sovereignty rules over all of creation. The problem begins in how Calvinists *apply* this truth in the context of salvation. They maintain that no one can resist God's saving grace: if it is God's decision to save you, then you *must* be saved; likewise, if it is God's decision to condemn you, then you *must* be condemned. God's decree concerning each human soul is made independent and regardless of that soul's own decision. Thus, if you are saved by God, you cannot be lost; and if you are condemned by God, you cannot be saved. Since God's sovereign decree cannot be altered or overruled, the saved cannot be lost and the lost cannot be saved.[108]

This is hugely assumptive, and it stands in glaring contradiction to practical application within the Scripture itself. For example, in the course of His ministry, Jesus was confronted by a wealthy young ruler (Mat. 19:16–22). This man wanted "to obtain eternal life." Jesus did not say, "It has already been determined that you will be saved or lost; there is nothing you can do about it." On the contrary, He said, "If you wish to enter into life, keep the commandments [of God, as codified in the Law of Moses]" (19:17, bracketed words added). Think about this: Jesus offered him eternal life based upon his *faithful obedience to the Law* and his willingness to *sacrifice his present life for a life with God*. Why was nothing brought up about God's sovereign will? Why did Jesus *never* talk about God's sovereign will as the determining factor for one's eternal destiny? Instead, He contradicted the idea of a forced election or reprobation—more accurately, the Calvinistic view of election contradicts everything He taught.

But someone might say, "Well, that was under the Law; Calvinism concerns the gospel of Christ." The fact is: *every person that has ever lived*, if he has been saved from his sins, has been saved *by* grace and *through* his faith (Eph. 2:8). While the Jew, from the time of Moses to the time that Jesus' church was established, was obligated to the Law of Moses, his *soul* was saved by God's grace and through that person's faith. The Law did not change what needed to be done for *salvation*, it only determined what a person needed to do to demonstrate his *faith*. Saving grace was given to *all* who demonstrated faith in God, whether prior to the Law, during the Law (for Israelites), or during the age of Christianity. "The righteous man shall live by faith" (Rom. 1:17, see Hab. 2:4) is consistent with what Jesus told the rich young man, and is consistent with what Paul preached to both Jews and Gentiles.

Furthermore, if God's sovereign will cannot be denied in His decree concerning the destiny of one's soul, then how can it be denied *at all?* In other words, every time a person sins against God, he denies what God decreed *ought* to have been done. If it is a sin for me to disobey God's specific commandment (e.g., do not lie, do not covet, etc.), then it is a sin for me to reject God's entire system of commandments—the gospel of Christ. When the apostle Paul preached to mixed audiences of Jews and Gentiles, some believed what he taught and others refused to believe it (Acts 13:42–48, 17:1–5, 19:8–10, et al). All those who disbelieved *violated* God's sovereign truth, which is to say they violated His divine decree to *believe* in the truth (John 3:16, 1 Tim. 2:3–4).[109] In other words, they did what God said *not* to do; they did the opposite of what God *wanted* them to do.[110] Not only this, but God Himself *permitted* this decision of theirs. That is what free will is all about: God making each person a free moral agent capable of deciding his own spiritual future. If we do not have free will, then there is no reason for us being alive on this earth at all: our stay here serves no purpose because we cannot change anything; our destiny is already determined; our earthly lives only postpone the inevitable.[111] What is the point of believing in the gospel when it does not change one's spiritual future? And, what is the harm in being disobedient to the gospel when it also changes nothing?[112]

Calvinism also maintains that a person is not just blinded by his sin (as stated in 2 Cor. 4:3–4), but is literally *unable* to respond (or "dead," as cited from Eph. 2:1) to God's gospel call. The reason why he is unresponsive is because of another man-made doctrine which Calvinism has absorbed, namely, the Doctrine of Original Sin.[113]

This doctrine maintains that Adam's sin (Gen. 3) infected the entire human race, and therefore every human soul is *born* sinful (i.e., guilty with Adam's sin) and cursed by God.[114] This condemnation/curse is what makes a person dead to God (from *birth*), and, just as a corpse cannot respond to the call of the living, so a "dead" person cannot respond to the call of God. And, since he cannot respond to God's call, it is up to God to regenerate him *apart* from his faith in Him. This leaves the decision to be *saved* or *left for dead* God's and God's alone. Thus, no one can have faith in the gospel of Christ until he has been "made alive" by God *first*. Such is the basic premise of Calvinism.

This teaching turns Paul's argument concerning faith on its head: instead of a person being credited with righteousness *because* of his faith (Rom. 1:17, 4:3), Calvinism teaches that a person cannot *practice* faith until he has first been regenerated by God.[115] A person cannot be "born again" by his own choice, but (according to Calvinism) only by God's choice—a choice that, once made, cannot be changed or rescinded. Allegedly, divine grace is applied "unilaterally and monergistically"[116]—i.e., by God's *sole* choice and His *sole* work—not as a response to one's calling upon the name of the Lord for salvation (as in Acts 2:21 and Rom. 10:11–13). This means that a person is not "born again" *after* hearing the word of God (because he is "dead" and therefore *unable* to hear it), but God must make him "born again" *first*. Once "made alive," a person can then respond rightly to God's commands for repentance, holy living, and good works.

Calvinism thus maintains that one's faith comes as a result of God's saving grace, rather than saving grace being God's response to his faith. In other words, he is saved from *being* "dead to God" before he even knows that he *is dead to God*. Those who are not called by God's grace will be punished for being in this condition (even though it is God who prevents them from being saved from it); those who *are* called by God's grace will escape all condemnation (through no act of faithful obedience on their own). Calvinism also necessarily implies that one who is "born again" retains all of his sins and guilt, since that person is taught to take the necessary steps of repentance and seeking forgiveness. He is not "born again" *pure* and *uncorrupted*, but is apparently re-born *in* his impurity and corruption, since his repentance follows his spiritual rebirth. This is all completely backward from what the New Testament actually teaches, yet millions of Calvinists today accept it without reservation.

Calvinists commonly cite the following passages in support of their doctrine. (The brief summaries after each citation are their own interpretations.)

- John 6:44, no one can come to God unless He first regenerates that man.

- Acts 13:48, no one can have eternal life whom God did not "appoint" beforehand.

- Rom. 3:10–18, no man does any "good" without God's having first regenerated him.

- Rom. 8:29–30, God "predestines" whomever He will; those whom He has not predestined are eternally lost.[117] No one can dispute God's having *not* called him, since His sovereign authority cannot be changed and must not be questioned.

- Rom. 9:10–18, God "calls" (saves) whomever He wishes, and does *not* "call" (or, does not save) whomever He chooses not to call. Thus, God called (saved) Jacob, but "hated" (did not save) Esau; God called (saved) the Israelites, but did not call (or, save) Pharaoh.

- Eph. 1:3–11 (and in every passage which speaks of God's "choosing" His people, His "choice," or the "elect"), God has "predestined" (or, foreordained the salvation of) those who are saved; thus, He has *also* predestined (or, foreordained the eternal condemnation of) those who will be lost. The entire matter rests upon God's own decision; each person can only accept whatever sovereign decree He has made concerning him, since he cannot change it.[118]

- Eph. 2:1–2, man is "dead" in sin, and thus is unable to respond to God's gospel until God makes him "alive" in Christ (2:4–5). His "dead" state makes him completely unable to have any faith in God until He makes him "born again" (1 Pet. 1:3).

- Eph. 2:8–9, man's "works" play no part in his salvation, but he is saved by divine grace *alone*.[119] "Faith" is what a person gives to God *after* (and *because*) he is saved.

The above citations do not *prove* Calvinism, but instead are "interpreted" *in light* of it. This is like an evolutionist "proving" evolution with fossils that he claims are the result of evolution! The *context* of each passage, and that of the entire New Testament, does not support the interpretations that the Calvinist has assigned to it.

Predestination is indeed a biblical doctrine, but it must be understood in the context in which it is used in the New Testament. When Paul speaks of "predestination" (as in Rom. 8:29–30 or Eph. 1:3–11), he *always* does so in reference of the entire *body* of believers, not of individual people. In other words, Christ's *church* is predestined for salvation and glory, but it is left up to each individual person to determine whether or not he will be *part* of that church, based upon his own response to the gospel (Rom. 2:4–11). In the case of Jacob and Esau, it is clear in the context—as well as throughout the Old Testament—that God's reference was to the *descendants* (or nations) of Jacob and Esau, not the two men themselves (Rom. 9:13). Neither God nor Paul speak of the *spiritual destiny* of each man, but how their posterity played out in history. God did not say, "Jacob's soul I will *save*, but Esau's soul will be *lost*." To turn Paul's example into a doctrine concerning each man's eternal destiny is to grossly misrepresent his point. His *point* (in Rom. 9) is that God's decisions concerning whomever He chooses to carry out His work in history are His, not men's. If God wishes to use Israel to bring Christ into the world, that is His choice; if He now chooses to allow Gentiles to benefit from this Messiah, that is also His choice. But He *never* says that He will decide who will be eternally saved or lost; that decision rests with the one who chooses to *believe* in God or not (John 8:24).

The TULIP Acronym

Calvinists are fond of appealing to church history as justification for their beliefs. Thus, they regularly cite the various religious councils (or, synods) in which landmark decisions have been rendered by a high court of church officials.[120] In some of these councils, Calvinism has been exonerated, while those who oppose it are summarily condemned as heretics. Two of these so-called heretics—Pelagius (354–420?) and Jacob Arminius (1560–1609)—are prominently described as "founders" of modern anti-Calvinistic teachings.[121] Thus, non-Calvinists who call themselves Christians are derogatorily referred to as "Pelagians," "semi-Pelagians," or "Arminians." This assumes, of course, that all such non-Calvinists are in full agreement with all that these men taught—a point which is neither true, necessary, or even relevant. No one should think that he is right with God simply because he refuses to identify himself with someone whom he thinks is wrong with Him. Two opposing belief systems cannot both be right, but they *can* both be wrong.

In bold response to Jacob Arminius' formal grievance (or, remonstrance) against Calvinism, Calvinists convened a historic council in the city of Dordrecht, Netherlands—commonly referred to as Dort (or Dordt)—from 1618 to 1619. In this council, Calvinists outlined a five-point statement of their beliefs, mnemonically referred to as "TULIP"[122]:

- **T**otal Hereditary Depravity: Since man's heart, emotions, will, mind, and body are completely affected by Adam's sin, he is born *sinful* and thus condemned. He is "dead" in his sins, and thus unable to respond to God's gospel. "We are not sinners because we sin; we sin because we are sinners. Since the fall [of Adam] human nature has been corrupt. We are born with a sin nature. Our acts of sin flow out of this corrupted nature."[123]
  - ◽ This assumes that all of human nature—i.e., *every human being*—is already corrupt upon birth, and that no one is *ever* innocent before God at *any* time in his (or her) life. This is what Calvinists say, but they fail to support it biblically. Their favorite verse is Rom. 5:12: "Therefore, just as through one man [Adam] sin entered into the world, and death through sin, and so death spread to all men, because all sinned." However, this verse does not teach what Calvinism says it teaches. In fact, it contradicts Calvinism: "because all

sinned" is the reason for the "death" of each soul, not Adam's own personal sin. Paul actually says this about *himself* a few chapters later (Rom. 7:7–11). Before he understood God's law, he was innocent: "I was alive apart from the Law [or simply, law]" (7:9). But once he understood God's law and what it revealed about what he was doing—i.e., once he became morally *responsible* to His law—"sin became alive and I died" (7:9). There is no mention of hereditary guilt or depravity; Paul "died" because *he* sinned against God, not because of Adam's sin. Paul had the free will to sin against God's law, just as you and I have the free will to do the same. "[F]or all have sinned"—i.e., we are guilty because of what *we* have done, not what Adam or anyone else did *to* us—"and fall short of the glory of God" (Rom. 3:23).

◻ "Total hereditary depravity" means that all babies and young children are sinful and hell-bound: they "bring an innate corruption from the very womb."[124] This means (if true) that if children die at an early age, they will suffer eternal punishment for actions for which they cannot possibly be held responsible. (Calvinists explain that those who die as infants or children may be "called" by God without us knowing it, so that their souls are saved. While a convenient rebuttal, this remains completely unsubstantiated.[125]) This must also mean that Jesus was born sinful, since He is the Son of Man ("born of a woman"—Gal. 4:4) as well as the Son of God. (Calvinists say that Jesus was exempt from hereditary depravity, but they will not say how or why.[126])

◻ Calvinists take Paul's "dead" reference (in Eph. 2:1) quite literally, but never really explain *what*, exactly, is "dead."[127] If it is one's soul, then how can that person function as a living being? If it is his spiritual awareness, then how can he have *any* consciousness? If it is his relationship (or fellowship) with God, *this makes sense*[128]—but the Calvinist wants it to mean so much more than this. The New Testament teaches: man *is* dead (or, "fallen"—Rom 3:23), but this refers to his inability to walk in fellowship with God. Yet, he is not *unable to respond* to God's gospel, for God has made it available to him for this very purpose (Rom. 10:5–13). If man is able—and *expected by God*—to "call upon the name of the Lord," then he most certainly has the God-given ability to *take the initiative* with regard to his salvation (Acts 2:21, 22:16).

- **Unconditional Election:** God does not base His "election" upon anything He sees in an individual person. He is unconcerned with what men do or do not do. He saves (or does not save) based solely upon His sovereign decision.[129] The Westminster Confession (1646), one of Calvinism's supportive creeds, says: "God, before the foundation of the world was laid, according to His eternal and immutable purpose, and the secret counsel and good pleasure of His will, hath chosen [human souls to be saved], in Christ, unto everlasting glory, out of His mere free grace and love, without any foresight of faith, or good works, or perseverance in either of them, or any other thing in the creature, as conditions, or causes moving Him thereunto."[130]

  ◌ This is a complete distortion of the meaning of "sovereignty of God." There is no question that it is God who regenerates the human soul, or that His grace—the atonement of Christ and the power of His Spirit—is the means of that regeneration (John 1:12–13, Titus 3:4–7, 1 Pet. 1:2, et al). But to place the *full responsibility* upon God for whether or not this regeneration takes place (and thus to deny man's free will) makes Him a "respecter of persons" and a God of partiality— exactly the opposite of what the Bible teaches (Acts 10:34–35, Rom. 2:11, Eph. 6:9, and Col. 3:25). If God justifies a person based upon his faith in Him, then He would be unjust to *deny him that opportunity* for which Christ has died (John 12:32, 20:31).

  ◌ To allow a person his free, independent will to *choose* this opportunity or *refuse* it is not questioning God's decision. His gospel stands intact, whether or not one chooses to obey it; His sovereignty remains unchallenged, whether or not one chooses to acknowledge it. As stated earlier, it is conspicuous that everyone who supports Calvinism is conveniently part of the "elect," and thus has no problem upholding God's decision to save *them*. This strongly indicates religious bias and conflict of interest. One loses all objectivity in interpreting Scripture when he believes that he cannot be wrong *in* his interpretation—and cannot be lost no matter what.

◻ In Rom. 2:4–11 (and 2 Cor. 5:10), Paul places the responsibility for the human soul's disposition in the afterlife upon what each person does, whether he is obedient or unrepentant. What would be Paul's point in this if the situation *could not be changed anyway?* According to Calvinism, this is unanswerable.

- **Limited Atonement:** "Jesus died only for the elect. Though Jesus' sacrifice was sufficient for all, it was not efficacious for all. Jesus only bore the sins of the elect."[131]

  ◻ This is based upon statements like Isa. 53:12 and Mat. 26:28, where it says Jesus died for "many," but not for "all." It is also based upon John 17:9, where Jesus prayed only for His disciples, but not for "the world." It is clear to any objective Bible student that when one uses passages like these in such a restrictive manner, the passage will only agree with the one who so interprets them but no one else.

  ◻ Jesus was *sent* to die for the entire world (John 3:16, 1 John 2:2). Just because the entire world does not rightly respond to His death does not mean that He did not *die* for all people. Passages that assert that Jesus died "for many" and not "all" cannot be construed to mean that Jesus' death was ineffectual for those not included in the "many," but only that those ("many") who *do* call upon His name for salvation will be atoned by His blood. Such language does not restrict His *work* on the cross, but only concedes that *not all* will appreciate that work.

  ◻ There is no question that the impartation of God's saving grace is conditioned upon one's personal and consistent faith—his belief who God is, his trust in what God promises to do for him through Christ, and his allegiance to Christ "unto death" (Rev. 2:10). The limitations of grace are not determined, then, by God's predestination of individual souls—and certainly not by Calvinist doctrine—but only by those who refuse to exercise such faith in Him.

◦ Paul wrote, "[God] desires all men to be saved and to come to the knowledge of the truth" (1 Tim. 2:4). It is impossible to get around this passage. One cannot conclude, "Paul only meant *Christian* men," because this violates the context of the full passage (1 Tim. 2:1–6); and it will never mean "only *Calvinist* Christian men," because the New Testament does not recognize such status. As far as God is concerned, He sent His Son to die for the *entire world*, but will only save those *of* the world who respond rightly to the "knowledge of truth" when they hear it in Christ's gospel (Rom. 10:17).

• **I**rresistible Grace: "When God calls His elect into salvation, they cannot resist. God offers to all people the gospel message. This is called the external call. But to the elect, God extends an internal call and it cannot be resisted."[132] Being "born again" is just like physical birth: the one being born has no part in the decision to be born.

◦ Such "interpretation" both misunderstands and misapplies what *is* taught in Scripture. In Phil. 2:12–13, for example, it says "God . . . is at work in you," which is straightforward enough. It does *not* mean, "God chooses salvation for you," but that God does things *for* the believer that he cannot do for himself. This is called *grace*, to be sure, but it is not irresistible. Calvinists say: "Though the irresistible grace of God in calling sinners is forceful and compelling, it works in such a way that the sinner's will is so renewed that he comes to Christ gladly and willingly."[133] Such reasoning is hugely presumptive; it only makes sense when a person buys into the premise of Calvinism in the first place, or when a Calvinist explains it. The reality is: if God's grace is truly "irresistible," then a person is *forced* to come to Christ, because he cannot do otherwise and he has no choice in the matter. Thus, God forces some to be saved, and also forces everyone else to be lost. Given Calvinism, there is no way around this. But where are the biblical passages that say, in clear language, that God's grace is "irresistible"?

◻ Calvinism says: "True Christians may fall seriously and radically, but they cannot fall finally from grace."[134] Yet, the New Testament teaches differently. People can receive grace "in vain" (2 Cor. 6:1–2); they can turn away from the Spirit of grace (Heb. 10:26–29); and they can *fall* from grace (Gal. 5:4). One cannot "fall" from something he never had in the first place.

◻ The New Testament clearly teaches that people *can* and *do* resist God's grace. This does not undermine God's sovereignty, but is a refusal of what His sovereign decisions have offered them. God's commandment is eternal life (John 12:50); but not everyone chooses to obey this command (Heb. 4:2). This does not make Him any less "God," but only makes those who refuse Him foolish people.

◻ "Born again" in the spiritual sense is an *analogy* to, not a literal *replication* of, one's physical birth. While it is true that I did not choose to be physically born, it is not true that my spiritual re-birth is held to this same condition. One is biological, the other is spiritual; one is natural, the other is supernatural; one regards my human (earthly) existence, the other regards my spiritual (eternal) existence. The two "births" may share some common features, but are not identical or interchangeable. Calvinists conspicuously avoid John 3:5: "Unless one is born of water and the Spirit." Being born of the *Spirit* is what God does for the believer; being born of *water* is what the believer does for God, in faithful obedience to what He has commanded. It is not only necessary that the believer participate in his born-again experience, but he is expected to initiate it through his demonstrations of faith (which includes his baptism).

- **P**erseverance of the Saints: "The doctrine of the perseverance of the saints teaches that . . . if by the Spirit of God you are regenerate [born again], justified, adopted into God's family, and sanctified, you cannot lose that salvation (1 Peter 1:5)."[135] Jesus said in John 10:27-28 that His "sheep" cannot perish; Paul said in Rom. 8:1 that the believer has passed out of condemnation, and therefore one's salvation is permanent and cannot fail ("once saved, always saved").

  - This point disregards the *conditional premise* of each passage being considered. God promises that He will never leave us (Heb. 13:5), but this does not mean we cannot leave Him (Heb. 6:4–8). Jesus will present every believer before the Father, but only *if* each person will "continue in the faith firmly established and steadfast, and not moved away from the hope of the gospel that you have heard" (Col. 1:21–23).[136] Even 1 Pet 1:5, which is cited in the quote above, is conditioned by *the rest* of 1 Peter, which requires Christians to live in holiness (1 Pet. 1:13–16) as a condition of their salvation. It is irresponsible to dwell on a given promise without also taking into account the conditions of that promise; the conditions are *part* of the promise, not something separate from it.

  - Calvinists also wrestle with passages like Rom. 11:22, which is unavoidably conditional.[137] They want to make *God's decree* the "condition," but Paul clearly teaches that man's faith is the variable. Paul (in Rom. 11:22) did not write to Gentiles who were guaranteed to be lost, but to those who had been saved: he warned them not to forfeit their salvation through unbelief. Thus, the burden is placed upon the believer to continue *in* his belief, not upon God to save someone regardless of his *unbelief*. God simply finalizes man's decision concerning his salvation; He does not make it unilaterally.

▫ When someone *does* "fall away" from the faith, the Calvinist claims that he was "never really saved at all," but only experienced "worldly sorrow" or a "dimension of enlightenment."[138] Such theology is convenient but not biblical; it is presumptuous and unprovable; simply put, it is plucked out of thin air. The New Testament teaches that not only *can* men fall away from the faith, but that some *will* (Acts 20:28–30, 1 Tim. 4:1, 2 Pet. 2:20–22, et al). This is not a fault of God, or the failure of His grace, but the decision of the one who rejects that grace and therefore bears the consequence of that awful decision (Heb. 10:26–31).[139]

⁓

Calvinism is a convoluted doctrine filled with double-speak. "They pray as if everything depended on God; and yet they preach and work as if everything depended on man."[140] Indeed, prayer, evangelism, good works, and benevolence are rendered pointless if God is going to do what He does and save whom He saves regardless of what people—believers and unbelievers alike—do or fail to do. (The Calvinist will respond: First, the non-elect are *permitted* to come to God, just not *able*—whatever that means. Second, since we do not *know* who the "elect" are, we are supposed to discover them through prayer and evangelism. Yet this smacks of arrogance and elitism, and is based on nothing more than a desperate attempt to justify one's position.) If God's will forces men to be saved against their own will, then they will be saved even without evangelism or prayer. And if we are *forced* to evangelize or pray or believe, then we are no longer intelligent human beings capable of choosing our own destiny, but are merely robots whose future is predetermined by God's sole decision.

Calvinism is not just a harmless interpretation of Scripture; it is an imposing and damaging one. It misrepresents both God and His plan of salvation. Even though its supporters claim to honor God's sovereign will, they handcuff the *application* of His will to their own interpretations of it. Listening to their arguments, they place high confidence in their champions of biblical interpretation—chiefly,

Augustine and John Calvin—but do not allow the Bible to speak for itself as a *whole* but rather in dissected and carefully selected pieces. They rely heavily on the conclusions of historical councils rather than on an objective study of Scripture. (Keep in mind that it was just such a religious council that condemned Jesus—Mat. 26:57–68.) The apostle Paul was not a Calvinist, nor was Christ. Calvinism came long after the fact; it was not a part of what was taught in the early church.

Summary Thoughts

Again, the reason for this excursus on Calvinism is because of this doctrine's huge influence on the subject of saving grace. Many, many people have been led to believe that Calvinism provides a biblical, accurate, and even meaningful explanation of grace, but this is not true. Calvinism does not teach what the New Testament teaches; it *changes* it in order to accommodate a certain theological perspective on God's sovereign will. The foundational premise of Calvinism *concerning* God's will is flawed, contradicts what God says about Himself, contradicts what *Jesus* and *Paul* say about Him, and therefore (and not surprisingly) withers under critical scrutiny.

God's saving grace—what it is, how it is imparted, who receives it, and whether or not it can be rescinded—is not left up to Calvinism, but is determined by God Himself. The study of grace in this book draws conclusions solely from the word of God, not a predetermined or denominational perspective. There has been no effort made to uphold a particular church's or religion's belief system. Quite frankly, it does not matter what any church or religion claims is true; it only matters what God *says* is true.

It should not be our desire to defend what men say about God and His salvation. Rather, it should be our earnest desire to believe, teach, and defend what God has said about Himself. This means that we, like any responsible Christian, should "[hold] fast the faithful word which is in accordance with the teaching, so that [we] will be able both to exhort in sound doctrine and to refute those who contradict" (Titus 1:9, bracketed words added). Any doctrine that challenges or maligns the gospel of Christ deserves to be exposed for what it is: a "different gospel" (Gal. 1:6–8).

Conclusion

Jesus once told a parable about the great wealth of riches which a person can discover in God. "The kingdom of heaven," He revealed, "is like a treasure hidden in the field, which a man found and hid again; and from joy over it he goes and sells all that he has, and buys that field" (Mat. 13:44).

I have often thought about that parable but have not always taken it seriously, or I have failed to appreciate its meaning. "Like a treasure"—yes, but greater than I can comprehend, the scope of which I cannot even fathom. "And from joy"—but I have not *always* felt joy over my participation in the kingdom. Sometimes I have felt despair, other times loneliness, anger, bitterness, even disillusionment. "Sells all that he has"—I have resisted this more often than not, for there have been things in my life which I did not release for the sake of the kingdom but to which I have clung with greed and tenacity. I am working on being closer to the Lord all the time, which means I will by necessity grow ever more distant from the plastic, useless, and hopeless treasures which seek to tether me to this world.

If I can be so challenged by a simple parable, then it is no wonder that the entire subject of grace has provided an even greater cause of struggle and self-examination. In my study of grace, I have attempted to ponder that which is really too wonderful for me to fully comprehend, much less explain to anyone else. I have been frustrated and disappointed by my own finite understanding, and especially by my unwillingness to subject myself completely and unfailingly to Christ's service. On the one hand, this seems perfectly natural, given my earth-bound circumstances. On the other hand, I feel that I ought to know more (and better) than I presently do, given the length of time I have been a Christian. The gospel of saving grace is, in its entirety, deep and profound, and I believe it will take even the greatest among us a lifetime to appreciate it appropriately. And even then, a person will not understand it in the way Christ understood it, nor as it is expressed in the infinite Mind of God.

Having said all that, I have no regrets whatsoever for the time and energy I have devoted to this majestic subject. I have grown immensely despite all my bewilderment and wonderment. Grace, and all it encompasses, is the most excellent gift God has given to mankind—and to me personally. In grace, all the promises and blessings of God are bequeathed to anyone who would prepare his heart to receive them. By the grace of God, all the prophecies in pre-Christian history are fulfilled; whatever yet remains to be fulfilled most certainly will be *because* of His grace. In grace, my own life has completion and purpose, my soul has acceptance and closure, and my hope has a distinct and meaningful future. If you are "in Christ," then God's saving grace will give you all these things as well.

Excellent things are worth striving for, and there is much to gain in the struggle itself. For example, in mining for gems or precious metals, a tremendous amount of common ore must be removed and discarded. Yet precious elements, though small in proportion to the whole, make the entire operation worthwhile. In like manner, God's gospel has been proclaimed to an often disinterested and unappreciative world. Many souls have resisted His message and will be cast away, but souls that respond to it are like jewels in God's hand. These souls, though few in proportion to the others, will have made the entire operation meaningful. The world will be saved in the same way that "all Israel will be saved" (Rom. 11:26): the relatively small number of Israelites who received Jesus as the Christ made all of God's dealings with Israel worthwhile. Grace is God's mining instrument, the human heart is the thing being mined, and one's obedience of faith is the precious treasure. While we seek the treasure of heaven, God seeks the treasure of our submissive heart. God is seeking us at the same time we are seeking Him (John 4:23–24). It is no wonder, then, when one has found the other.

Take time to reflect upon all that has been covered within the relatively short discourse of this book in order to appreciate the *manifold wisdom* of God's saving grace:

- Grace is anything and everything God does to compensate for our shortcomings and inability to be saved. Grace is God's activity in the human soul and earthly life of every person who lives by faith in God. Grace is God's part of a person's salvation—which includes forgiveness, peace, joy, hope, providence and every other spiritual blessing found in Christ—while obedient faith is that person's own part.

- Grace is not a burden but a blessing. Those who try to save themselves through their own efforts render useless the divine intention of saving grace in their lives.
- Grace is a gift and not a debt to repay. Our sins create an unpayable debt; God removes this debt when we appeal to Him for grace. Grace justifies us before God so that we can serve Him with obedient faith and gratitude.
- Access to saving grace is something that God determines, not people, churches, or religions. One who refuses to comply with His terms and conditions of saving grace will not receive it; those who do comply will not be denied it. While we are saved by grace and not human effort, God requires works of faith from all who claim to believe in Him and His ability to save them.
- God's saving grace is defined doctrinally, not personally or emotionally. The New Testament of the Bible is the sole and entire source of this doctrine. All gospels, religions, creeds, teachings, or versions of grace that are contrary to what has been revealed in the New Testament are unauthorized. God alone has the right to declare the terms of His covenant of salvation; we can only accept or reject those terms.
- Grace provides the means to be justified before God even though we sin *against* Him. Law cannot justify one who has sinned against it; only God's saving grace, when coupled with human faith *in* that grace, can restore human innocence. Grace does not remove the need for law, but provides recourse for law-breakers so that they can have fellowship with a holy God.
- As beautiful and beneficial as God's grace is, not everyone is willing to accept it. The reasons may vary, but they ultimately seem to boil down to these:

- They simply do not believe in God, His revealed word, or that He can perform in the manner that He has revealed to us. Even some who have claimed to believe may still greatly wrestle with *un*-belief.

- They are overcome with personal guilt and shame. Such people choose to listen to Satan's accusations, as well as those of their own heart, rather than to Christ's gospel of salvation. They fail to realize that grace is intended to remove guilt, not perpetuate or reinforce it.

- They observe all the abuses of (the doctrine of) saving grace in man-made religion and do not want to be associated with such abuses. Such people are driven by fear rather than piety; they fail to realize that God controls the imparting or withholding of saving grace, not churches or religious leaders.

- Human pride, in one form or another, always resists God's saving grace. Pride stands opposed to submission to Christ, obedience to His word, and the leadership of the Holy Spirit. No one will be saved by grace who refuses to surrender his pride to the will of God.

- While grace is a doctrinal teaching of the New Testament, the actual embodiment of grace is Jesus Christ. Everything we know about grace is inextricably bound to and made possible *by* Him. When we limit grace to an impersonal, abstract concept, we miss the personal relationship we are to have with Christ as a *necessary condition* of the grace-filled life. Grace will flourish in the believer's heart, however, when he allows Christ to live through him and determine his behavior.

- It is only because of grace that we are able to approach Christ's throne in prayer. The believer lays his gifts—praise, gratitude, petitions, and burdens—at the feet of Christ, the King and High Priest of God's kingdom. In response, Christ gives the free gift of grace to handle each and every situation that is too great for the believer to bear alone, according to His divine purpose.

- As we are *touched* by saving grace, so we are converted and transformed by it (Him). This requires our complete surrender to

Christ's will and allows Him to mold and complete us according to what serves His—and always our—best interest, as He prepares us for the life to come.

- God's saving grace is sufficient for all of our soul's needs. We are unable to make ourselves fit for His service apart from divine help; no amount of human effort can duplicate or replace what God alone is able to do for us. Whatever losses we incur in the course of this life will be abundantly compensated in the life to come.

- Grace is not something that only affects our spiritual circumstance, but must have a visible and remarkable effect on our earthly life. Not only does grace bring us into increasing conformity with Christ Himself, but it radiates outward to others so that they can see Christ in what we believe, how we live, how we love, and what we are working toward. The goal of grace is not only the forgiveness of our sins, but the full transformation of our hearts, which necessarily leads to a holy life.

- Calvinism (A.K.A. the Doctrine of Predestination), while originally intended to honor God's sovereignty, is a gross distortion of how His sovereignty is applied in the case of salvation. The review (and critique) of this doctrine underscores the need to remain true to God's gospel *in its context* in all matters of doctrinal teaching, and especially the teaching about how human souls are justified before God.

∽

By the grace of God, we are invited into the deepest, most intimate relationship possible on this earth: communion with the Father, Son, and Holy Spirit. By the grace of God, we are steadily being transformed into something we are not now—and someone better than *who* we are now. God invites us to be "partakers of [His] divine nature," but this can only be accomplished when we have "escaped the corruption that is in the world" (2 Pet. 1:3–4). The only way we can escape this corruption—really, *our* corruption—is through His saving grace. The only way we can receive this grace is to enter into a covenant relationship with God and become a follower of Christ—a *Christian.*

Yet, even though we become Christians, trouble still exists. Satan prowls about the earth looking for careless, compromising, and halfway-committed Christians who, in one form or another, resist the full measure of God's grace (1 Pet. 5:8). Others think that grace lessens the need for obedience, softens the danger of sin, or excuses them from responsibility to God's church. Actually, receiving saving grace does not make us *less* responsible (to ourselves, Christ, or His church), but requires us to be even *more* responsible than before. Not only this, but the gracious teachings of God's word show us exactly what this means and how it is to be carried out.

All the essential teaching on the gospel of grace—"everything pertaining to life and godliness" (2 Pet. 1:3)—is found within the revealed word of God, the Bible. This word is to be learned, studied, and implemented; we are to internalize this word in order to *live* it. At the same time, the process of studying alone will not bring us into the kind of relationship Christ desires of us. The gospel does not cleanse you of your sins, Christ does; the gospel does not make you holy, Christ does; reading the gospel does not transform your heart, *Christ* does—always with your consent, and always because of your submission to His will. The Bible is humankind's only direct revelation from God, but merely reading this revealed word is no replacement for the divine activity of God in the life of the believer. We are actually saved by grace and through faith—i.e., by what *God* does together with what He asks *us* to do—and not by knowledge alone.

The gospel of grace does not end here, even though this book does. There is still much more to explore and many more dimensions of fellowship with God to consider. I urge you to continue exploring just as I am continuing my own exploration. This book was never intended to exhaust all the different aspects of grace or take us to all the different levels of one's relationship with God. Instead, it was intended merely to provide a beginning point from which one *could* launch into a deeper study of these things. If you *keep* seeking the things above, where Christ is, then—by the grace of God—you will one day be *with* Him. This is a treasure worth pursuing.

If you are a Christian, then may the grace of God be with you always. If you are not yet a Christian, you can become one, and then you can enjoy all the benefits of those who are also in Christ. To such heaven-bound people, Paul writes: "Now may our Lord Jesus Christ Himself and God our Father, who has loved us and given us eternal comfort and good hope by grace, comfort and strengthen your hearts in every good work and word" (2 Thess. 2:16–17). Amen.

Endnotes

1   I will be citing from the 1995 updated edition of the New
American Standard Bible (NASB) throughout this book. The reason
for this is because I have found it to be an excellent study translation,
as it strives to stay as close as possible to a literal English rendering
of the original language of the New Testament (*Koine* Greek). I
would also recommend the English Standard Version (ESV) or the
New King James Version (NKJV). In my opinion, for the purpose of
studying, I recommend avoiding any paraphrased Bible (such as the
New Living Bible [NLB] or partly-paraphrased Bible (such as the
New International Version [NIV]). Such Bibles may be easier to read,
but in the process of re-wording the text *for* easier reading, original
meaning of the Greek text is compromised. It is also my opinion, for
what it is worth, that you should avoid the King James Version (KJV),
since it is written in 400-year-old English, which is not only difficult
to understand but is filled with archaic words and phrases.

2   If you like what you read in this book, I recommend that you
check out the other books I have written: go to www.spiritbuilding.
com/chad.

3   *Merriam-Webster's 11th Collegiate Dictionary* (electronic edition),
© 2003 by Merriam-Webster, Inc.

4   *NASB Greek-Hebrew Dictionary*, updated electronic edition
(Robert L. Thomas, gen. ed.; updated by W. Don Wilkins) [© 1998,
The Lockman Foundation]), #G2603a; James Strong, *Strong's
Dictionary*, electronic edition (database © WORDsearch, no date),
#G2603.

5   With reference to this, see Deut. 30:11–14, in which Moses
tells Israel that they did not have to "go up to heaven" to know the
commandments of God, but that He has made Himself available to
them. Paul picks up this idea and applies it to our salvation in Christ
(Rom. 10:5–13): we do not have to bring salvation down from heaven,
but Christ has brought salvation down to *us*.

6   Strong, *Dictionary* (electronic edition), #G5485; see also the root *chairo* (#G5463).

7   If there was no divine grace during the 1,500 years while Israel was "under Law," then there could not have been any unexpected kindness, any restraint, or any *forgiveness* from God toward the Israelites. This would undermine the entire sacrificial system, since the sacrifices were part of the forgiveness process; and it would undermine the entire priesthood, since the priests served as mediators between God and men in order for divine mercy and grace to be extended to God's people.

8   I go into the divine attributes of God in far greater detail in my book, *Seeking the Sacred* (Summitville, IN: Spiritbuilding Publishers, 2009); go to www.spiritbuilding.com/chad.

9   I have, for example, devoted an entire book to the subject of forgiveness, which is only one part of grace. I strongly recommend this book (*The Gospel of Forgiveness* [Spiritbuilding Publishers, 2011]) as a follow-up to the one you are reading now; go to www.spiritbuilding.com/chad.

10   For a deeper study on the subject of the Holy Spirit and His work in the individual believer as well as Christ's church, I strongly recommend my book, *The Holy Spirit of God: A Biblical Perspective* (Spiritbuilding Publishers, 2010); go to www.spiritbuilding.com/chad.

11   A "yoke," for those who may not know, is (usually) a wooden harness or coupling that straddles the necks of two animals such as oxen or horses, so that both animals can pull equally against a load. "Easy" is based on a Greek word that is difficult to translate into English (since it has several meanings at once), but "kindly" is perhaps a better sense of what Jesus means here. "Easy" implies effortless, whereas "kindly" implies "without intention to harm, but to help" (A. T. Robertson, *Word Pictures in the New Testament*, electronic edition [© 1960 The Sunday School Board of the Southern Baptist Convention; database © 2007 by WORDsearch Corp.], on Mat. 11:30).

12 The reference here is to Jesus' parable of the talents in Mat. 25:24–25; please read the entire parable (25:14–30) for context.

13 See 2 Pet. 2:1, where Peter uses this same language to describe false teachers.

14 "Law" refers to God's expectations of every person who has been made "in His image" (Gen. 1:27), inasmuch as we will give answer to Him for all that we have done (2 Cor. 5:10). For the unbeliever, "law" means the moral code by which a person ought to live that is consistent with God's own holy nature. For the Christian, "law" means this same moral code *and* whatever else is prescribed for him within the gospel of Christ—expectations that he agreed to when he became a Christian.

15 John Piper, *Future Grace* (Sisters, OR: Multnomah Books, 1995), 32.

16 Philip Yancey, *What's So Amazing About Grace?* (Grand Rapids: Zondervan, 1997), 62.

17 *Ibid.*, 25.

18 This is true whether or not the individual Israelite had knowledge of his sin and took care of it himself, or the sin was taken care of through a collective offering for the Israelite nation on the Day of Atonement (see Lev. 16).

19 These two words (pagan and polytheistic) are often used with reference to the ancient world, but seldom defined. "Pagan" technically refers to one who has little or no religion (i.e., heathens), and delights in sensual pleasures and material things (*Merriam-Webster* [electronic edition]). But historically, pagan has also referred to those who worship nature gods (i.e., the god of trees, the god of rivers, the god of a mountain, etc.), and whose lifestyle conforms to such nature-god beliefs. "Polytheistic" literally means "of many gods," and speaks of any people or culture that worships a variety of gods, whether gods of nature or otherwise.

20 The "Levitical sacrificial system" refers to the system of animal sacrifice prescribed in the Law of Moses, which was binding only upon the Israelite nation (and is described predominantly in

Leviticus). "Levitical" refers to the tribe of Levi, one of the twelve tribes of Israel, from which came the priests and high priests, and the Levites, who were responsible for teaching the Law to the people and helping to maintain the tabernacle for worship services.

21 *NASB Greek-Hebrew Dictionary* (electronic edition), #G7133a; see also Strong, *Dictionary* (electronic edition) for this root word [*qarab*], #G7126.

22 Many cite Isa. 53:4 ("Surely our griefs He Himself bore, and our sorrows He carried; yet we ourselves esteemed Him stricken, smitten of God, and afflicted") and assume that this means that God punished His Son on the cross on our behalf. This begs the question: why would the Father punish an innocent Man? And, what is to be gained by punishing His innocent *Son* for obediently carrying out His (the Father's) own will? It was not God who smote Jesus on the cross, but men; it was not God who afflicted Jesus, but instead, sent angels to *comfort* Him in His ordeal (Luke 22:43). Isaiah does not say, "God struck down His Son," but that "we *esteemed* Him as stricken, etc."— i.e., this is how things appeared to those who watched it happen. It was common in the ancient world to assume that if something bad happened to you, then you were be being *punished* by God (or, the gods); see John 9:1–2 and Acts 28:3–5. Thus, one who was hanged upon a cross *appeared to be* a sinner, the cross being his just punishment. But the fact remains that God was "well-pleased" with His Son (Isa. 42:1, Mat. 3:17, 17:5, et al), and there is no reason to believe that God would punish anyone who found favor in His eyes.

23 *Merriam-Webster* defines anarchy as: "absence of government; a state of lawlessness or political disorder due to the absence of governmental authority" (electronic edition). "Survival of the fittest" is a phrase that comes to us out of Darwin's *The Origin of the Species*, and which allegedly is one of the guiding principles of the theory of evolution.

24 Carl F. H. Henry, *God, Revelation and Authority*, vol. I (Wheaton, IL: Crossway Books, 1999), 29.

25 The same can be said for: forgiveness, being "at peace" with God, being righteous, being justified by faith (Rom. 5:1–2), being justified by grace (Titus 3:7), or having one's name in the Book of Life (Luke 10:20, Rev. 3:5), et al. All these words or phrases are equivalent to salvation or being "saved," as defined in the gospel.

26 I have written extensively on this doctrine in my book, *Being Born of God: The Role and Significance of Baptism in Becoming a Christian* (Spiritbuilding Publishers, 2014; go to www.spiritbuilding.com/chad).

27 For example, the covenant God made with Abraham was not the same as He made with Israel (Deut. 5:2–3). Likewise, the covenant into which one enters to become a Christian is a different ("new") covenant than that into which Israel entered (Luke 22:20, Heb. 8:7–13). Different covenants may require different expectations or rituals by which they are entered into, but these do not affect the unchangeable *moral* requirements of all covenants made with God.

28 Jesus' faith is not *exactly* like human faith, since He had conscious knowledge of His pre-existence with the Father, and therefore had seen what we cannot (John 1:18, 6:38, 17:5, et al). However, He still had to *demonstrate* His faith in the form of obedience, since He had to fulfill what had never been done before. Or, we could say, He had to prove His faithfulness as a Man, even though He had full knowledge, as a Divine Being, of that which was going to happen (e.g., Mat. 16:21).

29 This is completely at odds with the Doctrine of Original Sin, a man-made doctrine which is the backbone of Calvinism. We will deal with Calvinism in chapter 17.

30 "Reconciled" literally means "to be made friends with again," implying the restoration of a previous friendship, albeit on different terms. It is impossible to reconcile what did not exist in the first place. We are reconciled to God only through the blood of Christ (Rom. 5:10, 2 Cor. 5:18, 20, and Col. 1:19–22), which requires access to that blood.

31 While this citation from Hebrews does again mention Israel and Judah, it does so in an entirely different context than before. This "new covenant" will do what the old covenant could not do: provide for the forgiveness of sins through the blood of Christ. Those faithful to the first covenant were indeed forgiven by God, but only because Christ fulfilled that covenant with His blood, rather than with the inferior blood of animals (Heb. 10:1–10). We know that the Israelites were the first to be invited into this covenant (Rom. 1:16), but not the only ones (as we see later in Acts, with regard to the Gentiles). As it is, "in Christ," there is no distinction between Jew and Gentile (Gal. 3:28).

32 To better appreciate this, read Heb. 9:15–26. The writer is comparing the old covenant (that God had with Israel) with the new covenant (that we have with Him through Christ). There is a paradox involved here, inasmuch as under earthly circumstances, it is the father who dies and then his wealth is distributed based on the terms of his final will and testament. God the Father cannot die—however, His *Son* could, and did, so as to provide the blood (sacrifice) necessary to bring His covenant with us to life. Jesus' blood implies life, since He had to live to provide it; it also implies death, since He had to die in order to shed it. His sacrifice both *fulfills* and *supersedes* all of the sacrifices of the old covenant system. These sacrifices *typified* (or, foreshadowed) His, but could not *equal* His, even in their entirety (Heb. 10:1–10).

33 If someone else corrupts the two-party relationship of marriage, then *adultery* is committed. Adultery is not merely a sexual crime; it is a violation of one's covenant with someone else, even in the absence of sexual activity (Mat. 5:27–28). Likewise, when a Christian befriends the world after having committed himself to a covenant with God, he commits spiritual adultery against that covenant (Jas. 4:4).

34 For further explanation of all of this, I strongly recommend my book, *Christian Thinking* (Spiritbuilding Publishers, 2016); go to www.spiritbuilding.com/chad.

35 If you do *not* believe in Him, then "you will die in your sins"— John 8:24. We need to keep in mind that the same Savior who is speaking in John 3:16 is also speaking in John 8:24. To "perish," then, is to die in your sins.

36 When someone "breaks the law," it is really not the law itself that is broken, but the person who violates the law becomes broken. Many people can break the exact same law—all at the same time—and yet the law remains fully intact and has the power to condemn all those who violate it. (This is what is meant when Paul says, "The sting of death is sin, and the power of sin is the law"—1 Cor. 15:56.) When we die *to* the law, the law remains intact and capable of (still) condemning all those who violate it. Yet, the condemnation can be taken away if the penalty *for* violating the law is taken care of by someone else—in the case of faithful Christians, this is Christ.

37 Jesus said that we must be "born again," and that the process of being born again necessarily involves *water* and God's *Spirit*. Being born of water is what the believer is required to do; being born of the Spirit is something that only God can do. These two actions do not happen separately, but at the same time: as one is born of water (i.e., baptized into Christ), his soul is also sealed with the Holy Spirit, resulting in salvation (Eph. 1:13–14). One cannot be "born *again*"— i.e., undergo a second birth—until he first *dies*. A believer does not have two concurrent lives—one corrupted by the world, the other devoted to God—but *one* life that is devoted to God. He must die to the world *and* be born into this "newness of life" (Rom. 6:4) with the Lord. Just "asking Jesus into your heart" not only bypasses this entire process, it also defies what actually is written in the New Testament *and* poses as an acceptable means of entering into covenant with God, which is not true.

38 This paraphrase is compounded from at least the following verses: John 3:16, 8:24, 15:5, and Acts 4:12.

39 Jesus' final words before He died were, "It is finished" (John 19:30). "Finished" is translated from the Greek word *teleo*, which speaks to the fulfilling, completing, or accomplishing of something—

in essence, a goal that has been reached (Strong, *Dictionary* [electronic edition], #G5055). It also carries the idea of a debt that is *paid* (and thus, "finished"); the same Greek word is used in Mat. 17:24 and Rom. 13:6, both dealing with money being paid to satisfy a debt. In essence, Jesus' words are not limited to, "My *ministry* is finished"— although this is undeniable—but also, "The debt of all who call upon the name of the Lord for salvation is *paid in full*."

40 In having kept the Law of Moses perfectly, Jesus Christ was the only man who had never sinned against God's law. Thus, the Law— and the Lawgiver (God)—justified Him as a perfect, innocent, and sinless man. This is what made Him an unblemished (Lev. 22:17–33) and worthy sacrifice for our sins.

41 One of the counter-teachings to this is called "Calvinism," a subject which will be explored in some detail in chapter 17.

42 For further study on the Holy Spirit and the "fruit of the Spirit," I strongly recommend my book, *The Holy Spirit of God: A Biblical Perspective* (Spiritbuilding Publishers, 2010); go to www. spiritbuilding.com/chad.

43 See Rom. 5:16, 18, 2 Cor. 3:9, and Col. 2:13–14 (where the "debt" is this condemnation), for example. Paul *never* says that we are free from having to obey commandments once we are "in Christ." Such a position would invalidate the need for all the instruction of the New Testament to Christians! Not only this, but this contradicts what Jesus said: "If you love Me, you will keep My commandments" (John 14:15). It also contradicts what John said: "By this we know that we love the children of God, when we love God and observe His commandments. For this is the love of God, that we keep His commandments; and His commandments are not burdensome" (1 John 5:2–3).

44 Piper, *Future Grace*, 168.

45 This is often termed "Christian denominationalism," which is an oxymoronic phrase. There is nothing denominational about Christ, His church, or His gospel (John 17:20–22, Eph. 4:1–6). Paul asked incredulously of those Corinthians who were segregating themselves

by who had baptized them, "Has Christ been divided?" (1 Cor. 1:13). Ironically, the only time denominationalism is referred to in the New Testament is when it is being *condemned*.

46 Such sincere belief does not require the absence of any human doubt. The fact that we must "walk by faith, not by sight" (2 Cor. 5:7) necessarily implies that we have not yet *seen* that in which we have placed our faith. Even so, the convincing proofs that God has provided greatly outweigh the small pockets of doubt that a person may have concerning what is true but has not yet been fully realized.

47 There is no reason to believe that our resurrection will be different than Jesus'. As Jesus was literally and bodily raised from His death, so we will be raised from ours (John 5:28–29). As Jesus' body came out of His own tomb, so we will come out of ours (as foreshadowed in Mat. 27:52–53). Whether we are alive at His coming or have already physically died, we will *all* be raised "to meet the Lord in the air, and so we shall always be with the Lord" (1 Thess. 4:13–17).

48 Steve Farrar, *Point Man* (Sisters, OR: Multnomah Books, 1990), 111.

49 John Piper writes: "The sins of the unrepentant will be avenged in hell; the sins of the repentant were avenged on the cross" (*Future Grace*, 268). How *our* sins will be avenged will ultimately be determined by whether we listen to Christ or Satan.

50 A good companion to this citation is the parable Jesus gave concerning the slave who was forgiven an enormous debt, but who remained untransformed by this act of mercy and grace (Mat. 18:23–35). In that parable, the king who forgave his slave this huge debt *reinstituted* the debt when he discovered the slave's complete lack of gratitude. Jesus said, "My heavenly Father will also do the same to you" (18:35) who do not continue to meet the conditions of God's forgiveness in our covenant relationship with Him.

51 Dietrich Bonhoeffer, *The Cost of Discipleship* (New York: Simon and Schuster, 1995), 43ff.

52 "Charismatic" refers to the God-given *charisma* [lit., gifts] performed among the early church in the form of miracles (Rom. 1:11, 12:6, et al). In some cases, *charisma* refers to the "free gift" of God's grace (Rom. 5:15) (Strong, *Dictionary*, #G5486).

53 "Apostasy" is a word transliterated from the New Testament Greek [*apostasia*] which refers to a revolt against, defection from, or departure from (something). This word was used to describe those who refused to honor the Law of Moses (Acts 21:21, rendered "forsake" in the NASB); with regard to the gospel, it refers to a departure from divinely-revealed truth (2 Thess. 2:3). In a more general sense, apostasy refers to Christians falling away from that which they once believed to be true (1 Tim. 4:1–3, 2 Tim. 4:3–4; see also Luke 8:13, in principle). (The Greek word [*aphistemi*] is different in these latter citations, but the meaning is essentially the same as "apostasy.")

54 I have written much more on "change" and the healthy aspect of it in my book, *Christian Thinking* (Spiritbuilding Publishers, 2016); go to www.spiritbuilding.com/chad.

55 In his 2000 presidential campaign, Al Gore expressed the popular liberal view when said he would appoint judges "who understand that our Constitution is a living and breathing document," and that "it was intended by our founders to be interpreted in the light of the constantly evolving experience of the American people." This is an excellent summation of liberalism: authoritative, structural, and solemn documents, whether the U.S. Constitution or the New Testament, are to be flexible and changeable so as to allow people to live as they please. Thus, instead of the New Testament defining the Christian lifestyle, it is the modern *take* on the Christian lifestyle that defines and interprets the New Testament.

56 There are many Christians who will disagree with the idea that Jesus was a protectorate of the Law of Moses. They see Him as a revolutionary whose teaching *deliberately* sought the reform of the Law, often citing the "You have heard it said . . . but I say to you"

formula of the sermon on the mount (Mat. 5:21ff) as proof of this. But since Jesus had just finished vowing that He would *not* change the Law (Mat. 5:17–19), to view Him as a law-*changer* is to misrepresent Him entirely. Not only was Jesus "under the Law" (Gal. 4:4), but He was also (as a Jew) inducted into God's covenant with the nation of Israel upon His circumcision (Luke 2:21–24). Thus, He was bound to *keep* the Law, not change it, in order to *fulfill* the covenant, not violate it. It is impossible to reconcile a sinless Savior with that of a revolutionary law-changer. It is the Law of Moses that *validated* Jesus' sinlessness: He could not have violated the same law of God that honors His being innocent of breaking any of God's laws.

57 For the one who may not know, "Sabbath" [Hebrew, "rest"] refers historically to the seventh day, when God "rested"—that is, when He ceased to do any more *work* with regard to the Creation, since the Creation was *completed* (Gen. 2:1–3). God commanded the nation of Israel to observe this seventh day of the week as a "sign" of the covenant (Exod. 31:13) between Him and them, *and* to commemorate His having delivered them out of their bondage in Egypt (Deut. 5:13–15). Since Jesus was a Jew and was born "under the Law [of Moses]" (Gal. 4:4), He was obligated to keep the Sabbath. Thus, whatever He did *on* the Sabbath was permissible, since He never sinned against God. Not only this, but He was also "Lord of the Sabbath" (Mat. 12:8), and thus had the authority to know what could or could not be done on that day.

58 Jesus said that, unless they repented, He would "spit you [Laodiceans] out of My mouth" (Rev. 3:16). The word for "spit" here [*emeo*] literally means "to vomit" (Strong, *Dictionary* [electronic edition], #G1692). It is the same word from which we get "emetic" today—applied to ipecac syrup or something similar—which induces vomiting.

59 Paul's use of "malicious gossips" in 2 Tim. 3:3, for example, is from *diabolos*, the same Greek word from which we get "devil" and (transliterated) "diabolical" (Strong, *Dictionary*, #G1228).

60 Piper, *Future Grace*, 94.

61 This is a reference to the sad account of Ananias and his wife, Sapphira, who portrayed themselves falsely before the apostles and paid for this with their lives. Their crime was not that they held back some of what they profited from the sale of their property; rather, it was their pretending to donate the entire sale *while* keeping a part of it for themselves. Their pride turned something very honorable into something shameful (Acts 4:32—5:11).

62 We are not really physical beings with a spiritual soul; it is far more correct to say that we are spiritual beings with a physical body. The physical body is merely the way that our spiritual being (soul) participates in the physical world. But after the body dies, the soul lives on, and we become conscious and visibly aware of our spiritual existence. Much can be said on this subject, but it takes us beyond our present discussion. Even so, God promises to save the *whole* of "us"— i.e., spirit, soul, and body—in the final realization of our redemption (1 Thess. 5:23–24).

63 Jesus taught that there is no marrying in heaven (Mat. 22:30), and physical death terminates the marriage covenant we have with our wives and husbands on earth (Rom. 7:1–2). Likewise, whatever earthly relationships that are bound by human blood will be irrelevant in heaven. Instead, *all* believers will comprise the glorified "bride" of Christ (Rev. 21:9), and we will *all* be God's children forever (2 Cor. 6:18, Rev. 21:7).

64 "Levitical" refers to a priesthood derived from the tribe of Levi, one of Jacob's (Israel's) sons. (All priests of the Law had to be Levites, but not all Levites became priests.) God consecrated the tribe of Levi to minister to Him by way of the tabernacle service; they were denied an allotment of territory within the tribe of Israel so that they could devote themselves to this ministry, as well as to the teaching and explaining of the Law (Num. 3:1–13). Specifically, the high priest was derived from the lineage of Aaron (creating what became known as the Aaronic priesthood), who was also a Levite, and each high priest was ordained by Law through a ritual process (Lev. 8 – 9).

65 If you wish to pursue a thorough study of Hebrews, I recommend my *Hebrews Study Workbook* (Spiritbuilding Publishers, 2011); go to www.spiritbuilding.com/chad.

66 For a more detailed account of the tabernacle, priesthood and sacrificial system, I highly recommend Henry W. Soltau's classic work, *The Tabernacle: The Priesthood and the Offerings* (Grand Rapids: Kregel Publications, 1994).

67 This is especially true with regard to the Day of Atonement (Lev. 16) on which the high priest officiated as the sole intercessor between God and Israel—and to which the book of Hebrews makes considerable reference, directly and indirectly.

68 It is true that, *for a brief time* (40 years), God allowed a period of transition for the Jews to hear and receive the gospel of Christ. From the time of Christ's establishment of His church until the time when Jerusalem was destroyed (AD 30 – 70), the gospel of Christ was preached to the Jews as the fulfillment of God's ancient covenant with Israel. Those Jews who obeyed Christ prior to the destruction of Jerusalem were no longer bound to the Law of Moses; those Jews who had not yet heard this gospel were still obligated to continue under Law, since they knew nothing else. The destruction of Jerusalem, however, made the supremacy of the gospel *permanent* and *universal*, since the Law had been fulfilled, Christ's prophecy concerning Jerusalem had been fulfilled (Luke 19:41–44, et al), the Levitical priesthood was ended, the sacrificial system was inoperable, and God's break with the *nation* of Israel was finalized. No Jew living at that time could ignore the implications of this destruction, and thus no Jew could continue under Law unaffected *by* these implications.

69 The union of the two offices is also foreshadowed in the roles of Joshua (the priest) and Zerubbabel (a governor) in post-exilic Judea (Zech. 3 and 4), which are brought together by the same Spirit (i.e., these two offices are the two olive trees which are united in the one "lampstand"; the Spirit working through these two offices will provide light, hope, and stability for the spiritual Israel, which

is Christ's church). In Zech. 6:12–13, these two offices are said to be united in "the Branch," a prophetic reference to the Messiah (Christ).

70 We could also include here the role of the third Personage of the Godhead, the Holy Spirit. While Christ provides atonement for sin, the Spirit provides sanctification for service (1 Cor. 6:11, 1 Pet. 1:2).

71 This does *not* mean that we cannot lose our salvation, or that we cannot fall from grace. Since the righteous person lives by faith in God's ability to save him (Rom. 1:17), it is absolutely necessary that one's faith be continued in order for the promise of salvation to be honored. Jesus' blood reconciles us to God, but only *if* we "continue in the faith firmly established and steadfast, and not moved away from the hope of the gospel" (Col. 1:19–23). This means that salvation is conditioned upon faith, and will not be given in the absence of it.

72 This is the correct meaning of God providing us with a "way of escape" (1 Cor. 10:13). He will not provide a "way of escape" for those who are bent on sinning against Him, and who thus refuse to trust in His promises to shield us.

73 I have more to say on this subject in an upcoming chapter (on "The All-sufficiency of Grace"). Meanwhile, someone once described the difference between how American Christians pray and how African Christians pray. Americans tend to pray, "Lord, please remove this burden from me!"; Africans tend to pray, "Lord, please give me a stronger back to bear up this burden." We tend to seek personal comfort and (our version of) "normalcy" rather than learning to cope with—and, paradoxically, to *appreciate*—the pain of this world. No one wants to be burdened or in pain; at the same time, it is unrealistic to reduce God's grace to a mere pain-reliever rather than trust that He will walk us through this life *however He wants to*, which will never be more than we can handle.

74 "Advocate" [Greek, *parakletos*] in 1 John 2:1 is used elsewhere (John 14:16, 26, 15:26, and 16:7) to describe the work of the Holy Spirit among believers (Strong, *Dictionary*, #G3875). But in 1 John 2:1, it has clear reference to Christ. An advocate, in classical Greek usage, refers to one who is called alongside another, particularly in

a court of law, with the sole intent of helping that person overcome his ordeal (as before a judge). In the present case, John portrays the believer coming before the Father, helpless on his own to defend himself, and Christ serving as a friend of the court who intercedes between the believer and the Father. Whomever Christ defends, the Father forgives; and whomever the Father forgives has fellowship with both the One who interceded for him as well as the One who forgave him.

75 To underscore this point, see related passages: John 10:28, 1 Cor. 1:18, 15:18, 2 Cor. 2:15, 4:3, 2 Thess. 2:10, and 2 Pet. 2:9. It is interchangeable with being "dead" to God (Luke 9:60, 15:32, Eph. 2:1, 5, and Col. 2:13). In the most basic sense, to be "perishing" or "dead" to God means to be separated from His fellowship. Upon one's physical death, there is no longer any opportunity to address this situation, for there can be no demonstrations of repentance, obedience, or allegiance to Christ and His gospel in the afterlife. The time for these things is in this present life.

76 Strong, *Dictionary* (electronic edition), #G4762. Usually, the word is simply translated "turned," as in Mat. 16:23.

77 Stephen R. Covey, *The 7 Habits of Highly Effective People* (New York: Simon & Schuster, 2004), 105.

78 "Transformed," as in Rom. 12:2, comes from the Greek *metamorphoo* (from which we get "metamorphosis"), a compound word literally translated "with" (*meta-*) + "change" (*morph-*) (Strong's, *Dictionary* [electronic edition], #G3339).

79 There is an allusion here to Jesus' parable of the wedding guest (Mat. 22:1–14). Based upon the culture of the ancient Orient, if a king invited someone to a great event (such as the wedding of his son) who could not afford appropriate attire, then he (the king) would provide the attire himself, at his own expense. Thus, the wedding guest who was not dressed in wedding clothes had accepted the king's invitation, eaten the king's food, and mingled with the king's guests, but deeply offended the king by refusing to *dress the part*, especially when it was provided for him. So it is with Christians: we

are invited to a wedding feast (Rev. 19:7–9), but if we refuse to dress appropriately with the "clothes" *Christ* has provided us (through His grace), then we also will deeply offend Him—and this will not go well for us.

80 It is my understanding that the "gift of the Spirit" (in Acts 2:38) that is given to all who obey the gospel of Christ *is* saving grace. "The 'gift of the Holy Spirit' is that which is given to *all* persons who 'call upon the Lord' by repenting of their sins *and* being baptized into Christ (compare Acts 2:21 with 22:16). This 'gift' is *not* the ability to perform miracles, for this goes beyond the context of Acts 2:38. It cannot be limited to 'eternal life,' for this would conflict with other New Testament passages which speak of the Spirit's work in the church in the here and now. On the other hand, this 'gift' *must*: originate with God; be given by the authority of Christ; and have something to do with consecration and fellowship. . . . This 'gift' is one's *access to the Father* through the *agency of the Spirit* because of the *redemptive work of the Son*" (Chad Sychtysz, *The Holy Spirit of God* [Waynesville, OH: Spiritbuilding Publishing, 2010], 54–55, 57).

81 Christians do this same thing with, say, Phil. 4:13: "I can do all things through Him who strengthens me." Often, this is interpreted as: "Whatever I choose to do for the Lord, He will give me the strength to do it!" But this is a very proud stance, since it basically tells *Christ* what we are going to do for *Him* rather than allowing *Him* to tell *us* what He needs us to do. In context, this should mean: "Whatever Christ needs me to do for Him, He will also provide the strength to accomplish it."

82 For a general overview of the problem of evil and human suffering from a biblical point of view, I recommend Randy Alcorn's book, *If God Is Good* (Colorado Springs, CO: Multnomah Books, 2009).

83 Marvin R. Vincent, *Vincent's Word Studies*, electronic edition (database © 2014 by WORDsearch Corp.), on Phil. 2:15 (#G5458).

84 This is the position of a man-made religious doctrine called "universalism." This doctrine teaches that *all* will be saved in the end, even if they have to endure a form of "hell" of their own poor

decisions. According to this doctrine, God cannot deny salvation to those whom He loves, because allowing someone to be lost is not an act of divine love. Thus, the doctrine of salvation is not defined by what God actually said in His revealed word, but by imposing upon Him an emotional and subjective expectation of His love.

85   Some have mocked this view, saying, in essence, "God loves you *so much*, but if you do not love Him back, He will send you to hell!" This blasphemously misrepresents God's love *and* the reason for anyone being sent to hell. Jesus said, "If you love Me, you will keep My commandments" (John 14:15). Love and obedience are expected of those who have been given life and loved unconditionally by a benevolent Creator. Furthermore, it was Jesus' own love for and obedience to God that led Him to the cross on our behalf. This demands a humble and reverent response on our part, which is impossible apart from obedience (1 John 2:4–6). No one is sent to hell solely because he did not love God as he should have, but primarily because he violated God's laws and was thus condemned for such rebellion. His refusal to receive what God's love *offered* him—redemption and reconciliation—only compounds his spiritual demise.

86   The subject of forgiveness is huge—and hugely misunderstood. My brief comments in the course of this book deserve to be expounded upon, which I have done in another book, *The Gospel of Forgiveness* (Spiritbuilding Publishers, 2011); go to www.spiritbuilding.com/chad.

87   Some of the more general information on Calvinism in this chapter is from: *Amazing Grace: The History and Theology of Calvinism* (DVD), Apologetics Group, © 2004; and David N. Steele and Curtis Thomas, www.the-highway.com/compare.html (cited 2010).

88   Richard Price, *Great Christian Thinkers: Augustine* (Liguori, MO: 1996), 6–7. "Ordained," "priest," and "bishop" (in the context in which it is used to describe Augustine's position) are the words of denominationalists. In the New Testament, no one is formally

"ordained" to be anything; there is no separate priestly office; and "bishop" refers only to one of the elders of whatever specific congregation appointed them (1 Tim. 3:1–7, where "overseer" can also be translated "bishop"). Thus, by the 4th century, men had already begun to depart from the New Testament pattern laid down by Christ's apostles.

89 "A succinct characterization of Augustine is impossible, not only because his thought is so extraordinarily complex and his expository method so incurably digressive, but also because throughout his entire career there were lively tensions and massive prejudices in his heart and head. . . . He did not invent the doctrines of original sin and seminal transmission of guilt but he did set them as cornerstones in his 'system,' matching them with a doctrine of infant baptism which cancels, *ex opere operato,* birth sin and hereditary guilt. He never wearied of celebrating God's abundant mercy and grace—but he was also fully persuaded that the vast majority of mankind are condemned to a wholly just and appalling damnation. He never denied the reality of human freedom and never allowed the excuse of human irresponsibility before God—but against all detractors of the primacy of God's grace, he vigorously insisted on both double predestination and irresistible grace" (Dr. Albert C. Outler, "Introduction," *Confessions of St. Augustine,* electronic edition [database © 2007 by WORDsearch Corp.]). "Double predestination" refers to the predestination of the elect (saved) as well as that of the reprobate (damned).

90 Augustine, *Confessions* (electronic edition), 9.1.1.

91 Price, *Augustine,* 55; bracketed words are mine.

92 *Ibid.,* 56; bracketed words are mine.

93 *Ibid.,* 57. "All this is theological gobbledy-gook [*sic*] for 'I haven't a clue.' Augustine's inability to answer this crucial question is yet another weakness in his theory" (*Ibid.*). "Voltaire, in the article 'Original Sin' in the 1767 edition of his *Philosophical Dictionary,* described the doctrine [of predestination] as 'the wild and fantastic

invention of an African [Augustine] . . . who spent his whole life contradicting himself" (*Ibid.*, 58; bracketed words are mine).

94 *Ibid.*, 58.

95 W. Robert Godfrey, *John Calvin: Pilgrim and Pastor* (Wheaton, IL: Crossway Books, 2009), 16.

96 Godfrey, *John Calvin* (22). "Calvin rejected the medieval church's approach to the Bible where the Bible was honored, kissed, and carried in procession but was seldom opened or read by the people" (*Ibid.*, 170).

97 *Ibid.*, (33).

98 John Calvin, *Commentaries on the Epistle of Paul to the Romans* (3:22), as quoted in Godfrey, *John Calvin* (52). "The doctrine of predestination is no novelty of Calvin. Calvin believed strongly that this doctrine was taught clearly throughout Scripture and particularly by the apostle Paul. This doctrine was also taught by the great church father Augustine and by many medieval theologians, including Thomas Aquinas. The leading reformers including Martin Luther and Ulrich Zwingli also certainly taught it" (Godfrey, *John Calvin.*, 118).

99 *Ibid.*, 116.

100 *Ibid.*, 116.

101 *Ibid.*, 117.

102 *Ibid.*, 118.

103 Charlotte Methuen, *Luther and Calvin: Religious Revolutionaries* (Oxford, England: Lion Hudson, 2011), 149.

104 Godfrey, *John Calvin*, 126–127.

105 "The subject of predestination, which in itself is attended with considerable difficulty is rendered very perplexed and hence perilous by human curiosity, which cannot be restrained from wandering into forbidden paths and climbing to the clouds determined if it can that none of the secret things of God shall remain unexplored" (John Calvin, *Institutes of the Christian Religion*, electronic edition, trans. Henry Beveridge [database © 2007 WORDsearch Corp], 3.21.1). In other words, do not question God's decisions. And, if we

were dealing only with why God chooses one thing (or person) over another to carry out His will, this makes sense. But if we are dealing with what Calvin *says* God chooses (without sufficient explanation, and in defiance of biblical teaching), we are no longer questioning God but the man who thinks he can speak for Him.

106 Charles Spurgeon, in defense of unconditional election, says: "From the Word of God I gather that damnation is all of man, from top to bottom, and salvation is all of grace, first to last. He that perishes chooses to perish; but he that is saved is saved because God chose to save him" (quoted in Joel R. Beeke, *Living for God's Glory: An Introduction to Calvinism* [Lake Mary, FL: Reformation Trust, 2008], 62). What this misleading statement conveniently ignores, however, is that God's choosing the "elect" (through no decision of their own) also necessarily implies that He did *not* choose the "perishing." Thus, Spurgeon, and most Calvinists, want to exalt God's choice of the elect, but ignore (as much as possible) God's choice for those who cannot be elected. Thus, Spurgeon says that "damnation is all of man," but the truth is (according to their doctrine) God Himself is responsible for the damnation of every un-elected soul, since it was by His own alleged decree that they *cannot and will not be saved.*

107 Beeke, *Living for God's Glory*, 39.

108 "Calvin acknowledges that questions remain about reprobation as well as election to life but again calls Christians to be content with what God has revealed without trying to find reasons known only to God himself" (Godfrey, *John Calvin*, 122). Yet, it is not the "Christians" who should be worried about all this, if indeed they are saved and cannot be lost; it is the so-called "reprobates" who should question Calvinists as to why God would—for *any* reason—bring them into existence without any hope of redemption, fellowship, or future life with Him. Calvinism, for all of its wordy explanations, justifications, and selective expositions of the word of God, consistently fails to address this glaring and extremely slanted view.

109 "The problem, however, comes within the reach of [a] possible solution, if we distinguish between sovereignty as an inherent power,

and the exercise of sovereignty. God may limit the exercise of his sovereignty to make room for the free action of his creatures. It is by his sovereign decree that man is free. Without such self-limitation he could not admonish men to repent and believe. Here, again, the Calvinistic logic must either break or bend. Strictly carried out, it would turn the exhortations of God to the sinner [to repent and believe] into a solemn mockery and cruel irony" (Philip Schaff, *History of the Christian Church*, vol. VIII [Grand Rapids: Eerdmans Publishing Co., 1995], 573–574; bracketed words are mine).

110 As stated earlier in this book, breaking God's law does not literally undermine law itself, but destroys the person who does the "breaking." In reality, the sinner comes away broken; the law remains intact. And so it is with God and His sovereign decree: when one violates His decree or commandment, the sinner is broken (or, fallen; ruined; condemned), but God and His law remain fully, completely, and perfectly intact. Violating God's laws or decrees does not change God in the least; it only changes the one who does the violating.

111 Calvin says: no one has free will unless or until God makes him "born again" by visiting His saving grace upon him and making him alive to Him. "[I]t will be beyond dispute, that free will does not enable any man to perform good works, unless he is assisted by grace; indeed, the special grace which the elect alone receive through regeneration" (*Institutes*, 2.2.6 [electronic edition]). Thus, according to Calvin, no one has the free will to determine his own destiny, because this has already been determined by God's sovereign choice. Man has free will "not because he has a free choice of good and evil, but because he acts voluntarily [to sin], and not by compulsion" (*Ibid.*, 2.2.7). Conspicuously, Calvin's entire argument is devoid of any scriptural proof.

112 Calvin himself dismisses this challenge. God, he says, uses the preaching of His gospel to draw the elect to Him, and to "bring them to faith" (*Institutes*, 3.24.1 [electronic edition]). Thus, according to Calvin, preaching and service in the church are designed only to help those whom God has already elected to salvation, and offer no

permanent change—or *hope*—to those who are not elected. "But if this is manifestly impious," he chides, "let us have no doubt that the apostle [Paul] attributes all to the mercy of the Lord, and leaves nothing to our wills or exertions" (*Ibid.*). In other words, questioning Calvin's conclusions is tantamount to questioning God Himself, according to Calvin.

113 While based upon earlier teachings of Tertullian and others, what we know today as the Doctrine of Original Sin "was the happy invention of Augustine himself. The very term 'original sin' was probably coined by him, and it was through his influence that a strong doctrine of original sin became part of the common inheritance of western Christendom" (Price, *Augustine*, 57).

114 "All people are conceived in sin and born children of wrath, unfit for any saving good, inclined to evil, dead in their sins, and slaves to sin; without the grace of the regenerating Holy Spirit they are neither willing nor able to return to God, to reform their distorted nature, or even to dispose themselves to such reform" (*The Canons of Dort*, 1618, as cited in *Amazing Grace* [DVD]).

115 "For man to be able to choose the things of God, he must first be inclined to choose them. Since the flesh makes no provision for the things of God, grace is required for us to be able to choose them. The unregenerate person must be regenerated before he has any desire for God. The spiritually dead must first be made alive ('quickened') by the Holy Spirit before they have any desire for God" (R. C. Sproul, *What Is Reformed Theology?* [Grand Rapids: Baker Books, 1997], 159). Put more simply: "Calvin believed that it was God's action in instilling grace into a person's heart that made it possible for them to believe" (Methuen, *Luther and Calvin*, 157).

116 Sproul, *Reformed Theology*, 218; Beeke, *Living for God's Glory*, 107–108.

117 "By predestination we mean the eternal decree of God, by which he determined with himself whatever he wished to happen with regard to every man. All are not created on equal terms, but some are preordained to eternal life, others to eternal damnation; and,

accordingly, as each has been created for one or other of these ends, we say that he has been predestinated to life or to death" (Calvin, *Institutes*, 3.21.5 [electronic edition]).

118 "From all eternity God decided to save some members of the human race and to let the rest of the human race perish. God made a choice—he chose some individuals to be saved unto everlasting blessedness in heaven, and he chose others to pass over, allowing them to suffer the consequences of their sins, eternal punishment in hell" (Sproul, *Reformed Theology*, 166). Naturally, Sproul saw himself as an heir of "everlasting blessedness," but never offered any objective evidence as to how he—or anyone else—could know this for certain.

119 "By free, sovereign grace, therefore, we mean that the supreme God of heaven and earth . . . freely wills and applies saving grace [what is also known among Calvinists as *sola gratia*, "grace alone"] to guilty, contemptible sinners, transforming their lives so that they enjoy Him and live for His service" (Beeke, *Living for His Glory*, 135; bracketed words are mine).

120 Besides the Canons of Dordt, these include: Belgic Confession (1561); Heidelberg Catechism (1563); First Helvetic Confession (1536); Second Helvetic Confession (1566); Westminster Confession of Faith (1647); and the Calvinistic Baptist Confessions (mid-1600s) (Beeke, *Living for God's Glory*, 20–31). While Calvinism claims to be *rooted* in Scripture, Calvinists give more attention to their various councils and confessions than they do actual Scripture. Not only this, but we are left to wonder who put these "church officials" in positions of authority in the first place, since the New Testament pattern provides for no such "officials" greater than Christ's apostles, or the elders/shepherds of any given congregation. Apostles can make binding decisions and lay down church doctrine for Christ's church; elders cannot make binding decisions for Christ's church, and they can only cite and appeal to apostolic doctrine.

121 Richard Price, as head of the Department of Church History at Heythrop College at the University of London, wrote: "I would imagine that for at least a century every student of theology [at the

University of London] . . . has written an essay on why Pelagius
was a heretic. And yet almost none of these students actually read
Pelagius: after all, his surviving writings have only recently been
translated. Nevertheless, they were expected to condemn him
without a hearing; not even the Inquisition was so unjust" (*Augustine*,
45; bracketed words are mine). He makes an excellent point. Many
people condemn what they do not know, simply because it does
not (appear to) agree with what they have been taught to believe.
Pelagius, incidentally, was a contemporary of Augustine; he denied
that Adam's fall rendered human beings incapable of calling upon
God for salvation unless God called them through His grace. "Such
views seemed to him to subvert moral effort; salvation consists
not in piously twiddling one's thumbs waiting for an extraordinary
gift of grace, but in an active and generous response to the call of
the gospel" (*Ibid.*, 47). Some of Pelagius's teachings are indeed
questionable, or even unbiblical, but he appears to reject what we
now know as Calvinism for some of the same reasons that are put
forward in this present book.

122 Unless otherwise cited, summaries are from "Five Points of
Calvinism" by Matthew J. Slick, © 1998–2006 www.calvinistcorner.
com/tulip.htm), cited April, 2010.

123 Sproul, *Reformed Theology*, 139; bracketed words are mine.

124 Calvin, *Institutes*, 2.1.6, (electronic edition). "Hence, even infants
bringing their condemnation with them from their mother's womb,
suffer not for another's, but for their own defect. For although they
have not yet produced the fruits of their own unrighteousness,
they have the seed implanted in them" (*Institutes*, 2.1.8 [electronic
edition]). Thus, infants are allegedly born morally "defective," and
Adam is responsible for this.

125 In fact, Calvin himself seems to refute it: "Those who dream of
some seed of election implanted in their hearts from their birth, by
the agency of which they are ever inclined to piety and the fear of
God, are not supported by the authority of Scripture, but refuted by
experience" (*Institutes*, 3.24.10 [electronic edition]).

126 Actually, Calvin says: "We thus see that the impurity of parents is transmitted to their children, so that all, *without exception*, are originally depraved" (*Ibid.*; emphasis added). Inasmuch as Jesus was "born of a woman" (Gal. 4:4), He must have also been born *in sin*—a blasphemous thought, to be sure, but one that both the Doctrine of Original Sin and Calvinism cannot avoid and for which neither one has a biblical rebuttal.

127 Sproul uses Lazarus' dead body in the tomb that Jesus called forth (John 11:38–44) as an exact parallel of Paul's use of "dead" in Eph. 2:1 (*Reformed Theology*, 214). Yet, the two situations are hardly parallel. Lazarus' deadness had only to do with his physical body, not his spiritual soul; Paul is speaking about one's spiritual soul (or, spiritual fellowship with God), not his physical body.

128 This is perhaps best illustrated in the parable of the prodigal son (Luke 15:11–32). The prodigal son's fellowship with his father was severed by the son's own decision. Yet when the son "came to his senses," he returned to seek his father's forgiveness. The father's words are powerful: "This brother of yours **was dead** and has **begun to live**, and **was lost** and has **been found**" (emphases added). This father had always sought his son's fellowship; yet this fellowship could not have been restored until the son chose to initiate and pursue it.

129 Sproul tries to say that God already knows how a person is going to choose, live his life, respond to His gospel, etc., so that His sovereign decision *before that person is even born* is based upon this information (*Reformed Theology*, 166–168). He offers no biblical proof for this conclusion, however, because there is none.

130 Quoted in Sproul, *Reformed Theology*, 171; bracketed words are mine.

131 Slick, *Calvinist Corner* (internet citation).

132 *Ibid.* "If original sin involves moral inability [to respond to God's gospel according to one's own volition] . . . , then faith can occur only as the result of regeneration [i.e., being born again], and regeneration can occur only as a result of effectual or irresistible

grace" (Sproul, *Reformed Theology*, 227; bracketed words are mine). This assumes that "original sin"—namely, that we are all born guilty and condemned because of Adam's sin—is real, which it is not. It also contradicts all the passages in the New Testament that speak of those who obey Christ by hearing His gospel, not because God forced them, in effect, to be born again regardless of their own will.

133 Beeke, *Living for God's Glory*, 104.

134 Sproul, *Reformed Theology*, 247.

135 Beeke, *Living for God's Glory*, 116; bracketed words added.

136 Sproul cites 2 Pet. 1:10–12 as a proof-text of Calvinism, saying that true believers will "never stumble." But he wrestled with the "if—then" part of that promise: "as long as you practice these things" (from 2 Pet. 1:5–7). This puts a condition on that promise that must be upheld in order for the promise to be fulfilled. "Is the stumbling to which Peter refers so serious that we actually fall out of a state of salvation? Perhaps. Or is the apostle stressing the role of assurance in the believer's steady, sure-footed growth toward sanctification? Perhaps this is what Peter means, and his use of the term 'never' is a case of apostolic hyperbole. I do not know for sure" (*Reformed Theology*, 233). This is a big deal: Sproul staunchly advocates Calvinism, but here we have a verse that puts a nail in the coffin of it, and he admits he does not know what to do with it.

137 This is seen, for example, in commentaries by William Hendriksen (*New Testament Commentary: Romans* [Grand Rapids: Baker Book House, 1981], 375–376) and Albert Barnes (*Barnes' Notes*, vol. 10 [Grand Rapids: Baker Book House, no date], 252), both of whom were Calvinists.

138 *Amazing Grace* (DVD), on "Perseverance of the Saints." Sproul says that *all* who fall away from the faith were "not genuine believers in the first place" (*Reformed Theology*, 244). He cites Phil. 1:6: "For I am confident of this very thing, that He who began a good work in you will perfect it until the day of Christ Jesus." Taken by itself, this verse sounds like whatever God starts in a person, He will finish it. But throughout the New Testament are passages concerning the need

for sustained allegiance to Christ, which is not dependent upon the Lord Himself but the one who is required to "live by faith" (Rom. 1:17).

139 Beeke, for example, tries very hard to justify the Calvinist's position on this point (*Living for God's Glory*, 122–125). He cites John Owen's syllogistic logic: "The elect cannot fall away; [yet] some professors of faith do fall away; hence, those professors of faith are not elect believers" (*Ibid.*, 122). The huge flaw in this construct is in the major premise ("The elect cannot fall away"), which is put forward as a *fact*, when it is actually the thing being *proved*. Such circular logic always fails, and yet many Calvinists are quick to invoke it.

140 Schaff, *History*, vol. VIII, 571. The fuller quote reads: "No man is saved mechanically or by force, but through faith, freely, by accepting the gift of God. This implies the contrary power of rejecting the gift. To accept is no merit, to reject is ingratitude and guilt. All Calvinistic preachers appeal to man's responsibility. They pray as if everything depended on God; and yet they preach and work as if everything depended on man. And the Church is directed to send the gospel to every creature. We pray for the salvation of all men, but not for the loss of a single human being."

Sources Used for This Study

Amazing Grace: The History and Theology of Calvinism (DVD). © 2004, Apologetics Group.

Augustine. *Confessions of St. Augustine* (electronic edition). Database © 2007 by WORDsearch Corp.

Barnes, Albert. *Barnes' Notes*, vol. 10. Grand Rapids: Baker Book House, no date.

Beeke, Joel R. *Living for God's Glory: An Introduction to Calvinism.* Lake Mary, FL: Reformation Trust, 2008.

Bonhoeffer, Dietrich. *The Cost of Discipleship*. New York: Simon and Schuster, 1995.

Calvin, John. *Institutes of the Christian Religion* (electronic edition), trans. Henry Beveridge. Database © 2007 WORDsearch Corp.

Covey, Stephen R. *The 7 Habits of Highly Effective People*. New York: Simon & Schuster, 2004.

Farrar, Steve. Point Man. Sisters, OR: Multnomah Books, 1990.

Godfrey, W. Robert. *John Calvin: Pilgrim and Pastor*. Wheaton, IL: Crossway Books, 2009.

Hendriksen, William. *New Testament Commentary: Romans*. Grand Rapids: Baker Book House, 1981.

Henry, Carl F. H. *God, Revelation and Authority*, vol. I. Wheaton, IL: Crossway Books, 1999.

Merriam-Webster's 11th Collegiate Dictionary (electronic edition). © 2003 by Merriam-Webster, Inc.

Methuen, Charlotte. *Luther and Calvin: Religious Revolutionaries*. Oxford, England: Lion Hudson, 2011.

NASB Greek-Hebrew Dictionary (updated electronic edition), Robert L. Thomas, gen. ed.; updated by W. Don Wilkins. © 1998,   The Lockman Foundation.

Outler, Dr. Albert C. "Introduction." *Confessions of St. Augustine* (electronic edition). Database © 2007 by WORDsearch Corp.

Piper, John. *Future Grace*. Sisters, OR: Multnomah Books, 1995.

Price, Richard. *Great Christian Thinkers: Augustine*. Liguori, MO: 1996.

Robertson, A. T. *Word Pictures in the New Testament* (electronic edition). © 1960 The Sunday School Board of the Southern Baptist Convention; database © 2007 by WORDsearch Corp.

Schaff, Philip. *History of the Christian Church*, vol. VIII. Grand Rapids: Eerdmans Publishing Co., 1995.

Slick, Matthew J. "Five Points of Calvinism" (website). © 1998–2006 (www.calvinistcorner.com/tulip.htm), cited April, 2010.

Sproul, R. C. *What Is Reformed Theology?* Grand Rapids: Baker Books, 1997.

Steele, David N., and Curtis Thomas. www.the-highway.com/compare.html. (cited 2010).

Strong, James. *Strong's Dictionary* (electronic edition). Database © WORDsearch, no date.

Sychtysz, Chad. *The Holy Spirit of God: A Biblical Perspective*. Waynesville, OH: Spiritbuilding Publishers, 2010.

Vincent, Marvin R. *Vincent's Word Studies* (electronic edition). Database © 2014 by WORDsearch Corp.

Yancey, Philip. *What's So Amazing About Grace?* Grand Rapids: Zondervan, 1997.